EMINENT AMERICAN JEWS

BOOKS BY CHARLES A. MADISON

Eminent American Jews
Yiddish Literature
Book Publishing in America
The Owl Among Colophons
Leaders and Liberals in 20th-Century America
American Labor Leaders
Critics and Crusaders

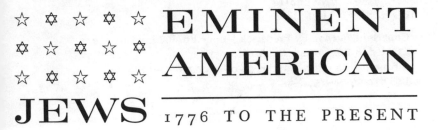

EMINENT AMERICAN JEWS

1776 TO THE PRESENT

CHARLES A. MADISON

FREDERICK UNGAR PUBLISHING CO.   NEW YORK

Copyright © 1970 by Frederick Ungar Publishing Co., Inc.
Printed in the United States of America
Library of Congress Catalog Card Number 74-125967
ISBN 0-8044-1576-5

PICTURE CREDITS

JUDAH PHILIP BENJAMIN
>   *From the Brady collection, Library of Congress*

FELIX ADLER
>   *Courtesy of the New York Society for Ethical Culture*

LOUIS D. BRANDEIS
>   *Zionist Archives and Library, New York*

ADOLPH S. OCHS
>   *The New York Times Studio*

STEPHEN S. WISE
>   *Courtesy of Justine Wise Polier*

HERBERT H. LEHMAN
>   *Pach Bros. and The Herbert H. Lehman Papers*

FELIX FRANKFURTER
>   *Zionist Archives and Library, New York*

Preface

ISRAEL ZANGWILL's idea of America as a racial and cultural melting pot was once widely popular. Certain social scientists, however, have long maintained that ethnic folkways, while losing their sharp distinctiveness in the process of reorientation, retain certain basic characteristics, so that American civilization is in fact a congeries of cultures. The early arrivals to the continent, predominantly British, naturally exerted a paramount influence on the colonial ethos. Yet from the first, other ethnic groups have continued to add to and modify the prevailing acculturation. Thus Dutch characteristics persist in New York, German peculiarities endure in Pennsylvania, and French elements are evident in Louisiana. Even more striking is the predominance of Irish influence in the once Puritan city of Boston.

As other European immigrants began to arrive in sizable numbers after the Civil War, and as Negroes moved gradually through the northern states, new ethnic characteristics were added to the folkways of the United States. Numerous national strands, persisting more or less vigorously within each group, give color and variety to the dominant cultural pattern. And all of these residual traits and qualities increase the vigor and vividness of the American ethos.

In this book I have aimed to show the contribution of the Jewish segment to American civilization. In view of the fact that Jews constitute less than 3 percent of the population and that they are relatively late arrivals, this contribution has been truly tremendous. They have exerted their great talents and persistent efforts to develop both the economy and the culture of the country; in business, in science, in scholarship, and in the arts not a few have attained first rank.

On the assumption that most readers find more interest in biographical studies of a few representative individuals than in a general survey of an entire group, I have selected for extended treatment fifteen men who, to me, best typify, both historically and individually, the significant Jewish contributors to American civilization. Whether it is the "honest broker" Haym Salomon, the secessionist Judah Benjamin, the eminent banker Jacob Schiff, the distinguished educator Abraham Flexner, or the great jurist Louis Brandeis, each man discussed here had a remarkable career, and his activities and attitudes are delineated in the light of his performance as Jew and as American. Although Jewish achievement in the arts has been considerable, I have excluded that field because my own interests lie rather in social history.

To provide background for each of the studies, and simultaneously to indicate the nature and extent of Jewish life in America from the first arrivals in 1654 to the present, I have prefaced each chapter with a brief historic or socioeconomic survey as well as miniature sketches of prominent Jews of the period under discussion. Each of these introductions relates fairly closely to the person treated in the chapter and thus serves to place him in his environment.

In the bibliography I have listed the books and articles used in the preparation of each chapter, and I hereby express my gratitude and obligation to their authors. May I also express my appreciation to the New York Public Library, and in particular to the staff of the Jewish Division, for supplying me with much of this material. I am indebted to Horace Friess, Jean Gottmann, James Gutman, William Liebmann, Lester Markel, Justine Wise Polier, and Fred Rodell for reading one or more of the chapters for critical comment. As in the past, my late wife, Edith H. Madison, read the entire manuscript with painstaking care prior to her illness, and I shall cherish her memory.

C. A. M.

FEBRUARY, 1970

Contents

JEWS ARRIVE IN
NORTH AMERICA

In the newly founded American colonies Jews, like Quakers and Anabaptists, were not welcome. Yet oppression in Europe caused a few of them, singly and in groups, to seek hoped-for asylum in the established towns of North America. The first Jewish immigrant of record, Jacob Barsimson, came to New Amsterdam from Holland in August 1654. A month later twenty-three fugitives from Brazil, after it was retaken from Holland, were brought to the same port by Jaques de la Motte, captain of the bark *St. Charles.*

Peter Stuyvesant, the irascible and dictatorial governor of the Dutch colony, was opposed to allowing the Jews to settle in New Amsterdam. In a caustic report to the directors of the Dutch West Indies Company, he urged that members of "the deceitful race be not allowed further to infect and trouble this new colony." Johannes Magapolensis, a minister of the Dutch Reformed Church, also advised the Classis in Amsterdam to reject "these godless rascals, who are no benefit to the country, but look at everything for their own profit." Both were overruled, however, by the directors, who stated that to expel the refugees "was inconsistent with reason and justice . . . especially because of the considerable loss sustained by the Jews in the taking of Brazil, and also because of the large amount of capital which they have invested in shares of the company."

With the British conquest of New Amsterdam came a greater tolerance, and the small Jewish settlement thrived. In the eighteenth century it formed the second largest Jewish congregation in the colonies. Moses Levy, a wealthy merchant, was active in community affairs and a leader among New York Jews. Hayman Levy was the largest fur trader in the colonies; in 1784 he employed young John Jacob Astor to beat furs at a dollar a day. When the British captured New York in 1776, most of the Jews, who generally favored independence, moved to areas within the control of the American army. With them went Rabbi Gershom Mendes Seixas, a friend of Washington and subsequently one of the incorporating trustees of Columbia College.

In 1658 a number of Jewish families of Portuguese origin who had found asylum in Holland, undoubtedly having learned of Roger Williams's religious tolerance, migrated to Newport, Rhode Island. Others soon followed, and during the eighteenth century the Jews of Newport became highly prosperous, largely through their international trade in sugar. One of them, Jacob Roderigues Rivera, introduced the use of sperm oil for candles. His son-in-law, Aaron Lopez, was instrumental in expanding American commerce with West Indies; he became a wealthy man and one of the city's leading citizens. When he moved to Massachusetts, after 1776, he became the first Jew to be naturalized in that state.

In 1760 Isaak Touro came to Newport from Jamaica to serve as rabbi. The synagogue which was erected for him three years later has been designated a national monument. When the Revolutionary War began, Newport had about 1,100 Jews, more than all the other colonies combined, but British occupation resulted in an exodus from which the congregation never recovered.

In early Massachusetts, where the patriarchs and prophets of the Old Testament were revered, living Jews were held in contempt. On May 9, 1649, *The Colonial Records of Massachusetts* mentions a Solomon Franco who was allowed six shillings a week for ten weeks while waiting for a boat to take him back to Holland. In 1674 there is a reference to Rolland Gideon, "ye Jue," and three years later one Robert Levy was whipped for attending a Quaker meeting. Yet in 1694 Increase Mather wrote to Joseph Dudley, "I know not that there were any Jew in Boston last winter." Three years later two Jews did arrive, and more came after 1700. Isaak Lopez became popular enough to be elected to the post of constable, which he declined and paid the required fine. Judah Monis (1683–1764) came to Cambridge as a young man. In 1720 Harvard College awarded him an M. A. for his Hebrew grammar—making him the first Jew to receive an academic degree in the colonies. Two years later he apostatized in order to become a teacher of Hebrew at Harvard.

Jews without means of support continued to be expelled from Massachusetts. Among them was Isaak Moses who later helped to supply the besieged American army in Boston during the Revolution; subsequently be became one of the foremost members of the New York Chamber of Commerce. Another Jew, Moses Michael Hays (1738–1805), a leading Boston merchant, was elected grand master of the Massachusetts Grand Lodge of Masons. He married Rabbi Touro's sister Reyna, and their son Judah was one of the founders of the Boston Athenaeum.

Jews began to arrive in Philadelphia in the 1700's. One of the early settlers was Nathan Levy. When a child of his died in 1738, he bought land and obtained permission to use it as a Jewish cemetery. Other Jews who gained prominence later in the century included Israel Jacobs, Moses Mordecai, and Bernard and Michael Gratz, two brothers of a distinguished rabbinical family. During the Revolutionary War Philadelphia harbored a number of Jewish patriots from New York and other places occupied by the British.

The struggle for independence was joined by most colonial Jews, the majority of whom had come from Central Europe, where oppression remained rife. Although a few of the wealthier ones retained their loyalty to England, most manifested intense devotion to the Revolution, deeply appreciative of the tolerance afforded them personally as well as of the ideal of political liberty. Thus in 1765 nine heads of the twenty-five Jewish families in Philadelphia signed the Non-Importation Agreement. When the war broke out ten years later, many joined the armed forces and several distinguished themselves on the field of battle and in other ways. Jared Sparks, the historian, refers to a Mr. Gomez, who at the age of sixty-eight undertook to enlist a company under his command. When members of Congress objected because of his age, he allegedly replied, "I can stop a bullet as well as a younger man." Among the Jewish patriots from Georgia, who had settled in the colony in 1733 despite the inimical attitude of the trustees, Mordecai Sheftall and David Emmanuel were especially active; the latter and his two brothers served as lieutenants in the army, and he himself became governor of the state in 1801. In South Carolina an English-born Jewish planter, Francis Salvador, was elected to the Provisional Congress in 1774 and died in battle in 1776.

Several Philadelphia Jews attained prominence as patriots and officers. Colonel Isaak Franks was an aide-de-camp to Washington, and in 1793, during the yellow-fever epidemic, rented him his substantial house in Germantown. Colonel David S. Franks came from Montreal and served as aide-de-camp to General Benedict Arnold before his defection; he also went on diplomatic missions in 1781 and 1784. Major Benjamin Nones, born in Bordeaux, came to America at the outbreak of the Revolution and served on the staffs of LaFayette and Washington; later he distinguished himself as an active Jeffersonian politician and Jewish leader.

1
Haym Salomon

H A Y M S A L O M O N is probably the best-known of the Jewish patriots. A real understanding of his part in the Revolutionary War requires separation of fact from legend. Ignored by some of the early historians and highly praised by others; involved in a fog of controversy by a son who sought to collect alleged debts from the United States government (and altered the wording of at least one document to bolster his claim), only to be repeatedly rejected by Congress; extolled by some more recent admirers and deflated by other critics, Salomon has become the subject of apocryphal legends spun by sentimental biographers and novelists. Based on the available record, however, he emerges as a patriot who was dedicated to the success of the Revolution and who used his financial talents for its crucial support.

Salomon was born in 1740 in Lissa, Poland. He received a modest Hebrew schooling, but little else is known about him before he reached New York in 1772. Most likely he left Lissa in his teens and spent a decade or more in several parts of Europe, where he gained a grounding in financial matters (although with little profit to himself) and learned several languages well enough to make good use of them subsequently. As a youth he probably had not mastered the writing of Yiddish, his mother tongue, well enough to communicate with his parents. In 1784 he had Eliezer Levy do the writing for him. In one letter he wrote,

> Pleased to mention to my father the difficulty that I have labored under in not having any learning, and that I should not have known what to have done had it not been for the languages that I learned in my travels, such as French, English, etc. Therefore would advise him and all my relations to have their children well-educated, particularly in the Christian language, and should any of my brother's children have a good head to learn Hebrew would contribute toward his being instructed.

In New York Salomon engaged in trade, with some success. He seems to have been alert to developing political events and he cast his lot wholeheartedly with the American patriots. Thus in 1776 Leonard Gansevoort recommended him to Major-General Philip Schuyler in support of Salomon's desire "to go suttling to Lake George." He wrote, "I can inform the General that Mr. Salomon has hitherto sustained the character of being warmly attached to America."

Later that year Salomon was arrested by the British, who had occupied New York, and put in the infamous Provost prison. His captors, sorely in need of interpreters to the Hessians and learning of his linguistic abilities, assigned him to Lieutenant-General Leopold von Heister, whom he served as interpreter and commisary. In these capacities, while remaining under strict surveilance, he had some freedom of action and was able to resume trading. He already possessed considerable capital, and by 1777 was well enough established to marry Rachel, the fifteen-year-old daughter of Moses Franks, one of the few prestigious Jews to remain in New York under British rule. All the while, Salomon took advantage of his relative freedom to help American and French prisoners to escape and to incite Hessian soldiers to desert to the American forces. On the verge of arrest as a spy in August, 1778, he managed to escape to Philadelphia, leaving behind his young wife and month-old son, and forfeiting his entire capital.

He reached Philadelphia, a stranger and penniless, and appealed to the Continental Congress for public employment. Describing his patriotic efforts in New York, he continued,

> Your Memorialist has upon this Event most irrevocably lost all his Effects and Credits to the Amount of Five or six thousand Pounds Sterling and left his distracted Wife and a child of a month old at New York waiting that they soon have an Opportunity to come out from thence with empty hands.
>
> In these Circumstances he most humbly prayeth to grant him any Employ in the Way of his Business whereby he may be enabled to support himself and family.

In the same document he pleaded for the rescue of a French prisoner. "This Monsieur Demezes is now most barbarously treated at the Provost's and is seemingly in danger of his life. And the Memorialist begs leave to cause him to be remembered to Congress for an Exchange."

The Congress ignored him. Without means, he most probably approached the Franks, relatives of his wife, for assistance. At any rate he soon managed to engage in trade, at first in staples and then increasingly in bills of foreign exchange, where his knowledge of languages and European financial practices gave him the advantage over his competitors. At his earliest opportunity he brought over his family.

For a time he had no office and made free use of advertisements in the local newspaper, stating that he could always be found at the "Coffee House between the hours of twelve to two." Later he established himself in an office on Front Street. He was not long in gaining a reputation for probity and fair dealing. His advertisement on February 18, 1781, read, "A few bills of exchange on France, St Eustasiay, and Amsterdam to be sold by Haym Salomon, Broker." About this time, having won the confidence and respect of Chevalier de la Luzerne, the French minister in Philadelphia, he was made the official broker of all French bills of exchange. In December, 1782, when he had also established an official relationship with Robert Morris, Salomon announced in an advertisement that he was "Broker to the Office of Finance and to the treasurer of the French Army, at his office on Front Street, between Market and Arch Streets."

The finances of the American government in 1781 were in a most deplorable state. Inflation was rampant. The army was ragged and hungry, officers and men were unpaid, and conditions in the country were desperate. "Continental currency," Robert Morris stated, "had sunk so low in public estimation that one dollar in specie could purchase from five hundred to one thousand dollars of it" (in paper). It was imperative that someone able to bring confidence and stability into the government's finances be put in charge of them, and the Congress chose Morris to undertake the tremendous task. He hesitated for weeks before accepting, aware of the difficulties he would encounter and the limited sources upon which to draw.

Morris struggled heroically to provide food and clothing and materiel to the suffering army. With the Continental Congress impotent to levy taxes, the government treasury remained empty and dependent on the loans from abroad. To cash these foreign bills of exchange, Morris made use of the available brokers. He soon found Salomon to be the most reliable and unselfish, as well as the most energetic and ingenious, of those he employed. With his aid he managed to keep government currency at a realistic level, selling bills of exchange at the highest possible prices in order to obtain enough money to buy flour, meat, guns, uniforms, lead, and other urgent necessities.

On June 8, 1781, a few weeks after Morris assumed office, he noted in his *Diary*, "I agreed with Mr. Haym Salomon the Broker, who has been employed by the officers of the most Chris'n Majesty to make sale of their Army and Navy Bills to assist me." On August 17 he wrote, "If Mr. Haym Salomon will call upon Mr. Robert Morris, tomorrow, at three o'clock, such business may be concluded which will be to their advantage and to the advantage of their country." In his *Diary* that day he noted, "Sent for Mr. Haym Salomon, the Jew Broker." In the course of time their relations became intimate and mutually respectful. Morris's *Diary* refers about seventy-five times to dealings with Salomon, of which the following are examples:

> Mr. Salomon the Broker came to negotiate about Bill I desired to know the Terms on which he can sell and encouraged him to think I shall draw.

> This morning I sent for Mr. Haym Salomon. He came and informs me that the interruption of our commerce and the losses of the merchants in this city had so dispirited the Purchasers of Bills of Exchange that he cannot make Sale at any Price.

> Haym Salomon came respecting Bills, &c. This Broker has been useful to the public Interest and requests leave to Publish himself as Broker to the Office to which I have consented. As I do not see that any disadvantage can possibly arise to the public service but the Reverse and he expects individual Benefits therefrom.

> Haym Salomon informs me that there is no sale for Bills of Exchange nor can he raise any Money for me.

Salomon the Broker came and I urged him to leave no stone unturned to find out Money—or the means by which I can obtain it.

Mr. Haym Salomon respecting Bills of Exchange. I consulted him about raising the Price he advises me to secure a good deal of Money first as he thinks an attempt to raise the Price will stop the Sale for some time and I am of the same Opinion.

Evidence of Salomon's successful efforts to provide Morris with money for his bills of exchange may be gleaned from a sworn statement by the cashier of the Bank of North America, which Morris was instrumental in establishing shortly after he assumed office, and of which Salomon was a shareholder and large depositor.

Respecting the examination of the deposition of the amounts charged in the undermentioned checks or drafts to the account of Haym Salomon, paid to Robert Morris and to the Superintendent of Finance:

August 1, 1782 to Robert Morris, $20,000; August 9, 1782 to ditto $10,000; August 27, 1783, $20,000; October 8, 1783 $6,000; October 13, 1783 $6,000; October 27, 1783 $2,000; October 30, 1783 $5,000.

The above, with thirty-three other orders, amounting to upwards of one hundred thousand dollars, exclusive of the above, of various dates and amounts, appear all charged as having been paid to Robert Morris, in the day book and ledger of the bank.

It is reasonable to assume that this money was not lent, as has been claimed, but represented sums which Salomon had obtained from the sale of bills of exchange, and deposited to his account, and later submitted to Morris. The fact that he charged only half of one percent commission, when other brokers required much higher fees, testifies to his devotion to the cause of the Revolution.

Salomon's skill as a broker was matched by his generosity to members of the Continental Congress and to officers of the army. Such magnanimity on his part was essential in view of the desperate financial straits caused by the increasing arrears of the government treasury. Shortly after his appointment, Morris wrote to the president of the Congress, "The Treasury was so much in arrears to the servants in the public offices that many of them could not without pay perform their duties. And must have gone to jail for debts they have contracted to enable them to live." So far as can be ascertained, these debts were owed mostly to Salomon. His liberality was apparently known to many, and doubtless few asked for loans in vain. Among the borrowers were James Madison, Edmund Randolph, James Wilson, Arthur Lee, Thomas Mifflin, and Arthur St. Clair. Henry Wheaton, an eminent jurist of the time, stated: "Judge Wilson, so distinguished for his labors in the Convention that framed the Federal Constitution, would have retired from public service had he not been sustained by the timely aid of Haym Salomon, as delicately as it was generously administered."

The excerpts from two letters Madison wrote to Randolph testify to this largess.

I cannot in any way make you more sensible of the importance of your kind attention to pecuniary remittances for me than by informing that I have for some time past been a pensioner on the favor of Haym Salomon, the Jew Broker. (8–27–1782)

I am almost ashamed to acknowledge my wants so incessantly to you, but they begin to be so urgent that it is impossible to suppress them. The kindness of our little friend in Front Street near the Coffee House, is a fund which will preserve me from extremities, but I never resort to it without great mortification, as he obstinately rejects all recompense. The price of money is so usurious that he thinks it ought to be extorted from none but those who aim at profitable speculations. To a necessitous delegate he gratuitiously spares a supply out of his private stock. (9–30–1782)

Salomon had apparently also been of assistance to Don Francisco Rendon, Spain's agent serving the American cause, who in 1783 wrote to the Governor General of Cuba,

> Mr. Salomon has advanced the money for the service of his most Catholic Majesty, and I am indebted to his friendship in this particular, for the support of my character as his most Catholic Majesty's agent here, with any degree of credit and reputation; and without it I would not have been able to render that protection and assistance to his Majesty's subjects which his Majesty joins and my duty requires.

The likelihood is that Salomon never was repaid by a number of his debtors, for his wealth was exhausted at the time of his sudden death. His generosity, indeed, extended in other directions as well. When specie payment was stopped and the city's poor were in dire need, he distributed $2,000 in cash. He made a sizable donation to the building fund of the synagogue he attended and presented it with a scroll of the Torah. He also sent a large sum of money to his parents in Poland. Yet he never considered himself a man of wealth, and to an uncle in London who had applied to him for help he wrote, "Your ideas of my riches are too extreme. Rich I am not, but the little I have, I think it my duty to share with my poor father and mother."

Haym Salomon continued to increase his brokerage activities and late in 1784 arranged to open an office in New York City in partnership with Jacob Mordecai. On January 1, 1785, advertisements in English and French announced the opening at 22 Wall Street and his readiness to function as "Factor Auctioneer and Broker." His health, however, had been failing for some time and six days later he died, leaving a widow with four young children. On January 11 the *Pennsylvania Packet* carried this obituary notice,

> Thursday last, expired, after a lingering illness, Mr. Haym Salomon, an eminent broker of this city; he was a native of Poland, and of the Hebrew nation. He was remarkable for his skill and integrity in his profession, and for his generous and human deportment. His remains were on Friday last deposited in the burial ground of the synagogue, in this city.

Death came unexpectedly, and Salomon died intestate. His financial affairs were in disorder, worsened by the suicide of McCrea, his chief clerk. On January 15 an announcement appeared that four administrators had been appointed to help Rachel Salomon, the administratrix. After considerable effort they found that, owing to the depreciation of many of the assets in his possession, largely in Loan Office Certificates and Continental currency, Salomon's estate was valued at $44,732; against it were debts amounting to $45,292. The family was left penniless, retaining only the household furniture.

For years thereafter Haym Salomon was a forgotten man, unmentioned by the historians who panegyrized the patriots of the Revolution. When his youngest son, Haym M. Salomon, began in 1827 to collect evidence to bolster his claim against the government for loans allegedly never repaid to his father, he found that many documents had been destroyed or lost. He did have the accounts of the executors which at their face value came to a total of $353,723.33. Adding the transactions with the Office of Finance, which were payments for bills of exchange rather than loans, he brought the total alleged debt to $658,007.43. When he submitted this evidence to the aged Madison, probably the last living "pensioner" of his father, he received an encouraging response. "The transactions shown by the papers you enclose were for the support of the delegates to Congress and the agency of your father therein was solicited on account of the respect and confidence he enjoyed among those best acquainted with him."

For thirty-five years, Haym M. Salomon pressed his claim upon Congress, and on several occasions the Senate Committee on Revolutionary Claims examined the submitted material and reported favorably, but no action was taken by Congress. In 1862, thirty-five years after the initial effort, the Committee again reported on the claim, repeating its earlier conclusions, and ended;

> Your Committee, in view of all the facts, and considering that his demand is just and reasonable, report the accompanying bill for the relief of the memorialist, limiting the amount to be paid to him to the sum of $100,000; which is in reality but a small portion of what is justly due him, but which he is willing to take, in view of his advanced years and the present condition of the country.

Again Congress refused to act, and Haym M. Salomon died unrecompensed three years later. In 1893 descendants of Salomon asked Congress to strike a gold medal in his honor in recognition of his services to the Revolution. This, too, Congress refused.

Salomon's patriotic services remained subject to controversy among historians. Ellis Paxson Oberholtzer, in his biography, *Robert Morris, Patriot and Financier* (1903), praises Morris for "his sensational operations with foreign bills, selling them for large sums through different bankers in different European cities, often without the slightest knowledge as to how they would be paid." Although his study of Morris's *Diary* must have shown him the extent of Salomon's services in this connection, he completely ignored him in his account of Morris's financial transactions. Another distinguished historian, Albert Bushnell Hart of Harvard University, generously praised Salomon's patriotic services. "All Americans may acclaim Haym Salomon as a patriot, a benefactor to this country, an inciter of patriotism to members of his race, to his countrymen and to later generations. It looks as though his credit was better than that of the whole thirteen United States of America."

In the 1920's the Federation of Polish Jews undertook to solicit funds for a statue of Haym Salomon and applied to the City of New York for a suitable public place in which to install it. The Municipal Art Commission, seeking to ascertain the legitimacy of the project, turned to Worthington C. Ford, an editor and historian of the Revolutionary period, for an evaluation of Salomon. His report, astounding in view of the available information, stated "that no one who has studied the finances of the Revolution has recorded or knew of such evidence; that the Morris papers give nothing, and that the story itself is incredible. . . . I see no reason for connecting Haym Salomon's name with the nation's history, and only as an estimable merchant has he claims to any recognition." On the basis of this opinion, the Commission refused to grant a public place for the statue.

About this time Max J. Kohler, an important Jewish scholar, learned about certain forgeries in the documents submitted by Haym M. Salomon to the Committee on Revolutionary Claims. Although the alterations pertained to the amount claimed and not to Salomon's services, Kohler reacted with indignation and urged the Federation to cease its efforts to erect the statue:

> Haym Salomon was a true and self-sacrificing patriotic citizen of our country, who rendered it valuable and important services in "the times that tried men's souls" of the American Revolution, though nothing seems to have been due to his descendants from our Government in dollars and cents, and I seriously doubt if he deserves a monument more than hundreds of patriots, to whom none was ever erected.

The Federation acted on this advice. A decade later, however, a group of Chicago citizens revived the project of the statue. Organizing the Patriotic Foundation of Chicago in 1936, the sponsors, headed by Barnet Hodes, a city official, collected $50,000 and engaged Lorado Taft, the sculptor, to design a statue of George Washington flanked by Robert Morris on his right and Haym Salomon on his left. When Taft died, his model was completed by his former student Leonard Grunelle, and on December 15, 1941, the gigantic bronze statue, erected in a prominent part of the city, was formally unveiled. Expressing the sentiment of the sponsors, Hodes said,

> It is felt that a monument showing Washington with Morris and Salomon would effectively symbolize not only the part played by Haym Salomon, but also the fact that all faiths participated in the making of America. While Haym Salomon happened to be of Jewish descent, the Patriotic Foundation is representative of all faiths because the sponsors of this monument believe that patriotism in America is universal among all the groups who make up our nation.

Under Salomon's statue the inscription reads:

HAYM SALOMON
Gentleman, Scholar, Patriot
A banker whose only interest was
the interest of his country

JEWS BECOME
AMERICANIZED

In 1789 American Jews, though few in number and scattered over the thirteen states, were flushed with patriotic zeal. Their six small congregations congratulated George Washington on his election to the Presidency in sentiments similar to those expressed in the letter from Moses M. Seixas, warden of the Newport synagogue.

> Deprived as we hitherto have been of the invaluable rights of free citizens, we now—with a deep sense of gratitude to the Almighty Disposer of all events—behold a government erected by the majesty of the people—a government which to bigotry gives no sanction, to persecution no assistance, but generously affording to all liberty of conscience and immunities of citizenship, deeming everyone of whatever nation, tongue or language, equal parts of the great governmental machine.

Each received Washington's appreciative acknowledgment; for, like the other Revolutionary leaders, he knew of the Jews' devotion to American independence.

Rooted prejudice dies hard, however, and the tolerance of religion that had been established by the Constitution and the Bill of Rights did not automatically nullify existing state laws and common practices. In several states the required oath affirming a belief in the New Testament long kept Jews from political office and certain legal activities.

Somewhat earlier, in an effort to establish the principle of religious freedom in the Constitution, Jonas Phillips, a patriotic Philadelphia Jew, had urged its adoption in an appeal to the Constitutional Convention

that all men have a natural and unalienable Right to worship almighty God according to the dictates of their own
Conscience and understanding . . . and that no authority
can or ought to be vested in or assumed by any power
whatever that shall in any case interfere or in any manner
Control the Right of Conscience in the free Exercise of
Religious Worship.

He had no way of knowing that the Founding Fathers had
already agreed on this principle of tolerance. Yet even after
enactment of the Bill of Rights several states continued to
adhere to a Christian qualification, and Phillips ran afoul of the
law in 1793 when he was fined ten pounds for refusing to testify
on the Sabbath. The Pennsylvania supreme court also upheld
the conviction of Abraham Wolf for "having done and performed worldly employment on the Lord's day, commonly
called Sunday." As late as 1833 the Supreme court of South
Carolina rejected pleas that Sunday laws contravened the Constitution, and upheld the conviction of Abraham Marks. The
Sunday problem indeed still remains moot.

In Maryland, too, legal discrimination remained on the
books for many years. In 1797 Solomon Etting initiated a campaign against it, but his petitions to the legislature were
repeatedly rejected. In 1818 Thomas Kennedy, a legislator and
Jeffersonian, submitted a bill "to extend to persons professing
the Jewish religion the same civil privileges that are enjoyed by
other religious sects." Known as the "Jew bill," it was finally
enacted in 1826.

Individual instances of anti-Jewish prejudice were not
uncommon. Uriah Phillips Levy, the first American Jew known
to pursue a naval career, suffered from the prejudice of his fellow officers. Born in 1792 of a well-established family, he ran
away to sea as a boy of ten and became master of a ship before
he was twenty-one. He saw active service in the War of 1812
and was for a time a British prisoner. In the years that followed
he was frequently ostracized by his superior officers and he
faced six courts-martial for agitating—with ultimate success—
against flogging in the Navy. Fortunately, he was repeatedly

vindicated, and promoted in rank, through the efforts of friends in the civilian administration and Congress. He was made a captain in 1844, and thirteen years later was given charge of a squadron in the Mediterranean in place of Commodore Lavclette, one of his detractors. At the time of his death in 1862 he was the highest-ranking officer in the Navy.

All things considered, however, American Jews enjoyed far greater freedom and fortune than did Jews in other countries. The relatively uninhabited continent was as open to them as to their fellow Americans for development and exploitation.

Some Jews speculated in western lands and acquired large tracts. In 1820 Benjamin Gratz, a young lawyer from Philadelphia, went to inspect the family possessions in the Indiana and Kentucky territories and was so pleased with what he saw that he decided to settle there. He became one of Kentucky's leading citizens and a founder of the Lexington and Ohio Railroad.

In the early 1800's Jewish pioneers penetrated the vacant lands of Michigan and farther west, seeking furs or trading with Indians. John Hays roamed over Illinois territory for adventure and Indian trade, married a local girl, was sheriff of St. Clair County for twenty years, and finally became collector of Indian Territory. In 1808 Samuel Solomon was established in the trading post of Saint Louis, and five years later he reported to General William Clark on the British activities in that region. In the South, Abraham Mordecai was the first white man to settle in the area of what is now Birmingham.

In 1817 Joseph Jonas, born in England in 1792, was the first Jew to reach the settlement of Cincinnati. As a skilled watchmaker, he readily found employment. Several other Jews from England joined him during the next two years, and David Israel Johnson came a little later from Indian territory. By 1824 the little group found it necessary to buy land for a cemetery, and organized a synagogue. Jonas thus became, as he later wrote, "the nucleus around which the first congregation might be formed to worship the God of Israel in the great western territory."

Similar settlements were established elsewhere over the rapidly developing land. In 1830 Jacob Gottlieb was the first

Jew to make his home in the hamlet of Chicago. A decade later enough other Jews had joined him to enable them to plan a united religious service. As the German-Jewish immigrants of the 1830's and later began to leave the Atlantic seaboard for the open spaces of the West, more and more found homes in the new states around the Great Lakes and to the south of them. The more isolated Jews, finding it difficult to observe the prescribed ritual in their new environment, tended gradually to adopt the ways of their neighbors. Not a few married locally and eventually lost their Jewish identity. Lewis N. Dembitz, a Kentucky pioneer and uncle of Justice Brandeis, wrote,

> Whoever came, came singly, found no one to pray with, and what is more, no one to mate with. Intermarriage of the newcomers with the daughters of the land followed naturally, and the descendants of the early Jewish settlers of Kentucky are known only by their Jewish family names and their Oriental features.

In the more populated eastern centers, Jewish congregations grew in number and prestige, and, as individuals, Jews gained the regard of their fellow citizens for their fair business and professional practices, their personal honesty, and their ready benevolence—although, of course, there was an occasional exception to this rule.

Deeply interested in politics, a number of Jews sought office wherever they were eligible. Most of them were Jeffersonians and were active in the campaign of 1800. In New York Solomon Simson was one of the founders, in 1794, of the Tammany Society, which was originally a liberal political organization, and served as its president in 1797; among the Grand Sachems were Noah Jackson and M. M. Noah. Jewish office holders in the early decades of the nineteenth century included Nathan Levy of Maryland, the American consul at St. Thomas; Morris Goldsmith of Charleston, a deputy U.S. marshal; and Benjamin Sheftall, who held several posts at Savannah.

Many Jews entered the professions. Moses Levy was a

lawyer and judge in Philadelphia, best known for his conservative ruling in the Cordwainers Case (1806), which established a landmark in anti-strike labor decisions. Naphtali Judah became a New York bookseller and publisher in 1797, and Abraham Hart, of the firm of Carey and Hart, was a leading book publisher in Philadelphia in the 1830's, greatly respected for his ingenuity and enterprise. Dr. Isaak Hays was an eminent ophthalmologist, and his *Hays Journal* was described by Sir William Osler as "one of the few great journals in the world." Among Jewish writers and editors the best known are Isaak Harby, a journalist, whose play *The Gordian Knot* was first performed in 1810; S. B. H. Judah, whose *The Mountain Torrent* was staged ten years later; and M. M. Noah.

The philanthropy of wealthy Jews was notable, and that of the Touro brothers was especially conspicuous. Brought up by their uncle Moses Michael Hays, they were both wealthy and generous. Abraham, the older, lived in Boston, and among the bequests he left at his death in 1822 were $10,000 to the Boston General Hospital, $15,000 toward the upkeep of the Newport synagogue, and sizable sums to other institutions, in addition to $100,000 to his brother Judah. Earlier he had donated $10,000 toward the preservation of the Newport Jewish cemetery.

Judah Touro settled in New Orleans in 1802 and was even more successful in his mercantile and financial undertakings. When the campaign for the Bunker Hill Monument lagged and no one responded to Amos Lawrence's offer of $10,000 if matched by a similar amount from others, Judah Touro donated the required sum and thus made possible the erection of the monument. He died a bachelor and without heirs; his will specified sixty-five sizable bequests totaling $387,000. Theodore Clapp characterized this will as one of exceptional broadmindedness. "With a generous profusion, he scattered his favors broadcast over the wide field of humanity. He knew well that many recipients of his bounty hated the Hebrews, and would, if possible, sweep them into annihilation." He was buried in the Newport Jewish cemetery, and the inscription on his tombstone reads, "By righteousness and integrity he collected his wealth. In charity and for salvation he dispersed it. The last of his name, he inscribed it in the book of philanthropy to be remembered for ever."

2
Mordecai
Manuel
Noah

POLITICIAN,
PLAYWRIGHT,
ZIONIST

MORDECAI MANUEL NOAH, the best-known American Jew of the early nineteenth century, achieved his fame less by reason of innate ability and exceptional accomplishment as by a flamboyant personality and a talent for controversy and showmanship. He was born in Philadelphia on August 19, 1785, the son of Manuel M. and Zipporah Noah. Little is known of his father. A native of Germany and an indifferent merchant in Charleston, he was apparently subject to melancholia and disappeared after failing in business there. His name is next found in the 1816 records of the New York synagogue. His mother was a daughter of Jonas Phillips, the Philadelphia merchant and civic leader. When she died in 1792, seven-year-old Mordecai was taken into his grandfather's home.

At the age of ten the boy was apprenticed to a carver and gilder. Although he had little schooling, he had a curious mind and spent much of his limited free time in the Franklin library, reading books on history and politics. His

23

assiduous reading attracted some of his elders in the library, and one of them, allegedly Robert Morris, helped free him from his apprenticeship contract and obtained a clerkship for him in the auditor's office of the United States Treasury. When the department was moved to Washington in 1800, Noah became a legislative reporter in Harrisburg. There he acquired the journalistic experience which he later used as editor of several newspapers.

From early boyhood Noah was strongly attracted to the theater. Later he wrote, "I seldom missed a night, and always retired to bed, after witnessing a good play, gratified and improved." He paid $18 for a season ticket, at that time an enormous sum for an impecunious youth. He became a member of a drama group in 1806 and wrote his first play, *The Fortress of Sorrento*, which was never produced but which was included in *Longworth's Dramatic Depository*—for which Noah received copies of all the plays on the publisher's list. Three years later he edited Mrs. Lenox's *Shakespeare Illustrated*, "With Critical Remarks and Biographic Sketches of the Writers by M. M. Noah." Of the projected edition, only the first two volumes were printed of the novels and histories on which Shakespeare based his plays.

By 1811 Noah, as a popular political journalist, applied to Secretary of State James Monroe for a consulship. Backed by his friend Joel Barlow, he was offered the post at Riga, then an important mercantile port. However, when he learned that war between France and Russia was imminent, he declined the office.

Instead he went to Charleston, where he studied law and worked on *The Charleston Times*. An active "War Hawk," he wrote a series of letters under the pseudonym of Muley Malack in which he agitated for war with England. His flair for invective and controversial rhetoric, which was to make him an influential and feared editor a decade later, aroused considerable opposition and he was apparently more than once challenged to a duel. In 1812 he was asked by a Mr. Young "to write a piece for his wife's benefit," she being a pretty local actress, and he produced *Paul and Alexis, or The Orphans of the Rhine.* He was amused by its success. "I was, at that period, a very active politician, and my political opponents did me the honor to go to the theatre the night it was performed, for the purpose of hissing it, which was not attempted until the curtain fell, and the piece was successful." In 1814 the melodrama was performed in London at the Covent Garden under the title of *The Wandering Boys.*

Still eager for a political appointment, Noah again applied for a consulship, this time to the Barbary States. He was assigned to Tunis—the first Jew to hold a major diplomatic post. Before he left, Monroe informed him that the crew of the brig *Edwin* was being held in captivity by Algiers and that he wished him to obtain its release by paying as much as "three thousand dollars a man, but a less sum may probably effect the object." Monroe further instructed him to conceal the government's part in the transaction and to act as if he were serving "the friends of the parties themselves." Noah knew, of course, of the piratical practices of the Barbary States and of the ransom and gratuities the American government had to pay as a consequence.

While on the high seas his ship was captured by a British man-of-war and he was taken to England as a prisoner. Released after several weeks, he proceeded to his destination in the slow and circuitous manner of the time. On the advice of Richard S. Hackley, American consul at Cadiz, Noah engaged Ricardo R. Keene, an American who had become a Spanish citizen and was on friendly terms with local potentates, to negotiate with Algiers for release of the captured Americans. After months of anxious waiting he received an eighteen-page report from Keene on how he managed to ransom two sailors as well as four men from New Orleans who spoke French but claimed American citizenship. Although Noah had no specific order from the State Department for their liberation, he did not see how he could refuse to ransom men who claimed American citizenship, and agreed to pay the required amount, which he was able to borrow because of his official position.

In the interim he handled American affairs with firmness and dignity. When the British consul protested against the disposal of British prize vessels captured by Americans, pointing out to the Bey of Tunis that his treaty with England prohibited such disposal by a Christian country, Noah argued that the United States was not a Christian power, referring the Bey to the American treaty with Tripoli which stated that "the government of the United States of America is in no sense founded on the Christian religion." He also upheld American rights of asylum and made himself generally respected by both the Tunisians and the European consuls.

He was therefore shocked to learn that the drafts for the money he had borrowed to pay Keene were protested because they exceeded orders. He was in this state of anguish and anger when he had to welcome Stephen Decatur, a one-time classmate, now in charge of an American naval squadron with power to establish the rights of American ships in the Mediterranean. Decatur greeted him warmly, then handed him a sealed letter from Monroe, which read in part;

> At the time of your appointment, as Consul at Tunis, it was not known that the Religion which you profess would form any obstacle to the exercise of your consular functions. . . . There are some circumstances, too, connected with your accounts, which require more particular explanation, which, with that already given, are not approved by the President.

"The receipt of this letter," Noah later declared, "shocked me inexpressibly . . . which at once stripped me of office, of rights, of honor, and credit." He considered it shameful, "after having braved the perils of the ocean, residing in a barbarous country, without family or relatives, supporting the rights of the nation, and hazarding

my life from poison or the stiletto," that his own government should not only treat him so shabbily but also insult
"the religious feeling of a whole nation."

Thinking quickly and sensing that Decatur was ignorant of the contents of the letter, he acted nonchalantly
as he explained to his friend how to force the Bey to pay
the prize money which he had permitted the British to obtain by selling the cargoes of captured American ships.
Decatur acted on this suggestion and forced the Bey to pay
the sum of $46,000. Noah appropriated the money and
paid the protested debt, sending the balance to Marseilles
to buy cargo for the injured American shipowners.

On his return to the United States Noah presented
himself to Monroe, only to find his reception "altogether
as ungracious as it was undeserved, and certainly unexpected, from a citizen possessing the character of Mr. Monroe." Noah thereupon prepared a pamphlet containing the
report of his activities as consul together with documentary
evidence and made it available to friends in Congress. Several personal friends, among them Isaak Harby and Naphtali Phillips, an uncle, wrote to Monroe in protest against
the religious disqualification. R. B. Jones, the American
consul at Tripoli, also wrote to praise Noah's firmness in
defense of American citizens and declared that Noah "had
reasoned wisely, and acted courageously."

For more than a year Noah's case remained in abey-
ance. In December, 1816 Attorney General Richard Rush
delivered his opinion to Monroe, stating that the ransom-
ing of the French-speaking Americans may have been unwise but was not dishonest. Acting on this grudging vindi-
cation, S. Pleasanton of the State Department wrote to
Noah to say that $5,216.57, "reported to be due you, will
be paid to your order." Noah's comment was,

> Thus ended my connection with the Government, and
> thus fell to the ground the charge "of going beyond
> orders"; nothing, then remained of the official charge but
> my religion, a subject which I had reason to believe the

President would have reconciled in a suitable manner, but which, after three years' delay, has not commanded his attention.

A year later, now out of office, James Madison did write to him

As your foreign mission took place whilst I was in the Administration, it cannot but be agreeable to me to learn that your accounts have been closed in a manner so favorable to you. . . . It was certain, that your religious profession was well known at the time you received your commission, and that in itself could not be a motive in your recall.

In 1819 Noah published *Travels in England, France, Spain, and the Barbary States in the Years 1813–14 and 15*. An elaborately detailed literary account of his journey to Tunis and back, with historical descriptions and cultural allusions to every place he visited, the long book is primarily a circumstantial account of his activities as consul and "a work of explanation and defense." Written in the leisurely and discursive style of the time, it is a travelogue of western Europe and northern Africa, with many piquant comments on people, places, and events, much of it acquired rather than experienced. Withal he revealed himself a keen observer and skillful narrator.

On his return from Tunis in 1816 Noah settled in New York as the editor of *The National Advocate*, owned by his uncle Naphtali Phillips. Long an intense Jeffersonian, he joined the Tammany Society and became one of its leaders. He quickly made his journal the vehicle of his political partisanship, and the gusto and fervor of his editorials made him a powerful and influential man. Political journalists at that time practiced without gloves, and with bare knuckles of prejudice and abuse tore into an opponent. Noah excelled in partisan attack, yet he professed to be devoted more to principle than to party, and once an election was over he was ready to work with the winners.

Thus when Andrew Jackson, whom he had championed, was beaten in 1824, Noah made an effort to cooperate with the Adams administration, causing *The United States Gazette* to comment in March, 1825, "Mr. Noah should have a pension from all lovers of order, as a most worthy pattern of zeal in the cause he adopts, and resignation to the results of his understanding."

In the early 1820's Noah became involved in a libel suit. More than two years previously he had an opportunity to purchase leases on six southern theaters. To obtain the required $10,000, later reduced to $7,000, he approached the directors of a bank friendly to Governor De Witt Clinton, whom Noah had opposed in the recent election. He offered to pay the current interest on the loan and allegedly agreed to cease his opposition to Clinton. The loan was refused and the project failed to materialize. When Noah running for sheriff in 1821, William Coleman, editor of the New York *Evening Post*, charged him with selling himself to Clinton for $7,000. Noah challenged this accusation, and Coleman printed a letter by Silvanus Miller, a journalistic adversary of Noah, relating the details of the incident of the proposed loan. Noah's response was to call Miller a liar and "a profligate old man." Miller sued for libel, but the jury disagreed and the case was dropped.

Primarily the journalist and the politician, Noah was also a playwright. In his autobiographical sketch for William Dunlap's *A History of the American Theatre*, published in 1832, he stated, "My 'line,' as you well know, has been the more rugged path of politics, a line in which there is more fact than poetry, more feeling than fiction." Yet the theater was his first love, and although he realized his artistic inadequacy, he enjoyed concocting plays and was skillful enough to give them dramatic interest.

As was the custom then, new plays were usually produced as benefits for interested parties. Thus Noah wrote one in 1819 for the accommodation of Miss Leesugg (Mrs. Hackett), an attractive English singer and actress. "Anxious for her success," he explained, "I ventured to write a play for her benefit, and in three days finished the patriotic piece of *She Would Be a Soldier, or The Battle of Chippewa*, which, I was happy to find, produced her an excellent house." The next year this play was the biggest success of the season in Philadelphia. In the preface to the printed version he admitted that the reception of this "dramatic bagatelle . . . far exceeded its merits." It tells the old story of a father arranging the marriage of his daughter to a wealthy lout and her successful union with the man she loves, a patriotic soldier. Although the plot was hackneyed even then, the dialogue is fairly lively and the suspense well sustained. It was also the first play by an American on an American theme.

To help out his actor friends Price and Simpson, he informed Dunlap, "I ventured upon another attempt for a holiday occasion, and produced *Marion, or The Hero of Lake George*." Without even seeing it, William Coleman, his political antagonist, wrote that it was "the most wretched stuff that ever insulted an audience."

The Siege of Tripoli was produced in 1820 for his own benefit at the Park Theatre, a play based on his own experiences while in the Barbary States. The crowded house assured the play's success and Noah's financial reward, but a fire broke out near the end of the final act and the theater was gutted. According to James Rees in *Dramatic Authors in America* (1845), "Noah, notwithstanding his own pecuniary wants, and they were many at the time, returned every fraction of the amount, and caused it to be divided among the performers who had been stripped of their little all by the fire."

Grecian Captive, or The Fall of Athens was written in 1822 for his uncle Aaron Phillips, a respected actor; to enhance its appeal the action included a live elephant and camel on the stage. A mock-heroic tragedy, full of intrigue and bombast, it contains a number of effective lines and a modicum of suspense to the very end, when the Greek rebels rout the oppressive Turks. His frank evaluation of himself as a playwright was stated in the preface to this work.

I believe I should apologize for this play being, after all but a poor play, but then the reply will be, why did you not write a better one? So let it take its chance with the rest of my little bantlings, which are vagabonding over the Union, played in big and little theatres, adding a trifle to my reputation and nothing at all to my fortune.

Noah was a deeply conscious Jew. Brought up by his pious grandfather, a leader of the Jewish congregation, he retained in maturity a closeness to his fellow Jews and an identification with their beliefs and interests. His observation of the harsh medieval squalor among the Jews in the Barbary States, made him wish he could lighten their lot and enlighten their minds. Monroe's anti-Jewish manifestation shocked him into an awareness that even the land of his birth was not yet wholly free of religious prejudice. On his return to the United States he grappled with the problem of how to better the lot of his fellow Jews. Gradually he became convinced that only by returning to the land of their forefathers and establishing their political independence could the oppressed majority of Jews free themselves from prejudice and persecution. "We will return to Zion as we went forth," he declared rhetorically, "bringing back the faith we carried away with us. The temple under Solomon which we built as Jews we must again erect as the chosen people."

Noah was one of the first American Jews to embrace the ideal of Zionism. In April, 1818, he delivered a discourse at the consecration of the Shearith Israel synagogue in New York; in it he eloquently enlarged upon the tenets of Judaism and expressed his sanguine hopes for Jewish amelioration.

Never were prospects for the restoration of the Jewish nation to their ancient rights and dominion more brilliant than at present. There are upwards of seven million of Jews known to be in existence throughout the world, a number greater than at any period in our history, and possessing more wealth, activity, influence, and talents than any body of people of their number on earth.

He distributed the printed sermon among leading Americans, and a number responded respectfully and encouragingly. Stimulated by this favorable reaction, he conceived the idea of bringing the more oppressed Jews of Europe to the United States, where they could live in freedom and comfort until it became possible for them to enter the land of Israel. Assuming that the wealthy European Jews would assist their oppressed brethren to migrate to America, he wished to approach them in person and applied to John Quincy Adams, then Secretary of State, for an appointment as chargé d' affaires in Vienna. He did not get the appointment, but the more he pondered the idea of a Jewish colony in America the more it gripped his imagination.

> This is the only country where the Jew can be completely rejuvenated, where the enjoyment of perfect civil and religious liberty, free from the operation and effect of national or religious prejudices, under the protection of the laws, their faculties could be developed, their talents and enterprise encouraged, their persons and property protected and themselves respected and esteemed, as their conduct and deportment shall merit.

Unable to go to Europe, he broached the project to a number of prominent European Jews. Several ridiculed it as visionary and fantastic, but a few reacted sympathetically. In 1822 Edward Ganz and Leopold Zunz, both of Berlin, wrote to him,

> The better part of the European Jews are looking with eager countenance of hope to the United States of North America, happy once to exchange the miseries of their native soil for public freedom, granted there to every religion; and for that general happiness which, not the adherents of a privileged faith alone, but every citizen is entitled to share.

Clinging to his idea despite unexpected discourage-
ment, he reduced it to a token when applying to the New
York legislature for a grant of land on uninhabited Grand
Island in Niagara River near Buffalo. When this was refused, he persuaded his friend Samuel Leggett to purchase
2,500 acres on the island for the purpose of making it a
"City of Refuge for the Jews." He named the area Ararat
and broadcast a proclamation calling upon the wealthy
Jews of Europe to expedite the exodus of the oppressed
poor to the new world. The inauguration of Ararat took
place in September, 1825. Because of the difficulty of passage to the island, the numerous celebrants met in the small
Episcopal church in Buffalo. Noah had brought with him
the cornerstone, properly inscribed, and spoke at length
about his plans for the colony. Simulating a Biblical pa-
triarch, he empowered himself, "by the grace of God, Governor and Judge of Israel," and formally proclaimed Ararat
as a haven of the Jews of the world.

> It is my will that a census of the Jews throughout the
> world be taken. . . . A capitalization tax of three shekels in
> silver, *per annum*, or one Spanish dollar, is hereby levied
> upon each Jew throughout the world, to be collected by
> the Treasurers of the different congregations, for the pur-
> pose of defraying the various expenses of reorganizing the
> government, of aiding emigrants in the purchase of agri-
> cultural implements, providing for their immediate wants
> and comforts, and assisting their families in making the
> first settlements.

To manage the emigration from Europe he named as
commissioners the most prominent religious and lay leaders of world Jewry—all of whom promptly rejected the
scheme. On his return to New York Noah reacted to the
repulse with proud silence. Nothing subsequently remained
of his extravagant hope but the cornerstone, which for a
time leaned unnoticed against the wall of the church and
is now kept as a relic at the Buffalo Historical Society. The
incident did not, however, diminish Noah's stature within

the compact Jewish community of New York, and in 1827 he married Rebecca Esther Jackson, daughter of a well-to-do Jewish merchant, and through the years became the father of six sons and one daughter.

All this time and later Noah was engrossed in politics and journalism. In 1821, he was the successful Tammany candidate for sheriff of New York County. In reward for his service during Andrew Jackson's campaign for the Presidency, he was appointed surveyor of the Port of New York in 1829. An accepted but non-practicing lawyer since 1823, he was made a judge of general sessions in 1841.

His journalistic career was equally varied. When his position as editor of *The National Advocate* became untenable owing to a difference of opinion with one of its new owners, he started *The Inquirer*. In 1829 he merged this with *The Courier*, later selling his share to his partner, J. W. Webb. In 1834 he began to publish *The Evening Star*, but disposed of it when appointed to the judgeship. Temporarily free of journalistic work, he wrote a play, *Natalie, or The Frontier Maid*, for Celeste, the currently popular French danseuse. Off the bench in 1842, he began to edit *The Union*, which he subsequently made into a weekly and named *Noah's Sunday Times and Messenger*. His Jeffersonian zeal had by this time become fairly well attenuated and he wrote, according to Philip Hone, like "a conservative inclining to Whiggism." Although he now favored slavery, and was even ready to edit a pro-slavery daily if provided with financial support, he remained a stanch unionist.

In 1845 he published *Gleanings from a Gathered Harvest*, a distillation of his nonpolitical journalistic writings over the previous decades. In a series of informal essays, the book presented his views on the nature of morality and ethics. Although of not unusual literary distinction, the essays have the merit of clarity and sagacity.

His Ararat fiasco notwithstanding, Noah continued to take an active part in New York Jewish affairs. He favored reform of the synagogue service and preached in its favor in the new Shearith Israel synagogue in 1834. When the Damascus blood accusation agitated world Jewry in 1840, Noah joined in its condemnation. He also wrote the preface and made possible the publication of the *Book of Jasher*, a medieval forgery which he believed authentic and important.

In the fall of 1844 he delivered two lectures on Zionism, later published as *Discourse on the Restoration of the Jews*. In the preface he made clear his continued belief in the re-establishment of Zion and called upon the civilized world to help. He appealed directly to "citizens and Christians" to do justice to the Jews, "to feel for their suffering and woes," and to help restore them "to the land of their forefathers and the possession of their ancient heritage." He based his plea on the fact that the United States had favored freedom and independence in South America, Greece, Africa, and other places and should therefore also aid Israel. He further explained why the Jews did not accept Jesus as the messiah. "The Jews, my friends, were but the instrument of a higher power, and in rejecting Jesus of Nazareth we have a great and overwhelming evidence of the infinite wisdom of the Almighty" (since this rejection had brought Christianity into existence). He also abjured Christian missionaries to cease their evangelizing among Jews and to help them return to Israel, intimating that by furthering the return of the Jews to their ancient home they would expedite the second advent of Jesus.

It is your duty, men and Christians, to aid us peaceably, tranquilly, and triumphantly to repossess the land of our fathers, to which we have a legal, equitable, perpetual right, by a covenant which the whole civilized world acknowledges. . . . The second advent, Christians, depends upon you. It cannot come to pass, by your own admission, until the Jews are restored, and restored in their unconverted state. If he is again to appear, it must be to his own people, and in the land of his birth and his afflictions—on the spot where he preached, and prophesied, and died.

Unlike Theodor Herzl, who was possessed by a similar dream and gave his life to its realization, Noah now appeared satisfied with the emotional expression of his vision. When his fellow Americans failed to respond, he let the aspiration languish.

During the ensuing six years, until a paralytic stroke proved fatal, Noah pursued his various activities, basking in the enjoyment of his accrued distinction. As "the Nestor of the press" and "one of the prominent men of New York," he was, as stated by Samuel Lockwood, "indisputably a gentleman, urbane and polite, affable, and ever ready to take by the hand the youthful aspirant."

JEWS IN THE
CIVIL WAR

Most Jews have been ardent patriots of the countries in which they lived. This was evident even where they were harassed and persecuted, and more so where relative tolerance and equality prevailed. During the Civil War most of the American Jews eagerly pledged allegiance to the section of the country in which they lived.

Between 1840 and 1860, the number of Jews in the United States swelled from 15,000 to nearly 200,000 as a result of the large migration from Central Europe. While the vast majority made their home in New York and other eastern cities, the more adventurous scattered over the Middle West and South where they were not long in assimilating the propensities and prejudices of their neighbors. In the South most of them accepted the institution of slavery, despite the fact that Jews have opposed it since biblical times. The few who found it repugnant but did not move north suffered severely during the years of secession and war.

Although there were not many Jews in the South, a number did achieve prominence in politics and public affairs. In 1845 David Levy Yulee, an active advocate of slavery and secession, became the first elected Senator from Florida. Three Louisiana Jews were elected to high office—Senator Judah P. Benjamin; his cousin, Lieutenant-Governor H. M. Hyams; and Speaker of the House Edwin W. Moise. All three were strong defenders of slavery.

When, after 1860, the conflict with the North became "irrepressible," Jews in the South responded loyally to the call to arms. No complete records are available, but at least 1,200 are known to have joined the Confederate forces, and twenty-one became staff officers. Moise, who would be wounded at Gettysburg, spent ten thousand dollars to outfit 120 cavalry-

37

men under his command. Major Raphael J. Moses of Charleston, a fifth-generation American, was on General Longstreet's staff and sat at General Lee's mess table. Abraham C. Meyers of Georgia was quartermaster-general of the army—until he was displaced because of derogatory remarks made by his gentile wife about Mrs. Jefferson Davis. Julius Ochs, father of the future owner of the New York *Times*, was an army captain. Simon Baruch, father of Bernard, served as a doctor and was twice captured while tending the wounded on the battlefield. Captain David C. De Leon became surgeon general, and Edwin De Leon, lawyer, journalist, and American consul to Egypt, was Jefferson Davis's personal agent in Europe.

Isaak Hermann, who had migrated from France to Georgia in 1855, distinguished himself in battle as "Captain Ike." When still a private he came to Richmond on a Saturday to collect his pay for several months. He arrived on a Saturday —only to find the treasurer's office closed until Monday. Without money, he expressed his distress to a man in the building and was given a ten-dollar bill. When he received his pay on Monday, he approached his benefactor, to return the loan. When the man refused the money, Hermann argued that he did not "like to take presents from strangers." Whereupon he was told, "We are no strangers; my name is Judah P. Benjamin."

The case of Philip Phillips, born and raised in Charleston, is an instance of divided loyalties. Opposed to nullification in 1832, he moved to Mobile, where he practiced law and was elected to Congress in 1853. Although he declined a second term, he remained in Washington. Opposed to seccession in 1861, he had no influence on his wife and daughter, who openly espoused it. The latter two were arrested soon after the outbreak of war, but were released through the intercession of Phillips's friend Edwin M. Stanton and permitted to leave for New Orleans. When the city was captured by General Benjamin Butler, Mrs. Phillips was imprisoned on a disease-infested island for three months. Though she never relinquished her devotion to the South, after the war she and her husband returned to Washington, where he resumed his successful law practice.

At least 6,000 Jews joined the Union forces, 7 were awarded Congressional Medals of Honor for displaying unusual courage under fire. Jews in the northern states had long disapproved of slavery, and the few who owned slaves had manumitted them. A number were active abolitionists. Best known was Ernestine L. Rose, who was born in Poland and came to New York in 1836 via England, where she had been befriended by Robert Owen. A prominent feminist as well as abolitionist, her success as a lecturer earned her the sobriquet, "queen of the platform."

Another Jewish abolitionist was August Bondi, who had come from Austria to St. Louis in 1848. Bondi, Theodore Weiner, and Jacob Benjamin went to Kansas where they fought with John Brown. Isidor Bush of Prague settled in Missouri in 1849, from which he later served as an antislavery delegate and was active in state politics.

Abraham Lincoln's election in 1860 was hailed by northern Jews. Lewis N. Dembitz, uncle of Justice Brandeis and a lawyer and journalist in Louisville, was proud to have helped nominate him. When Lincoln started for Washington, Abraham Kohn, city clerk of Chicago, presented him with a silk flag bearing the Hebrew inscription of verses 3–9 from the first chapter of Joshua. The last verse read: "Have I not commanded thee? Be strong and of good courage; be not afraid, neither be thou discouraged; for the Lord thy God is with thee wherever thou goest."

Many of the Jewish army volunteers were recent immigrants with little knowledge of English but with a clear understanding of the nature of the conflict. A number distinguished themselves in action, rising from the ranks to become officers. Edward S. Solomon fought heroically at Gettysburg and was referred to by General Carl Schurz as "Lieut-Col. Solomon of the 82nd Illinois, who displayed the highest order of coolness and determination under very trying circumstances." He was a brigadier general at the end of the fighting, and in 1870 President Grant appointed him to a four-year term as governor of Washington territory. Frederick Knefler rose from private to major general. Among others who achieved high rank were General Leopold Blumenberg, General William Mayer, Brigadier General Philip J. Joachimsen, and Assistant Adjutant General Louis A. Gratz.

Jews in civilian life supplied the armed forces with clothing, provisions, and other necessities and helped to raise money by selling bonds and arranging for loans in this country and abroad. Mayer Lehman in the South and the Seligman brothers in the North exerted themselves not only for personal profit but also to serve the sections in which they lived. The Seligmans in particular produced army uniforms by the tens of thousands and handled loans and bonds in European centers, placing about half of the total bonds sold abroad. August Belmont, although a Democrat in politics and handicapped by the reluctance of the Rothschilds, his employers, to risk their millions on Northern victory, did what he could with European financiers and diplomats on behalf of the Union.

Profiteering has always been a concomitant of war. Fighting and closed frontiers create scarcities of essential goods and result in inflation stimulated by greed. In 1863 Jefferson Davis stated, "The passion for speculation has seduced citizens of all classes from a determined prosecution of the war to a sordid effort to amass money." Jewish merchants were not immune from this acquisitiveness, although they were not among the conspicuous culprits. Nevertheless, latent anti-Jewish prejudices singled out Jews allegedly guilty of profiteering. In the small town of Talbotton, Georgia, a grand jury "indicted" the Jewish merchants for profiteering. Since the community had only one Jewish storekeeper, the eminently scrupulous Lazarus Straus, his indignation at the unjust accusation made him decide to move away. The townspeople, badly in need of his services, assured him the indictment was not aimed at him, but he would not be placated. He remained in Columbus until the end of the war, then moved to New York.

General Butler, shortly after obtaining control of New

Orleans, railed at the immense fortunes supposedly acquired by "army contractors, principally Jews," although he did not mention his own brother-in-law, who made a profit of $200,000 out of such contracts.

Anti-Jewish sentiment was also evident in the North, and most newspapers readily exploited it. When Benjamin, while still in the Senate, defended the Southern position on slavery, Senator B. F. Wade of Ohio accused him of being "an Israelite with Egyptian principles." Simon Wolf, an 1848 arrival, who long acted as spokesman for Jews in Washington, wrote to the New York *Evening Post* attacking the preposterousness of the accusations. "The war now raging," he pointed out, "has developed an insanity of malice that borders on the darkest days of superstition and the Spanish Inquisition." On reading this communication, Lincoln stated, "No class of citizenship in the United States (was) superior in patriotism to those of the Jewish faith." Nevertheless, Colonel L. C. Baker, head of the detective bureau of the War Department, arrested Wolf as a member of the "disloyal organization, the B'nai B'rith," which, he said, had "secret ramifications in the South and was helpful to the traitors." War Secretary Stanton, aware of the baselessness of this accusation, quickly set Wolf at liberty.

Years later, J. M. Rogers published an article in the December, 1891, issue of *The North American Review*, in which he maligned Jewish patriotism during the Civil War by asserting, "I cannot remember meeting one Jew in uniform or hearing of any Jewish soldier." Simon Wolf thereupon assembled documentary evidence demonstrating that "the enlistment of Jewish soldiers, North and South, reached proportions considerably in excess of their ratio to the general population." It is unlikely, however, that this factual information persuaded Mr. Rogers or others who wished to believe otherwise.

3
Judah
Philip
Benjamin

THE BRAINS
OF THE
CONFEDERACY

ACCORDING TO Justice David J. Brewer, "Benjamin was called 'the brains of the Confederacy,' and in acuteness of intellect he probably surpassed most men of his time." Certainly Benjamin was the most prominent Jew of the Civil War generation. Born in St. Croix of Anglo-Jewish parents on August 6, 1811, he was brought to Wilmington, North Carolina, two years later and grew up in Charleston. In 1817 he entered Fayetteville Academy and eight years later Yale College. A very bright student, he was the winner of the Berkeleyan book prize, inscribed by Yale's President Day "For excellence in scholarship." But he was expelled from the Calliopean Society late in 1827 and left college.

The abrupt departure from Yale of the sixteen-year-old Benjamin is shrouded in mystery. Nearly thirty-four years later, after he had resigned from the Senate to join the Confederacy, the abolitionist *Independent* accused him of having been dismissed for cheating and stealing. Benjamin, who had habitually disregarded personal criticism, was incensed enough to sue for libel and engaged northern lawyers to act for him, but the outbreak of war two weeks later made the suit an impossibility. To a colleague he wrote at the time, "I have determined to yield to the advice of my friends, and let a lifelong career of integrity and honor make silent and contemptuous answer to such an attack." Yet his assertion that he had left Yale because of his father's indigence does not square with the facts. Available documents indicate that the youthful Benjamin had boisterously violated some of the rigid college rules and left without being formally expelled. Shortly after his return to Charleston, on January 14, 1828, he applied to President Day for reinstatement: "I beseech you, Sir, not to attribute my improper conduct to any design or intentional violation of the laws of the college, nor to suppose that I would be guilty of any premeditated disrespect to you or any member of the faculty." President Day apparently did not reply, nor did he reinstate him.

Benjamin left home to make his way in New Orleans. He worked for a notary, gave private lessons in English, and studied law in his free time. In December 1832, at 21, he was admitted to the bar. Two months later he married Natalie St. Martin, an attractive girl of French-Catholic parentage, whom he had taught English in exchange for French lessons. Her dowry consisted of two girl slaves and 3,000 piasters. Their marriage was not a success. Benjamin had simple tastes, devoted himself to his work, and had no interest in religion; Natalie had a commonplace mind, was inclined to extravagance, and was extremely pious. In 1845, when their daughter Ninette was five years old, Natalie took her to France to be educated, and remained there. In 1858, at Benjamin's urging, she came to Washington to live with him in a house that he had sumptuously outfitted, but she left for Paris very soon after. Benjamin visited her almost annually and maintained her and Ninette in great comfort.

In 1834, while still a fledgling lawyer, he and his

friend Thomas Slidell, future chief justice of the Louisiana supreme court, prepared the volume *Digest of the Reported Decisions of the Late Territory of Orleans and of the Supreme Court of Louisiana.* It proved very useful to lawyers and judges and greatly increased Benjamin's legal practice. He specialized in commercial law, and his thoroughness and competence helped him win case after case. In 1842 the *Creole* suit gave him a national reputation. It concerned a shipment of slaves from Norfolk to New Orleans. On the high seas nineteen of the slaves mutinied, killed the agent, wounded the captain, and forced the crew to sail for Nassau. There the British held the nineteen for murder and released the remainder. Benjamin represented the insurance companies and won in the Louisiana supreme court.

Active in politics, he was elected to the Louisiana legislature in 1842. Two years later he was chosen as a member of the state constitutional convention and was particularly concerned with the section on education. By then, as a leader of the rising commercial group in opposition to the radical agrarians, he reacted sharply to the current antislavery agitation in the North: "The course of events within the last few months proves that we must rely upon ourselves and our Southern comrades to maintain our rights and cause them to be respected—and not upon the stipulations in the Federal compact. We must insist on ample security for these rights."

Severe eye strain forced Benjamin to lessen his legal work, and he devoted himself to sugar culture on the plantation he had acquired some time earlier. He pioneered in agricultural and chemical experimentation and was one of the first in the South to produce pure cane sugar commercially. Early in 1847 he brought his mother and older sister from South Carolina to live with him. His mother died later that year, but his sister remained close to him, and he supported her and other members of the family to the end of his life. His sister acted as his hostess during his lavish week-end entertainments.

When his eyes improved, he renewed his law practice. In 1848 he served as presidential elector from Louisiana and went to Washington for the inaugural. While there he was admitted to practice before the Supreme Court. His activities involved him in various commercial projects, including a railroad across Mexico to the Pacific. In 1852 a severe flood destroyed his sugar crop, and when he found himself obliged to make good as endorser on a note for $60,000, he sold his share of the plantation.

By this time Benjamin had become the most eminent lawyer in Louisiana and a dominant figure politically. He was elected to the Senate by a large majority in 1852, and it is significant that he declined President Fillmore's offered appointment to the Supreme Court in the belief that he could serve the South more usefully in the Senate. A hard worker and an astute thinker and debater, he delivered his sharpest thrusts in a gentle and friendly manner and in a voice, according to Senator Thomas Bayard, "of singularly musical timbre, high pitched, but articulate, resonant and sweet." Guy C. Lee, editor of *The World's Best Speeches*, considered him one of the most effective speakers of the century.

When the Senate began to debate the Kansas-Nebraska bill, Benjamin was chosen to present the southern position. That his speech was highly effective may be gathered from the reaction of General Lewis Cass, one of his opponents. "I listened to him, as did the Senate, with the deepest interest. I have rarely witnessed, in my Congressional experience, an effort marked with higher powers of oratory."

Benjamin at no time tried to conceal or minimize his Jewish background; on the contrary, he esteemed it and did not hesitate to strike back at senators who cast slurs on his Jewish appearance and allegedly Semitic traits. Nor did he hesitate to present to the Senate a memorial of Jewish citizens protesting discrimination in Switzerland against Americans of the Jewish faith. On the whole, however, he thought of himself more as an American than as a Jew, and more as a Southerner than as an American.

While in Washington he again argued cases before the Supreme Court, then a common practice among senators. Benjamin's practice had gradually expanded internationally and commanded the highest fees, his annual income reaching $50,000. He particularly distinguished himself in the New Almadan case, concerning ownership of the California quicksilver mine.

In 1856 Benjamin reluctantly left the disintegrating Whig party and joined the Democrats. In May of that year he made his notable speech on Kansas, successfully matching wits and oratory with Senator Seward. He stressed the point that the South would not again agree to a compromise and would thereafter insist on the conditions of the original compact.

> She looks to those contained in the Constitution itself. By them she will live; to them she will adhere; and if those provisions which are contained in it shall be violated to her wrong, then she will calmly and resolutely withdraw from a compact all the obligations of which she is expected scrupulously to fulfil, from all the benefits of which she is ignominiously excluded.

He further maintained that Congress could not exclude slavery from "the common territory" and that the right of revolution was as valid in 1856 as it had been in 1776.

Shortly thereafter he was influential in defeating President Fillmore for the Democratic nomination in favor of James Buchanan, who was more acceptable to the South. In 1858 he declined President Buchanan's offer of the ambassadorship to Spain, again convinced that he would be of greater usefulness in the Senate. The Dred Scott decision that year, attacked by Seward as biased and without warrant, drew Benjamin's most eloquent retort. J. L. M. Curry in *Civil History of the Government of the Confederacy* wrote,

His magnificent speech . . . was a masterpiece of polemic discussion, and placed him in the foremost rank of the parliamentary orators of our time. Calm and courteous in manner, with a voice as musical as silver bells, with marvellous lucidity of statement and power of analysis, with merciless logic exposing sophistry; in precise and guarded language charging misrepresentation, evasion and perversion, every sentence a rapier bringing blood; holding auditors, friend and foe, in breathless attention, he added new luster to the great council chamber, which for fifty years has been the theatre of oratory and statesmanship.

Re-elected for another term in the Senate in 1859, Benjamin watched with increasing concern and anxiety the rift between the two sections widening and deepening. As a boy of eleven he had witnessed the Negro insurrection in Charleston, led by Denmark Vesey, and he had never forgotten the subsequent hangings. As an owner of slaves on his plantation he had come to think of them as property: an essential concomitant of the Southern way of life, too deeply ingrained in the culture and too firmly rooted in the economics of the South to be eliminated without draining its very lifeblood. He was opposed to secession to the very end, but he insisted that the North must allow the South to deal with its own problems without interference. As late as October, 1860, he promised "to repel the absurd and self-contradictory charge that we seek to dissolve the Union." But the election of Abraham Lincoln and the prevailing distemper on both sides forced him to acquiesce in the movement for secession. He made a passionate defense of the Southern position, but he pleaded for a peaceful separation in a calm and quiet voice.

> You may carry desolation into our peaceful land, and with the torch and fire you may set our cities in flame . . . but you never can subjugate us; you never can convert the free sons of the soil into vassals, paying tribute to your power;

and you never, never can degrade them to the level of an inferior and servile race. Never! Never!

Most Northern newspapers, echoing his opponents in the Senate, accused him of demagogic insolence, but so important a daily as *The Philadelphia Bulletin* admitted the effectiveness of his speech.

> He went over the whole ground of Southern causes of complaint against the North as coolly and dispassionately as if arguing a case before the Supreme Court. . . . [His] reiteration of the word "never" was as free from emotion as if he had been insisting on some simple point of law, which could not be decided in any different way. But, free from emotion as it was, it produced the greatest effect. The whole gallery, on all sides, burst out as one voice, in uncontrollable applause.

The Southern states, led by South Carolina, began to secede one after another. Benjamin was fully aware of the possibilities as he made his farewell speech in the Senate on February 4, 1861, urging caution and contemplation.

> Men do not war against their benefactors; they are not mad enough to repel the instincts of self-preservation. I pronounce fearlessly that no intelligent people ever rose, or ever will rise, against a sincere, rational, and benevolent authority. No people were ever born blind. Infatuation is not a law of human nature. When there is a revolt by a free people, with the common consent of all classes of society, there must be a *criminal* against whom that revolt is aimed.

When Dennis Murphy, official reporter in the Senate for forty years, was asked to name the best-equipped and ablest senator in his experience, he answered without hesitation, "Judah P. Benjamin of Louisiana."

Fearful of arrest if he lingered in Washington, Benjamin left for New Orleans, where he remained only briefly.

When Jefferson Davis was chosen provisional President of the Confederacy, in Montgomery in February, 1861, he appointed Benjamin attorney general because he "had a very high reputation as a lawyer, and my acquaintance with him in the Senate had impressed me with the lucidity of his intellect, his systematic habits and capacity for labor." Before leaving for Montgomery, Benjamin told a group of Louisiana soldiers that "our independence is not to be maintained without the shedding of our blood. . . . Yet fearful as is the ordeal, and much as war is to be deplored, it is not an unmixed evil which many consider it to be."

Assuming that conflict was unavoidable, he at once proposed to the cabinet that the Confederacy buy 100,000 bales of cotton and ship them to England before a blockade became effective so that it could purchase munitions with part of the proceeds and keep the remainder for contingent needs. The other members did not believe that the North would actually resort to armed force and rejected the proposal.

It was Benjamin's fate to be assigned tasks beneath his talents or impossible of fulfillment. As attorney-general he had little to do, since the Southern states had not yet established their judicial systems and the exigencies of war made legal refinements irrelevant. Eager to serve, he sought to be useful to the harassed and overworked Davis. His buoyant behavior and calm, smiling presence tended to soothe Davis; his exceptional capacities for work and his acute advice made the President dependent upon him in matters that required careful action. Mrs. Davis, a close and intelligent observer of both men, stated, "Mr. Benjamin was always ready for work; sometimes with half an hour recess, he remained with the Executive from ten in the morning until night." And Gamaliel Bradford, not an admirer of Benjamin, explained Davis's intimacy with him by stating, "He seemed to have a kind of electric sympathy with every mind with which he came into contact, and very often surprised his friends by alluding to something they had not expressed nor desired him to interpret."

The capture of Fort Sumner made the War Department of the Confederacy most crucially important. Secretary L. P. Walker, however, was neither a well man nor a good administrator, and the work of the department went from bad to worse. The tremendous task of organizing and providing a large army greatly exceeded Walker's capacities, and Davis soon began to ask Benjamin to assist in various ways. By September, 1861, Walker admitted his inability to cope with the situation, and Davis made Benjamin acting secretary of war and soon *de jure* head of the department.

Confronted with the task of procuring men and munitions and forming an army large enough and strong enough to meet the Northern challenge, Benjamin worked heroically to turn "farmers into gunsmiths." He did bring order into the department, but he could neither obtain adequate arms from abroad nor have them manufactured in quantity at home, and this lack became more acute with the passing weeks. The generals, naturally antagonistic to direction by a civilian, blamed him for failure to equip their armies. He also had to contend with governors who considered the protection of their states more urgent than that of the Confederacy. Yet men in a position to know the facts agreed that he was fulfilling his task as well as possible. Robert Toombs of Georgia wrote to Vice-President A. H. Stephens that "Benjamin's administration of the War Office gives great satisfaction here. People can now get things settled one way or the other, and a bad way is infinitely better than no way at all. By this I do not mean to say that he does not discharge his duties well, for I have seen nothing to complain of."

Benjamin's unpopularity, inevitable under the circumstances and intensified by those who resented his intimacy with Davis, was climaxed by the fall of Roanoke Island. General Henry A. Wise, who had lost the battle, blamed Benjamin for not supplying him with the required guns, unaware that Benjamin had none to give him. Both congressmen and generals accused Benjamin of "gross acts of official misconduct." Henry S. Foote of Tennessee, who was later found guilty of treasonous action when he offered Seward a plan for the South's defeat, called Benjamin an "unprincipled minister of an unprincipled tyrant" and shouted "Judas Iscariot Benjamin!" The Confederate congress ordered an investigation. With neither Benjamin nor Davis willing to reveal the shortage for fear of exposing the weakness of the army to the enemy, the committee accused Benjamin of responsibility for the capture of the fort. "It is the deliberate judgment of this House that the Hon. Judah P. Benjamin, as secretary of war, has not the confidence of the people of the Confederate States, nor of the Army, to such an extent as to meet the exigencies of the present crisis."

Davis, aware that Benjamin's position in the war office had become untenable, appointed him secretary of state before congress acted on the committee's report. Mrs. Davis wrote that "the President promoted him with a personal and aggrieved sense of injustice done to the man who had become his friend and right hand." The elevation was unpopular with a number of Confederate leaders. E. A. Pollard in *The First Year of the War* made a stinging attack on Davis's action, calling it an "ungracious and reckless defiance of popular sentiment." Robert E. Lee, however, commented generously, "The trouble with him is that his first thought is not to be polite but right—and what he thinks at the start is usually what others think last."

Benjamin was more suited to his new office than he had been to his previous assignments. Opinions of course differed. James G. Blaine, long his political adversary, considered him "the Mephistopheles of the Rebellion, the brilliant, learned, sinister Secretary of State." The historian James Schouler thought he was "sanguine and serene in bearing through all mutations of fortune and misfortune." Mrs. Davis admired his extraordinary capacity for work and his impertubable poise. "Both President and Secretary of State worked like galley slaves, early and late. Mr. Davis came home fasting, a mere mass of throbbing nerves, and perfectly exhausted; but Mr. Benjamin was always fresh and buoyant."

From the outset Benjamin was aware that recognition by European powers was essential to the survival of the Confederacy; he based his foreign policy on the belief that "cotton is king" and that England's urgent need of it would force her to recognize Southern independence. To quote Senator Vest, "he devoted all his talents and energy sending abroad diplomatic agents who would manage successfully the cause of the Confederacy at foreign courts, and especially with the wealthy commercial interests abroad." James M. Mason, John Slidell, H. Hotze, Edwin De Leon, and others functioned individually and in conjunction to achieve his objective. Prodded and prompted by Benjamin, they resorted to every argument, even to bribery, to move the English government—only to fail, for it was faced by national moral fervor against slavery. Benjamin was able to comprehend this moral superiority over material well-being only years later when he acknowledged to his journalistic friend Sir W. H. Russell, "I admit I was mistaken! I did not believe that your government would allow such misery to your operatives, such loss to your manufacturers, or that the people themselves would have borne it."

With the passing of time Benjamin perceived with greater objectivity than did any of his colleagues that only a radical change of policy might still save the Confederacy. With Northern armies growing comparatively stronger and more aggressive, he was inclined to enroll Negroes as soldiers, with the promise of freedom. The proposal, made on February 9, 1865, being tantamount to emancipation, deeply antagonized most Southerners. Senator Hunter exclaimed, "If we didn't go to war to save our slaves, what did we go to war for?" On February 13 the Senate divided evenly on a resolution declaring that "J. P. Benjamin is not a wise and prudent Secretary of State, and has not the confidence of the country." Two days later the house sustained the same resolution. Benjamin submitted his resignation, but Davis would not accept it.

By this time, of course, it mattered little who was secretary of state. The Northern armies were pressing hard on all sides and approaching Richmond. On April 2 General Lee reported that he could not hold the line much longer and urged Davis to leave Richmond without delay. This Davis and the cabinet did. They stayed for a week in Danville and then went farther south, fearful of capture. On May 3 Benjamin, determined not to be taken alive, parted with Davis, who was going west, and went toward the Florida coast. Using disguises and hiding with sympathizers, he managed to reach the shore and obtain a small, open boat to take him to the Bimini Islands. There he transferred to a larger vessel going to Nassau; after an accident that nearly cost him his life, he was taken in a British ship to England. His estate having been confiscated, he was almost penniless on arrival, but he had to his credit a hundred bales of cotton, which he promptly sold for $20,-000. The sudden failure of the bank in which he deposited the money, however, left him with only a small fraction of the amount.

Benjamin was now fifty-four-years old, a fugitive from the land in which he had achieved extraordinary prominence, and without funds or means of livelihood. Opportunities, however, were not lacking: while in Paris visiting his wife and daughter, whom he had not seen in over five years, he was invited to join a Parisian financial concern. It was his aim, however, to return to the practice of law, and England seemed to him the best place.

On his return to London he was befriended by Baron Frederick Pollock, the eminent elderly jurist, who found him "a charming companion, an accomplished brother lawyer, and a true friend, one I could not easily replace." When Benjamin enrolled in Lincoln's Inn, the baron induced his son Charles to take him into his chambers, stating, "Benjamin has no need to learn the law; all he needs is to see some of the practice of our courts, and to obtain some introduction to the English Bar."

To maintain himself while at Lincoln's Inn—he lived often on cheese and bread in order to continue supporting his wife in Paris and his sisters in New Orleans—Benjamin wrote weekly editorials on international affairs for the *Daily Telegraph*. At the urging of a number of prominent lawyers who had come to know him, his term of enrollment was reduced from the usual three years to six months. He was admitted to the bar on June 6, 1866, and chose to practice in the northern circuit, which included Liverpool.

With few clients in the first two years, he devoted most of his time to writing a book entitled *Treatise on the Law of Sales of Personal Property, with Reference to the American Decisions, to the French Code and Civil Law* which was published in 1868 and soon became a standard authority. Generally referred to as *Benjamin on Sales*, it appeared in several editions in both England and the United States.

The number of Benjamin's clients greatly increased, and he became established as a leading lawyer in the commercial and maritime fields. Lord Chancellor Cairns was so impressed by Benjamin's argument in one suit that he proposed to make him Queen's Counsel for the County Palatine of Lancaster, an appointment Benjamin accepted. In 1872 he argued his first case before the House of Lords (Rankin *vs.* Potter), and the Lord Chancellor, Lord Hatherby, was so affected by his presentation, which stressed not so much the client's case as abstract justice, that he bestowed upon Benjamin the high honor of a patent of precedence, thus ranking him above other Queen's Counsels. He also became the leading lawyer in the Privy Council, where his knowledge of foreign legal systems was very useful. In the ensuing decade before his retirement, he handled 136 major cases. He was one of the highest-paid lawyers in England; his income from fees in 1880 was nearly 16,000 pounds. One authority stated that "the success of Benjamin at the English Bar is without parallel in professional annals."

In 1880, while visiting his family in Paris, Benjamin fell from a rapidly moving tramcar and was badly injured. Although he recovered quickly and resumed his work, his health became impaired by diabetes and other effects of age. He announced his retirement in 1883 and was given a dinner in the Inner Temple by the leaders of the bench and bar. The London *Times* reported it as "an event without parallel in the long history of the Bar." Lord Selborne, the Lord Chancellor, said, "No man within my recollection has possessed greater learning or displayed greater shrewdness or ability, or greater zeal for the interests entrusted to him." Benjamin went to live in Paris, where he died on May 6, 1884.

Although he was buried in a Catholic cemetery, Benjamin had to the end of his life remained a Jew. He accepted his religious heritage, as he did his Semitic features and short stature, as a natural part of himself. Although he had early ceased to observe the Jewish ritual, and although Natalie wished him to become a Roman Catholic, he never converted—probably a reason for their continued separation. He remained fond of her and supported her generously, but he visited her only briefly. He provided his daughter with an annual income of three thousand dollars upon her marriage to a French officer, but her Catholicism undoubtedly placed a barrier between them. His association with his own family, which remained traditionally Jewish, was both devoted and close. His letters to his sisters evidence great warmth and love, relating at length his experiences and affairs and expressing concern for their personal well-being.

Benjamin's position in the history of his time is secure. Generally accepted as an accomplished lawyer and statesman, he failed to achieve stellar distinction. A product of Southern slavocracy, steeped in client-oriented loyalties, exerting his great powers in defense of an institution denying human equality, he was more the astute lawyer than the dedicated leader, more the practical politician than the inspired statesman. By becoming "the brains of the Confederacy" he carved for himself a smaller niche in American history than his talents seemed to warrant.

JEWS IN
AMERICAN BANKING

Contrary to common assumption, Jews in modern times, and certainly in the United States, control only a minor fraction of the banking business, and this mostly in the investment field. For centuries, the rulers of Europe deliberately limited the precarious livelihoods of their Jewish subjects to trading and money lending, and a few Jews did achieve influential, if self-abasing positions as financiers to kings, nobles, and bishops. Beginning with the Fuggers in the fifteenth century, when the Church removed the ban on money lending by Christians, Jews ceased to dominate the money market. Although such Jewish banking families as the Rothschilds, the Speyers, and the Warburgs gained a certain prominence in the nineteenth century, their financial dealings formed only a small part of world banking.

In the United States, the first well-known Jewish banker was August Belmont, born Schoenberg. In 1837, only 21 but already well-trained in finance, he was sent by the Rothschilds to New York to look after their American interests. Although he soon opened an office of his own, he continued to take full advantage of his Rothschild connection. He sloughed off his Jewishness, married the attractive daughter of Commodore M. C. Perry, and became one of the social leaders of New York. In 1844 he served as American general council to Austria, and after 1853 he was chargé d'affaires and minister, respectively, to the Hague. During the Civil War he acted in behalf of the North to obtain loans from European financial circles, and later became influential in the Democratic circles.

Philip Speyer, of an old German banking family, also entered American banking in 1837. He floated government bonds during the Civil War and later specialized in loans to railroads and foreign governments. His nephew, James Speyer, who joined his firm in 1885 and became senior partner four years later, worked strenuously to control the panic of 1893, and was involved in the financial reorganization of such railroads as the Baltimore and Ohio and Central Pacific. Although he married a non-Jewish wife and was accepted by the exclusive social set of the city, he felt too conscious of his family history to renounce his Jewishness. He was a founder of the Provident Loan Society, contributed to the Museum of the City of New York and Mount Sinai Hospital, and with his wife established the Ellen Prince Speyer Animal Hospital.

The eight sons of David Seligman were partners in J. & W. Seligman and Company. Joseph, the eldest, came to the United States in 1837, peddled notions from door to door, and saved the money to bring over his younger brothers. They joined him in peddling, trudging their way through rural America, and soon graduated into storekeeping. Shortly before the start of the Civil War they bought a large clothing factory and were soon producing army uniforms by the thousands. They also engaged in banking, and their successful placement of government bonds with European investors was later rewarded with the fiscal agency for federal loans in this country and abroad. By 1869 the partnership had a working capital of six million dollars.

Following the Rothschild pattern, Joseph made his seven brothers equal partners. Seligman branches were established in leading European cities as well as in San Francisco, with one or more of the brothers in charge. They marketed government bonds as well as railroad and industrial issues. Joseph gained the gratitude of the Navy when he let the financially hard-pressed department hold up a large payment for a year without interest. President Grant, a friend of the family, offered him the office of Secretary of the Treasury, but he declined it.

In 1877 Joseph Seligman was the best-known Jew in the United States. He and his brother Jesse had founded the Hebrew Orphan Asylum in 1859 and had contributed generously to its maintenance. Both were also active in other Jewish charities and in civic affairs, and Joseph was the first president and a financial supporter of the Society for Ethical Culture.

The refusal in 1877 of rooms in the Grand Union Hotel in Saratoga because of his religion was a severe blow to his ego. Judge Henry Hilton, who operated the hotel for the A. T. Stewart estate, had instructed the clerk to say, "Mr. Seligman, I am required to inform you that Mr. Hilton has given instructions that no Israelite shall be permitted in the future to stop at this hotel." The scandal was widely publicized in the newspapers, and was condemned even by those who were not fond of Jews. Henry Ward Beecher preached against it in a sermon that was extensively reprinted and read. One effect of the vulgar incident was the precipitous decline of the Stewart department store.

The death of Joseph Seligman in 1880 made his brother Jesse head of the firm. He floated numerous railroad securities as well as stock in other enterprises. He, too, suffered the indignity of anti-Semitism in 1883 when the Union League Club, of which he had long been a member, changed its policy and blackballed the application of his son Theodore, causing him to resign in protest.

By the late 1890's other Jewish banking firms had spurted ahead of the Seligmans in initiative and ability. However, the Seligmans got a windfull when Will Durant, having been rejected by G. W. Perkins of the Morgan company and told to seek "a Jewish house," arranged with them to organize the General Motors Corporation.

Goldman, Sachs and Company began as modestly as the Seligmans. Marcus Goldman started out as a peddler of notions on reaching this country in 1848 but soon opened a clothing store in Philadelphia. At the end of the Civil War, persuaded by his wife to move to New York, he opened a part-time banking office in a cellar. He visited merchants in jewelry and leather goods during the morning, lent them cash on promisory notes at a discount, tucked the notes into the inner band of his capacious silk hat, and then called on commercial banks to dicker about the purchase of his notes. Before long he was able to sell up to five million of commercial paper annually, and six times that amount by 1880. Goldman took Samuel Sachs, his son-in-law, into his firm.

After Henry Goldman had replaced his father as head of the company, he arranged with his friend Phillip Lehman to cooperate in the financing and reorganization of industrial companies. Among the numerous corporations they refinanced were Underwood, Studebaker, Woolworth, and Continental Can. Henry's pro-German bias during World War I produced a rift between him and Samuel Sachs, causing a severance of the partnership. Not till much later, when Sidney Weinberg, who had risen from office boy, became head of the firm, did Goldman, Sachs again become a prominent banking house. It was Weinberg, after Henry Ford's death, who arranged for the large private issue of Ford stock and devised the complex nature of the relationship between the corporation and the Ford Foundation. His influence in Wall Street and in Washington was notable to the end of his life in 1969.

Henry, the first of the Lehman brothers, arrived in Mobile in 1844 and opened a dry goods store. By 1850 his younger brothers Emanuel and Mayer had joined him and engaged in cotton brokerage in Montgomery. Henry died of yellow fever in 1855, but the younger brothers continued to expand their enterprise and Emanuel opened an office in New York to handle the commercial bills of exchange which they obtained from their sales of cotton. The Civil War almost stopped their marketing of cotton; Emanuel received only small amounts shipped north through the blockade. Both brothers favored the South, and Emanuel went to London to sell Confederate bonds.

After the war the brothers resumed their cotton brokerage, with offices in Montgomery and New Orleans as well as New York. In 1868 Mayer joined Emanuel in New York, where much of the financing of cotton was handled. They well supplemented each other—Emanuel was cautious and Mayer bold. From cotton they expanded their activities to such other commodities, as coffee, petroleum, rubber, and automobiles. When Philip, Emanuel's son, took control of the firm, he greatly broadened its scope and, as we have seen, he collaborated with Henry Goldman, of Goldman, Sachs, in the refinancing of large corporations. Over the years the firm of Lehman Brothers remained a highly successful and increasingly prestigious investment banking house.

Of the several other existing Jewish banking houses—among them J. S. Bache and Company; Hallgarten and Company; Carl M. Loeb, Rhoades and Company; and Wertheim and Company—the one destined to become largest and most prominent, Kuhn, Loeb and Company, was started in 1867 by four partners: A. Kuhn, J. Netter, S. Loeb, and S. Wolf, all related by marriage. Solomon Loeb was from the first the most active member of the firm. He had emigrated from Germany to Cincinnati in 1849 and was soon a successful clothing merchant. After the Civil War, his young and ambitious second wife objected to living in "Porkopolis," as Cincinnati was then called, and insisted on moving to New York, where her husband could enter banking. Indeed, Solomon then had a capital of a half million dollars. With the nation recuperating from the terrible war and expanding in every direction, the new investment house shared in the hectic prosperity. Loeb's caution, however, limited the scope of the firm's business. In the 1880's Jacob Schiff succeeded him as senior partner, and under him Kuhn, Loeb and Company soared into the upper reaches of American finance. The four partners most intimately connected with Schiff were Otto H. Kahn, Felix M. Warburg (who was married to Schiff's daughter), Paul M. Warburg (who was married to Loeb's daughter), and Schiff's son, Mortimer.

Otto H. Kahn (1867–1934), born in Germany, went to London in 1888 to work in the Speyer bank. Five years later he was transferred to New York, and in 1897 joined Kuhn, Loeb. A shrewd banker, he was deeply interested in music and the theater and lavished his money in support of the Metropolitan Opera House and various theatrical enterprises. Judaism had only a feeble hold on him, but Hitler's harangues in the 1920's kept him within the fold.

Felix M. Warburg (1871–1937), who entered the firm in the same year as Kahn, was both an able banker and a warmhearted Jew. Scion of an old and distinguished banking family, he worked for his maternal grandfather, a jewel merchant. In

1895 he married Frieda Schiff and joined Kuhn, Loeb at the invitation of his father-in-law. More than any other partner he devoted himself to philanthropy. While serving as a commissioner of education he was instrumental in bringing trained nurses into the New York public schools. For years he was president of YMHA. He was chairman of the Joint Distribution Committee from 1914 to 1932 and a founder of the Palestine Economic Corporation.

Paul M. Warburg (1868–1932) studied finance in London and Paris before entering the family bank in 1895. He married Nina J. Loeb and joined Kuhn, Loeb in New York in 1902. Some years later he worked with Senator Nelson W. Aldrich on the proposed federal reserve system, a monumental project enacted into law in 1913. Shortly after World War I he founded the International Acceptance Bank. He was active in philanthropic causes and wrote three outstanding studies of banking.

Schiff's son Mortimer (1877–1931) did his best to live up to his father's expectations both as banker and philanthropist. In the 1900's he assumed more and more of his father's functions on the boards of various institutions, and after the latter's death Mortimer emulated him in his role as the most generous philanthropist in American Jewry.

These several bankers and other wealthy Jews of the period very early began to contribute to philanthropic and cultural institutions, having from childhood been indoctrinated to consider charity as a moral obligation. They enjoyed luxury and indulged their appetites, but they also made literature and music an integral part of their leisure. Intensely loyal Americans, they took pride in the freedom and tolerance they were enjoying in the land of their adoption; traditionally devoted to family life, they practiced an exceptional intimacy with their numerous relations. Prince André Poniatowsky, who visited New York in 1892, was impressed by the striking differences between the Jewish and non-Jewish banking communities:

I was profoundly surprised at the time by the contrast that their private lives offered to those of most bankers and businessmen of Anglo-Saxon ancestry whom I met in

America that year. In Wall Street, their financial power placed them all on an almost equal level with the big Anglo-Saxon bankers. Money itself, however, had no significance for them outside of business. Any observer would have taken them for good *rentiers*, given to sport, literature, art, and especially to music, who contributed generously to charity.

4
Jacob
H.
Schiff

FINANCIER
AND
PHILANTHROPIST

JACOB H. SCHIFF was a member of an illustrious German-Jewish family, with a recorded history of five centuries. Among his forebears were Meir Schiff (Maharam), a brilliant Talmudic scholar of the seventeenth century, and Tevele Schiff, chief rabbi of London's Great Synagogue in the eighteenth century. His father, a broker for the Rothschilds, was a strictly religious man who inoculated his piety in his children.

Born on January 10, 1847, Jacob went to an Orthodox school, where he studied Hebrew and the Old Testament along with German grammar and other secular subjects. At fourteen he went to work in a mercantile house and then later with a banking firm. When he was eighteen he wrote to a friend of his father in St. Louis to ask about employment in the United States where he could keep the Sabbath "because I am inclined by principle to devout religious observance."

64

He reached New York in 1865 and began to work for the brokerage house of Frank and Gans. A year later he and a friend opened their own office under the name of Budge, Schiff and Company. The business thrived, and in 1870 Schiff became an American citizen; two years later he joined the Chamber of Commerce. The partnership was dissolved in 1873 because both men decided to return to Germany for family reasons, Schiff to visit his recently widowed mother. In Frankfurt he met A. Kuhn, who invited him to return to New York and join Kuhn, Loeb, which he did in 1875. That May he married Loeb's daughter Therese and received a full partnership as a wedding present. His increasingly successful activities during the ensuing decade placed him at the head of the firm when his father-in-law retired.

Between the end of the Civil War and the 1900's the railroads dominated the activities of the leading investment houses. Readily available European capital was used to expand railway mileage in every part of the country and to juggle companies and managements for greater concentration and more centralized control. In the unavoidable rivalry new railroads and branches were laid in competition with existing ones, in more than one instance stretching out over uninhabited prairies and doomed to failure. Financiers found ready backers even for these needless railroads and investors suffered from unscrupulous manipulators and executives. Regardless of eventualities, however, the investment bankers usually received their commissions and special emoluments. The chief financial underwriter for the railroads was J. P. Morgan, who combined solid knowledge with bold action; his biggest rival was Jacob H. Schiff.

Schiff had begun early to concentrate on railroad developments. He rode on trains in every direction, talked to employees and managers, evaluated the prospects of each line as well as its shortcomings. Simultaneously he studied the men heading the various railroads and cultivated the friendship of the most dynamic leaders. His exceptional grasp of economic conditions made his business judgment supremely accurate.

As early as 1877 he became intimate with the president of Chicago and Northwestern; he refinanced the railroad successfully; was awarded a fee of a half million dollars, and soon became the financier of more than a dozen railroads, large and small.

In 1894 Kuhn, Loeb financed the purchase of Chesapeake Securities by Illinois Central, of which E. H. Harriman was a vice-president. Schiff had known Harriman for a decade and respected his great ability and greater ambition. A year later, when Harriman went after control of the Union Pacific, the transcontinental railway which had been financed by the federal government, and which now owed it $60 million and was in difficulties—a "battered, bankrupt and decrepit" railroad. Schiff undertook the financial reorganization of the railroad, which took three years to accomplish but became a highly profitable operation and placed Kuhn, Loeb among the leading investment houses. Schiff then helped Harriman obtain control of the Southern Pacific and other adjacent railroads, which he united with the Union Pacific.

Schiff was in the middle of the titanic struggle at the turn of the century between James J. Hill and Harriman for control of the northwestern railroads. In the resulting compromise he enhanced his prestige as a banker and fighter. Although Hill and he had been close friends since 1886, and the bouncy magnate had often dined in the Schiff home, Hill was not always a man of his word and dealt mostly with Morgan. When Harriman sought to acquire the Chicago, Burlington and Quincy to keep it from competing with the Union Pacific, Hill tried to outmaneuver him. Schiff, who believed in cooperation rather than in competition and preached the principle of "community of interest" to both men, tried to enlist Morgan's help to stop the increasingly ruinous rivalry, but the latter made no effort to control Hill. Schiff and Harriman thereupon decided to undercut Hill by buying heavily into Northern Pacific. Hill, with Morgan's help, bought every available share, driving the price up and causing a panic among speculators who were caught short. Schiff was in a good position to benefit from this scurry for shares, but for the sake of peace he halted the panic and the men compromised, Harriman gaining a seat on the board of the newly formed Northern Securities Holding Company. To Ernest Cassel, his intimate banking friend in London, Schiff wrote in November, 1901: "I believe the whole arrangement is of the greatest importance and advantage to the Union Pacific, and justifies in every way our attempt last spring to preserve the Union Pacific from damage." In 1903, when the government sought to dissolve the Northern Securities Holding Company as a trust, Theodore Roosevelt called Schiff to the White House for consultation.

Schiff handled a total of a billion dollars in the financing of the Pennsylvania Railroad in the 40 years of his association with its several successive executives. He was certain that the railroad's entrance into New York would redound to everyone's benefit and readily financed the tunnel under the Hudson River and the magnificent station at its terminal. He even placed a bond issue of $50 million on the Paris Bourse.

Kuhn, Loeb and Company also took part in the financing of a number of mining companies, among them Anaconda Copper Company, and Schiff advised the Guggenheims in their defense against and subsequent conquest of their adversaries on the American Smelting and Refining Company. Kuhn, Loeb also marketed stock issues for street and subway railroad companies, Canadian Pacific, Mexican firms, and various other enterprises. By 1920 it had issued more good investments and fewer bad ones than any other banking house in the United States. Since the securities it handled added up to the billions—1.75 billion during 1900–1905 alone—this record is indeed remarkable.

Heretofore Schiff had been in all his financial transactions primarily the perspicacious investment banker, concerned with enhancing the country's economic growth, benefiting both his clients and the public, and employing his astute investment sense for his own profit. In his loans to Japan during the Russo-Japanese War in 1904 he was as much "the prince of Israel" as he was the private banker. For many years deeply grieved by the persecution of Jews in Russia and outraged by the government's callous encouragement of Jewish oppression, he was determined to take no part in any loans to Russia and to discourage other bankers from making them. In April, 1904 he wrote to Lord Rothschild,

> I pride myself that all the efforts which at various times during the past four or five years have been made by Russia to gain the favor of the American market for its loans, I have been able to bring to naught. . . . May not a like position be counted upon as far as the influential and important banking houses all over Europe are concerned? Unfortunately heretofore, this, you know my Lord, better I do, has not been the case.

In reply Rothschild informed him that his house had refused Russian loans since 1875, but that certain Continental bankers were sometimes compelled by their governments to participate in them.

Schiff was in London when Baron Korekiyo Takahashi came to negotiate a loan to Japan. Conditions in 1904 were not favorable to it, as the outcome of the Russo-Japanese war was still in doubt. When Schiff learned of Takahashi's efforts, he offered to underwrite $50 million, half of the requested loan, thereby assuring its success. His daughter Frieda later explained that it was "not so much my father's interest in Japan, but rather his hatred of Imperial Russia and its anti-Semitic policies that prompted him to take the great financial risk." Later Schiff floated other loans to Japan, totaling $200 million, and Japanese victory made these issues profitable to their investors.

When the Russian emissaries came to Portsmouth, New Hampshire, to arrange the peace terms with the Japa-

nese, certain American Jews thought the occasion oppor-
tune to discuss the problem of the Jews with the Russian
diplomats. Schiff thought otherwise and wrote to Philip
Cowen,

> I have been urged to meet Mr. Witte and Baron Rosen, to
> discuss with them Jewish affairs, but I have fought shy of
> them. First, because I know it can do no good; secondly,
> because I do not wish to have it said that I went to discuss
> Russian finance with Mr. Witte. There is one thing we
> can do: To give as hard knocks to Russia as we can, when-
> ever the opportunity offers, to accept no promises in return
> for our aid, when this is asked for, and to do nothing for
> Russia until she has *actually* given civil rights to her Jew-
> ish subjects.

In 1905 the Japanese government awarded Schiff the
Star of the Second Order of the Sacred Treasure. The next
year, it invited him for an extended visit to Japan, where
the most important government and banking officials extended their hospitality to him. He was the first private
citizen of a foreign country to be invited by the emperor
for a personal interview and official lunch. On this occasion
he was invested with the insignia of the Order of the Rising
Sun. On his return home he took along Takahashi's fifteen-
year-old daughter and made her a member of his household
during her three years of attendance in American schools.

Staunch in his anti-Russian attitude, Schiff was prepared to suffer financial loss as a consequence. In 1915,
with the war in Europe in full swing and news of Jewish
pogroms and persecution coming from every part of the
Russian war front, Lord Reading came to New York to arrange for a loan to the Allies. Otto Kahn and Mortimer
Schiff were strongly in favor of participating in the loan,
but Jacob Schiff said he would agree to it only if assured
that none of the money went to Russia. When Lord Reading could not give the assurance, Schiff told his junior
partners, who favored the loan,

I realize fully what is at stake for the firm of Kuhn, Loeb and Co. in the decision we are going to make. But come what may, I cannot run counter to my conscience, I cannot sacrifice my profoundest convictions for the sake of whatever business advantage. I cannot stultify myself by aiding those who in bitter enmity have tortured my people and will continue to do so, whatever fine professions they may make in their hour of need. I cannot sacrifice my profoundest convictions. This is a matter between me and my conscience.

When Japan entered the war on the side of Russia and sought simultaneously to dominate China, Schiff resigned from the Japan Society, of which he was a founder.

Although Schiff had veered from the orthodoxy of his youth to Reform Judaism, he persisted in keeping the Sabbath, and no business was urgent enough to disturb him on that day. He recited the Friday evening prayers at home, attended services on Saturday morning, and fasted on Yom Kippur to the end of his life. In his general behavior, indeed, he followed the traditional precepts and practices of Judaism.

Brought up in the belief that the world rested on the three pillars of study, prayer, and benevolence, he considered it his religious duty to give a tithe of his income to charity. Usually he gave much more than that, since he considered only that part in excess of the tenth of his earnings to be philanthropy. Great as was his generosity, he shunned publicity. Moreover, unlike those rich men, who start dispensing their wealth only after they have devoted a lifetime to its accumulation, he began giving money to causes he valued as soon as he had it to spare. As early as 1880 his contribution to the United Hebrew Charities headed the list of donations. Thus his philanthropic largess during his active life exceeded in amount his final bequests. In addition, he contributed his time and thought to numerous organizations, serving on their boards to assure their efficient functioning.

Almost no philanthropic cause was omitted from his benevolence. "Long before he had reached the age of fifty," *The Literary Digest* commented at the time of his death, "he was known not only throughout the country, but throughout the world, as one of the greatest financiers and one of the greatest philanthropists." He was particularly interested in the Montefiore Home and Hospital for Chronic Diseases, which he helped establish in 1884 in honor of Moses Montefiore's 100th birthday, and of which he was president to the end of his life. He visited with the patients every Sunday morning he was in the city. On his seventieth birthday he reflected that "I have probably derived greater satisfaction from the work I have been permitted to do in Montefiore Home than from anything it has been my privilege and good fortune to accomplish in my life."

Schiff early became concerned about the plight of Jewish immigrants, who began arriving in increasing numbers after 1880 and experiencing great difficulty in establishing themselves. In 1893 he and several other public-spirited men organized the Educational Alliance, a settlement house in which immigrants were taught English and provided with cultural facilities. The next year he donated a fountain to Rutgers Square, an open square crowded by the East Side poor on summer days. He also supported the Henry Street Settlement and made possible the expanded activity of the Visiting Nurses Service. In 1907, when large numbers of Jews came to this country in their flight from pogroms, he established the Jewish Immigration Information Bureau to encourage newcomers to settle in the less crowded areas of the United States.

Although he gave much time and wealth to the poor and the sick, he was equally generous to religious and educational institutions. In 1886 he volunteered to help the struggling Jewish Theological Seminary, stating that he considered it a privilege to further the advancement of Hebrew scholarship. He was later instrumental in raising a half million dollars for its endowment—providing most of it himself—in addition to giving the money for a new building. When Cyrus Adler tried to evade the presidency of the Seminary because of his work at the Smithsonian Institution, Schiff made him change his mind when he said, "If I can make sacrifices, so can you."

Schiff was a founder of and large contributor to the American Jewish Historical Society and the Jewish Publication Society. He financed the English translation of the Old Testament and established a fund for the publication of Jewish classics, provided money for books to the Jewish Division of the New York Public Library; donated the Semitic Collection and the Semitic Museum building to Harvard University, and the Semitic library to the Library of Congress; established a chair in social economy at Columbia University, and gave Barnard College money for its Student Hall; contributed generously to New York and Cornell Universities. In addition his philanthropy benefited the Salvation Army, the Red Cross, YMCA, YWCA, and other general social services.

Reports of Jewish persecution both angered him and quickened his sympathy for the victims. He contributed large sums for relief after the Kishinev pogrom in 1903 and condemned the outrage in public meeting, calling upon the American government to protest to Russia. Jewish suffering during World War I caused him to open his purse wide. When Henry Morgenthau, American ambassador to Turkey, cabled from Constantinople about the plight of Jews in Palestine, Schiff quickly collected $50,000 for their relief. With the funds of the Jewish Colonization Society blocked in Germany, he advanced the society $200,000. A founder of the Joint Distribution Committee, formed to assist Jewish war sufferers, he gave more than half a million dollars and collected a large amount from others, including $100,000 from the Rockefeller Foundation. As conditions worsened he called to "all Jews of every shade of thought, irrespective of the land of their birth," to contribute with the "utmost generosity."

In all his philanthropy Schiff sought to efface himself and refused to permit his name to appear on buildings he donated. This attitude he explained on his 70th birthday: "Nothing it was my privilege to do during my life originated in a desire to earn gratitude, nor do I feel that such has ever been owing to me."

Personal friends of Schiff met frequently at one another's homes. Because they gathered at a different house each time, they called themselves the "Wanderers." All were men of wealth, and all were concerned about the increased evidence of anti-Semitism, in particular the Dreyfus case in France, the anti-Jewish agitation in Germany, and even more the Kishinev pogrom in Russia. Out of these informal meetings came a call for a nationwide organization of an American Jewish Committee "to prevent infringement of the civil and religious rights of Jews, and to alleviate the consequences of persecution."

Most of the members of the Committee were of Germanic origin and tended to patronize the afflicted East-European Jews they sought to protect. As often happens in such relationships, they soon generated an emotional and intellectual dichotomy between themselves and the mass of Jews who resented their patrons' condescension. The cleavage was deepest on the subject of Americanization. A half century and more of residence in the United States, with concomitant prosperity, had developed in the German Jews an intense loyalty to their adopted land, and a tendency toward assimilation. Jews from Eastern Europe, most of whom came to the United States after 1900 and had brought with them keen memories of persecution along with their deep-seated Jewish aspirations, were much slower to undergo the Americanization process. They clung to their Yiddish speech, delighted in the efflorescence of Yiddish writing, voiced radical ideas, and dreamed of Zionism, much to the annoyance of their patrons. The more articulate of the Russian Jews, sensitive to the implied superiority on part of the Committee, became openly antagonistic.

Although more tolerant than most of his fellow members toward the cultural mores and aspirations of the Russian Jews, Schiff was too much the loyal American to acquiesce in the Zionistic agitation, fearing that it might be construed as un-American. To him Jewishness was primarily a religious concept. Writing to Professor Schechter in 1904 about the death of Theodor Herzl, the Zionist leader, he said, "What poor Doctor Herzl believed he had accomplished amounted to naught—and that the plans he wished to carry through were entirely impracticable and utopian." Later, having learned that Schechter had joined the Zionist movement, he wrote,

> Speaking as an American I cannot for a moment concede that one can be at the same time a true American and an honest adherent of the Zionist movement. . . . The Jew should not for a moment feel that he has only found an "asylum" in this country; he must not feel that he is an exile and that his abode here is only a temporary or passing one.

For all his genuine good will toward his fellow Jews, he failed to perceive the complexity of modern Judaism. Moreover, his objections to Zionism, while arising from laudable motives, were more emotional than realistic. It was common knowledge that Palestine was not only very difficult to obtain as a homeland for the Jews but was able to support only a fraction of the then twelve million Jews; at most it could serve only as an asylum for those who had become second-class citizens in the lands of their birth. Yet opposed as Schiff was to Zionism, in 1908 he contributed $100,000 to the establishment of the Technium in Haifa, and gave money to other worthy projects in Palestine.

The cleavage between the Germans and Russian Jews

came into the open with the intensification of World War I and the increased suffering of the Jews in the Russian war zone. With Turkey fighting on the side of Germany and ripe for dismemberment, Zionists everywhere—and they now included Jewish leaders throughout the world—were exerting themselves to obtain an Allied promise of a Jewish homeland in Palestine. In the United States, in 1915 the strongest neutral power, the Zionists and other Jewish groups wanted to call a congress of all Jewish organizations to discuss the problems of relief and rehabilitation. The American Jewish Committee opposed the idea, feeling capable of handling such matters by itself and fearing that the discussion of Zionism would bring the accusation of hyphenism, or lack of loyalty to America.

Schiff, the Committee's most prominent member, who had been accused of being pro-German and therefore was acutely sensitive about his American loyalty, publicly stated his opposition to both the congress and Zionism. "We stand at the parting of the ways," he maintained. "Are we to be American Jews or Jews who happen to dwell in America? . . . I feel, my friends, that unless we live our Judaism as a religion, and as a people in America feel that we are Americans, our posterity may become subjected to great prejudice and to great moral suffering." Then, according to his biographer Cyrus Adler, he added, "If the Jews in Russia and the Jews of Poland would not have been kept as a separate people by themselves, by discriminatory laws, the prejudices and persecution to which they have been subjected would not have reached the stage to which we all regret it has unfortunately come." The newspaper version of this statement, in both English and Yiddish, was quite different: "If the Jews in Russia and the Jews in Poland had not kept themselves apart, had not insisted on a separate language, the tragedies and persecution to which they had been subjected would not have reached such stages."

The cruel irony of the published version infuriated the Russian Jews who knew from bitter experience that they had been forcefully confined in the Pale of Settlement and compelled to live in practical isolation. The Yiddish press reacted vehemently in denunciation.

Schiff was stunned by the attack and rejected it with bitterness. "Think of my being accused of disloyalty—I who for twenty-five years, single-handed, struggled against the invasion of the Russian government into American money markets and to this day have staved them off." In his anger he stated that although he had all his adult life "been seeking the good of my people" and would persist in serving them,

> I say this by way of valedictory: I have been hurt to the core, and hereafter Zionism, Nationalism, and the Congress movement, and Jewish politics, in whatever form they may come up, will be a sealed book to me. . . . I shall continue to work for the uplift of my people; I shall continue to cooperate as far as I can in procuring full civil rights for our brethren in the war zone, especially in Poland, Russia, Rumania, and Palestine, for they are all flesh of my flesh and bone of my bone. But beyond this, my friends, my duty ends.

On rethinking the situation, he concluded that, with the core of Judaism in Eastern Europe practically destroyed, Palestine would be a logical asylum for the survivors. Continuing to reason in religious terms, he insisted on "Zion" without the "ism." In writing to Israel Zangwill at the time he said that in view of "these unexpected occurrences," it might be desirable to have in Palestine "a gathering together there of the best elements among our people, to give them an opportunity to further develop all that is so desirable for the great world to get from the Jews." He expressed this revised attitude in an address in April, 1917.

> It has come to me, while thinking over events of recent weeks—and the statement may surprise many—that

the Jewish people should at last have a homeland of their own. I do not mean by that there should be a Jewish nation. I am not a believer in a Jewish nation built on all kinds of issues, with egotism as the first, and agnosticism and atheism among the others. But I am a believer in the Jewish people and in the mission of the Jew, and I believe that somewhere there should be a great reservoir of Jewish learning in which Jewish culture might be furthered and developed, unhampered by the materialism of the world, and might spread its beautiful ideals over the world.

And, naturally, that land should be Palestine. If that ever develops—and the present war may bring the development of this ideal nearer—it will not be accomplished in a day or a year, and in the meantime it is our duty to keep the flame of Judaism burning brightly.

His opposition to political Zionism he maintained to the end. In March, 1919 he wrote to Simon Wolf to assure him he was no Zionist, adding, "However, I have always strongly sympathized with certain phases of Zionism, those which tended to stimulate interest in Judaism among Jews who would otherwise have been entirely indifferent to Jewish history, Jewish life, and Jewish traditions." He praised the Zionist leaders, "from Herzl down," for having "awakened in the Jew self-respect, self-consciousness, and perfectly justifiable race pride," but maintained that the task ahead was economic rather than political if the homeland was to become a reality.

Schiff was able to give his time to civic and philanthropic interests because he had trained his younger associates to relieve him of all routine affairs. In the late 1890's he wrote to Cassel, "I do not trouble myself much any more about the daily routine, and I must say that the younger partners, Heinsheimer, Kahn, Felix Warburg and James Loeb, take great pains to relieve me of details." This was especially true of Felix Warburg and, after 1900, of Schiff's son Mortimer, both of whom participated in his philan-thropic activities and often represented him on boards and at meetings.

In August, 1919, on his annual vacation in Maine, he overstrained his heart while mountain climbing, but per-sisted in his usual activities. In September, 1920 he de-termined to fast on Yom Kippur despite his debilitated con-dition. He died two days later. The funeral service at Tem-ple Emanu-El attracted tens of thousands, many of them bearded Jews from the East Side who had come to honor and mourn the man who had long been their benefactor and friend. Comments from every part of the world and from men in the highest stations paid tribute to the pass-ing of a great man. Most apt, perhaps, was the one from Charles W. Eliot, long an intimate friend.

I have never met a keener intelligence, a more sym-pathetic yet discriminatory maker of gifts large and small, a truer disciple of the nameless Good Samaritan, or a more grateful patriot, Jewish and American combined.

JEWS AS
BUSINESS LEADERS

In the second half of the nineteenth century many Central-European Jewish immigrants started their lives in America as peddlers, subsequently to become owners of clothing factories and department stores, helping to revolutionize American dress, shopping practices, and the general consumer economy. These immigrant peddlers filled a need in the life of farmers and villagers who had no ready access to stores. In the South particularly, where the plantation economy did not further the development of urban shopping centers, the peddler, on foot and with horse and wagon, enjoyed the hospitality and patronage of both the planter's family and his slaves.

Before long the more enterprising peddlers opened stores in central locations, both in sparsely populated county seats and in the larger, established cities. Their emporiums expanded in size and in the variety of goods along with the growth of the nation as a whole.

The Civil War, and the demand for tens of thousands of uniforms to fit men of various dimensions, encouraged a rough standardization of sizes for men, and in time for women as well. As a result, most men and a good many women ceased patronizing tailors and dressmakers, buying ready-made clothes at less cost. By the end of the century, men's suits and overcoats, for instance, were being manufactured by such familiar firms as Hart, Schaffner & Marx, Kuppenheimer, Hickey-Freeman, Stein-Bloch, and Rosenberg's Fashion Park—all owned and operated by Jews. "Levis," trousers of exceptional strength originally produced by Levi Strauss for California miners, became popular on farms and in factories. This general sartorial development caused class distinctions in dress practically to disappear, so that there came to be little difference in appearance between clerk and manager.

As some of the more ambitious Jewish storekeepers gradually added to their wares, their small shops became large department stores. They were not of course alone in this form of enterprise, as was evidenced by such non-Jews as A. T. Stewart and R. H. Macy in New York, John Wanamaker in Philadelphia, and J. L. Hudson in Detroit. Compared to the population as a whole, however, Jews loomed large in the field of merchandising. Of the current 50 largest department stores in the United States, at least half were founded or taken over by Jews.

Adam Gimbel (1817–1896) migrated from Bavaria in 1835, peddled notions in the Mississippi Valley, and opened a general store in Vincennes, Indiana. As his seven sons grew up he helped them establish stores in other cities. Jacob and Isaak went first to Danville, Illinois, then to Milwaukee, where they started one of the first modern department stores in the Middle West. In 1894 they opened another store in Philadelphia, with their brother Charles in control. And in 1910 the brothers established a large store in New York. They bought Saks and Company in 1923, and three years later Kaufman and Baer in Pittsburgh. Even earlier they had opened their store in Chicago; subsequently they established a branch of Saks-Fifth Avenue in Beverly Hills. Best known among the younger members of the family were Charles Gimbel (1861–1932), who was active in Jewish philanthropy in Philadelphia, and Bernard F. Gimbel (1885–1959), son of Isaak, who headed the family interests after 1927, and became a nationally prominent citizen and benefactor.

Benjamin Bloomingdale also came from Bavaria, in 1837, and also started out as a peddler. After the Civil War his son Lyman (1841–1905) joined him in the manufacture of hoop skirts. In 1872 Lyman and his brother Joseph (1842–1904) opened a dry goods store in New York, which was gradually expanded into the Bloomingdale Brothers department store in 1886. Lyman was active in Jewish charities and founder of a tuberculosis sanitarium. Joseph, equally generous-spirited, was a founder of the Hebrew Technical Institute and of Barnard College, and an active trustee of the Young Men's Hebrew

Association. Emanuel Bloomingdale (1852–1928), joined his older brothers in the management of the business, practiced law, and participated in politics and local charities.

Benjamin Altman (1840–1913) was a successful merchant of quality goods. After working in his father's small dry-goods store, he and his brother Morris opened a store of their own; upon Morris's death in 1876, Benjamin became sole owner. In 1906 he was bold enough to move his store to its present location at Fifth Avenue and 34th Street, at that time a considerable distance from the city's central shopping center. He was an art collector whose works of art were valued at $20 million at the time of his death in 1913. He bequeathed his collection to the Metropolitan Museum of Art, together with an endowment of $150,000 for its maintenance. He also established the Altman Foundation, with stock worth $30 million, for assistance to charitable and educational institutions, and left numerous bequests to individual employees.

Louis Bamberger (1855–1944) and Felix Fuld (1869–1929) were brothers-in-law who opened a small department store in Newark in 1892. By aggressive promotion they succeeded in making it the largest and most successful department store in New Jersey, with sales reaching $35 million in 1928, a year before they sold the business to R. H. Macy and Company. Bamberger was a generous employer as well as a benevolent citizen. He established a pension system for the store's employees, and in 1939 distributed a million dollars in cash and annuities to 236 of the older workers. He contributed $700,000 to the Newark Art Museum and $100,000 each to Beth Israel Hospital and the Jewish Agricultural Corporation. In 1930, a year after Fuld's death, he and Mrs. Fuld donated $5 million to the establishment of the Institute of Advanced Study in Princeton; additional amounts were added later. Fuld, too, was generous during his lifetime, giving around $2 million to hospitals and other charitable institutions.

Edward A. Filene (1860–1937), director of William Filene and Sons Company, the large Boston Department store founded by his father, was distinguished as a reformer and philanthropist. During his first two decades in business he had concentrated on the successful operation of the store. Thereafter, for more than thirty years, he devoted much of his time to civic reform and charity. In 1904 he pioneered in the establishment of credit unions. One of the founders of the U. S. Chamber of Commerce and the International Chamber of Commerce, he was a prime mover in the advocacy of ethical practices in business, and his work for peace brought him honors from several countries.

In 1922 he established the Twentieth Century Fund for the purpose of making social and economic studies. A decade later he gave a million dollars to the Consumers' Distribution Corporation to further consumer cooperatives. He was an active founder of the Good Will Fund, the American Association of Labor Legislation, the National Institute of Public Affairs, the Society for the Advancement of Management, and was president of the National Recovery Board of New England in 1933–34.

His younger brother A. Lincoln Filene (1865–1959) was equally active in the direction of the family business, becoming chairman in 1941, and long warmly interested in civic and communal affairs.

Louis E. Kirstein (1867–1942) was closely affiliated with the Filene brothers, joining them in 1911 as the firm's vice-president. A member of the original National Labor Board, he was also associated with NRA and an adviser to the Department of Commerce. An outstanding Jewish leader, he was chairman of the executive committee of the American Jewish Committee (1941–42) and active in the United Jewish Appeal, the Jewish Welfare Board, the Graduate School of Jewish Social Work, and other institutions. He donated the Kirstein Memorial Public Library, specializing in business subjects, in memory of his parents.

The most prominent of the merchant families was fathered by Lazarus Straus. His Alsatian grandfather, Jacob Lazar, was a member of the Sanhedrin convoked by Napoleon in 1806. He was a wealthy landowner who took the name of Straus when the French government ordered each family to

give itself a cognomen. In 1852 his grandson Lazarus, impoverished and discouraged after the 1848 revolution, in which he
had been a participant, decided to migrate to the United States.
After a brief period as a peddler in Georgia, he settled in the
town of Talbotton, where he opened a store and, within two
years, saved enough money to bring over his wife and children.
The only Jew in Talbotton, he carried on his merchandising
with unquestioned honesty and saw to the education of his
growing boys. In 1863, irritated by the emergence of anti-
Jewish feeling among his townsmen, previously mentioned, he
moved to Columbus, where he remained until the end of the
war; when Northern soldiers and local rabble pillaged his cotton goods, he decided to settle in New York.

Lazarus's oldest son Isidor (1845–1912) had gone to
Europe in 1863 as secretary to a Confederate mission, which
failed. On his own and possessed of a keen sense of business,
he managed to sell Confederate bonds and participate in other
projects, so that by the time he returned to New York at the
end of the war he had saved a considerable sum. With this
capital he and his father entered the crockery and glassware
business. In 1874, Isidor and his brother Nathan (1848–1931)
obtained a concession in the basement crockery department of
the store owned by R. H. Macy. When Macy retired in 1887,
the brothers bought his equity and became owners of the entire store. Thereafter they expanded the business in every direction until it became the largest and one of the most profitable
stores in the world. The two brothers also became partners in
the Abraham and Straus department store, started in Brooklyn
in 1888.

Isidor actively engaged in civic affairs and politics. As a
friend of Grover Cleveland, he helped his campaign for the
Presidency in 1884, and he himself served in Congress in
1894–95. He was a founder of the Reform Club and a vice-
president of the New York Chamber of Commerce. In the
Jewish community he was president of the Educational Alliance from 1893 to the end of his life, a trustee of Montefiore
Hospital, and a founder of the American Jewish Committee.

A passenger on the *Titanic*, he and his wife refused to be saved at the expense of others crowning a useful life with a noble ending.

The death of his older brother caused Nathan Straus great anguish and hastened his decision to yield the direction of the stores to younger members of the family. He began his public career as park commissioner of New York in 1889–1893. During the depression of the early 1890's, he developed a system of relief which combined assistance with a modicum of self-respect: providing food and coal at a cost of only five cents for each. In 1914–1915, when unemployment was again severe, he arranged to serve one-cent meals to many thousands.

His campaign for pasteurized milk made the city of New York, and gradually most of the world, conscious of the need for pasteurization. Appointed health commissioner in 1897, he organized a sterilization plant on Randall's Island and no doubt saved the lives of many children by providing them with germ-free milk. By 1920 there were 297 milk stations in 36 cities.

He became interested in Palestine when he visited there in 1904. Six years later, he initiated public health work to prevent and cure such common diseases as malaria and trachoma, and in 1913 he started a Pasteur Institute in Palestine. In 1915, with war conditions aggravating the poverty of the local Jews, he sent provisions worth $50,000 for their consumption and the next year he sold his yacht to aid war orphans in that country. He also helped establish Hadassah's Child Health Welfare Stations, and later opened health centers in Jerusalem and Tel Aviv. His total donations to the country came to $2 million.

The sons and grandsons of the Straus brothers have carried on both the gigantic business enterprise and some of their philanthropic interests. Jesse I. Straus, son of Isidor, on graduation from Harvard in 1893, joined the store of Abraham and Straus but changed to Macy's three years later and remained there until he headed the firm, resigning in 1933 to assume the American ambassadorship to France. He and his brothers were active in civic and political affairs and gave Straus Hall to Harvard in memory to their parents. Herbert and Percy gave a million dollars to New York University. Jesse's sons Jack and Robert have been active members of the firm and likewise followed the family tradition in benevolence.

Nathan Straus, Jr., distinguished himself as a housing expert and headed the U. S. Housing Authority from 1937 to 1942. His brother Hugh Grant was active in Brooklyn philanthropic institutions. Roger W., son of Oscar Straus, married a Guggenheim daughter and later became president of American Smelting and Refining Company. His son Roger entered the book publishing business and has made a name for himself as the active head of a quality house.

5
Oscar S. Straus

CIVIC LEADER AND DIPLOMAT

OSCAR SOLOMON STRAUS, younger son of Lazarus, was the most distinguished member of his family. Born in Alsace on December 23, 1850, he was brought to Talbotton four years later. His schooling during the eleven years he lived in Georgia was mediocre, and he had to do remedial study in New York to meet the requirements of Columbia College in 1867.

With the support and encouragement of his father and Isidor, Oscar entered Columbia Law School on graduation from college. He received his law degree in 1873, and went into practice with James S. Hudson, a classmate. With some changes in partners he worked hard and successfully, mostly as a trial lawyer, for the next six years. In 1880 his health had so deteriorated—his weight was reduced to 105 pounds—that his doctor urged a change of occupation. After a long rest, he joined the family's china and glassware company, which by that time had expanded considerably making Oscar's legal knowledge a definite asset. Settled in his new career, he married Sarah Lavanburg in 1882 and in time became the father of two daughters and a son.

Oscar Straus early interested himself in civic and Jewish affairs. In 1874 he was a founder of the Young Men's Hebrew Association and was active in its development over the years. Like his older brothers, he also participated in other Jewish activities. His political concern was aroused in 1882 when Tammany leaders refused to renominate Mayor W. R. Grace, and he worked for Grace in opposition to the Tammany candidate. Two years later he campaigned to help Grover Cleveland win the Presidency.

Straus had an aptitude for scholarly research along with a deep interest in the origins of American government. In 1884 he presented the results of his reading and reflection in a discourse at the YMHA entitled "The Origin of the Republican Forms of Government." Encouraged by its favorable reception, he developed his thesis into a book under the same title. It was published in 1885, and was well received.

In his book Straus traced the development of church-state relationships from the time when Constantine united them, through the cynical arrangement during the Reformation of *"cujus regio, ejus religio"* (who governs, his religion), to the opposition of the Puritans to both the Church of England and the king, and finally to the American Revolution and the Constitution. The burden of his discussion was that the development of American government was definitely influenced by the Hebrew Commonwealth at the time of the Judges.

At this early period of mankind—1500 years and more before the Christian era, before Rome had obtained a foothold in history, 500 years before Homer sang, and 1000 years before Plato had dreamt of his ideal republic, when all Western Europe was an untrodden wilderness— the children of Israel on the banks of the Jordan, who had just emerged from centuries of bondage, not only recognized the guiding principles of civil and religious liberty that "all men are created equal," that God and the law are the only kings, but also established a free commonwealth, a pure democratic republic under a written constitution, "a government of the people, by the people, and for the people."

Pursuing this argument, he maintained that the Puritans, believing implicitly in the divine origin of the Old Testament, sought to emulate the ancient Hebrews in the practices of their political theocracy; that their early intolerance was moderated to a vanishing point by the time of the Revolution. (In a later essay he wrote that to the Puritans "Moses was their law-giver, the Pentateuch their code, and Israel under the Judges their ideal of popular government. . . . With the American Puritans especially the Mosaic code and the Hebrew Commonwealth were living realities, so intense was their interest, so earnest was their religious life.") He quoted Samuel Langdon, president of Harvard College, who in 1775 had preached on the nature of the Hebrew Commonwealth: "The civil polity of Israel is doubtless an excellent general model, allowing for some peculiarities; at least, some principal laws and orders of it may be copied in more modern establishments." This sermon had been sent to each minister in Massachusetts as well as to each member of the Congress. To stress the fact that this was a general trend, Straus cited sermons of other important ministers who extolled the democracy of the Hebrews and urged its tenets upon the political leaders.

Straus's interest in religious liberty led him to a study of Roger Williams. Although he continued to give full time to his business affairs, in his leisure hours he steeped himself in the life of the seventeenth-century both in England and New England, reading source materials pertaining to the political and religious perturbations and Williams's role within them, and completing his book on him in 1894. Years later he reminisced, "Of all my books, the *Life of Roger Williams* contains the greatest amount of work in the way of research and study; but the amount of pleasure it gave me in the doing was commensurate."

Straus, having conceived a profound admiration for Williams as a man and libertarian, concluded his study with this encomium:

> We call those men great who have devoted their lives to some noble cause, and have thereby influenced for the better the course of events. Measured by that standard, Roger Williams deserves a high niche in the temple of fame, alongside the greatest reformers who mark epochs in the world's history. He was not the first to discover the principles of religious liberty, but he was the first to proclaim them in all their plenitude, and to found and build up a political community with those principles as the basis of its organization.

Senator A. P. Gorman was so favorably impressed with Straus's book on the origins of American Government that he recommended him to President Cleveland as American minister to Turkey. The president, a friend of the Straus brothers, inquired among Protestant missions to see whether a Jew would be agreeable to them as guardian of their interests in Asia Minor. Henry Ward Beecher replied, "Of his *fitness* there is a general consent that he is personally, and in attainments, eminently excellent." And he continued,

> But I am interested in another quality—the fact that he is a *Hebrew*. The bitter prejudice against Jews, which obtains in many parts of Europe, ought not to receive any countenance in America. It is because he is a Jew that I *would* urge his appointment as a fit recognition of this remarkable people who are becoming large contributors to American prosperity and whose intelligence, morality, and large liberality in all public measures for the welfare of

society, deserve and should receive from the hands of our government some such recognition.

Cleveland's appointment of Straus in 1887 was, moreover, a rebuke to Austria-Hungary for rejecting A. M. Keiley as American minister because his wife was born of Jewish parents. When Straus hesitated to accept the post because of the financial cost, he was assured by his brother Isidor, "Take care of the Turks and the dollars will be looked after in New York."

In Constantinopole Straus at once confronted pressing problems, among them that American missionaries and their schools were being mistreated and persecuted by government officials. Straus quickly perceived that in dealing with Turks, from the Sultan down, one had to be "patient, pleasant, persistent . . . eternally vigilant." By intelligent employment of these qualities he succeeded in gaining their respect and friendship, and thus obtained more favorable treatment for Americans residing in the Turkish empire.

Late in 1887 Baron Maurice de Hirsch, who had built a railroad connecting Constantinople with European cities, came to negotiate a financial controversy between the Sultan and himself. Abdul Hamid suggested to de Hirsch that they employ Straus as the arbitrator at a fee of a million francs. Although the State Department was agreeable, Straus refused the fee but offered his services gratis. His handling of the claims was accepted by both men. Now favored, he had no difficulty in obtaining the Sultan's permission for a Babylonian excavation by Dr. J. P. Peters of the University of Pennsylvania. Later, when nearly 300 American schools were in danger of being closed by a new interpretation of a Turkish law, Straus persuaded the Grand Visier to waive the new requirements.

When Straus visited Palestine late in 1887, he learned that some 300 Jews of foreign birth were arbitrarily imprisoned in Jerusalem. When the vali of that city wished to honor him, Straus rejected the offer and told him that the jailing of these men was contrary to the treaty with the great powers and threatened to report the vali to the Sultan. The hapless Jews were liberated and Straus entered Jerusalem in the proferred carriage. In a meeting with the vali he obtained assurance of fair treatment of Jews in the future.

Straus's friendly association with Baron de Hirsch brought about the American establishment of the Baron de Hirsch Fund, the Trade School, and the Clara de Hirsch Home for Working Girls, with millions of dollars donated to help Jewish immigrants to become farmers or craftsmen.

When President Cleveland failed of re-election in 1888, Straus resigned his post, despite many requests from American missions that he remain. He had been spending nearly $40,000 a year on a salary of $7,500 and felt it was time to return to his place in the family business. Shortly before he was to leave Constantinople the Russian ambassador invited him to visit Russia on the way back. When Straus reminded him that as a Jew he would not be allowed to do so, the ambassador secured for him a special passport reading, "The Jew Oscar Straus is permitted to enter Russia for three months." Straus did not take advantage of this special favor.

By now a man of national prominence, Straus found himself involved in various current affairs. He served on a committee of leading Jews who called on President Harrison urging him to protest against Russia's maltreatment of Jews. In 1891 he was instrumental in incorporating the clause on silver in the New York Democratic platform, and he helped nominate Cleveland for the Presidency in Chicago a year later. He was a founder of the American Jewish Historical Society in 1892 and served as its president until 1898.

During this period he also found time for research and writing, completing his study of Roger Williams and a companion work entitled *Religious Liberty in the United States* (1896). Here he once more lauded Williams for accomplishing what no one before him "had the courage and wisdom, combined with the conviction of the broadest liberty, even to attempt: to found a purely secular state."

As an advocate of sound money, Straus opposed the nomination of William Jennings Bryan and broke with the Democratic party by voting for William McKinley. When the massacre of Armenians in 1897 shocked the civilized world, McKinley, who had been consulting with Straus on occasion, told him it was his duty to return to Turkey as American minister, as he was "the only man in the United States who could save the situation." McKinley also asked his advice on the Cuban situation, then greatly agitated, and Straus suggested Spanish suzerainty over Cuba as a likely solution, but the sinking of the *Maine* precipitated war with Spain.

Meantime American relations with Turkey had further deteriorated. The Sultan refused American claims for property destroyed during the massacres, and Americans in Turkey were clamoring for American warships to back up their claims. McKinley again requested Straus to take the post. Straus, who had been reluctant, now accepted, fearing another *Maine* incident if American ships were sent there, and certain that the difficulties with Abdul Hamid could be resolved by diplomacy alone. McKinley agreed to be advised by him so far as Turkey was concerned. "I shall be guided by you; I shall support you; I have confidence in your ability and foresight. No vessel will be sent to Turkey unless you demand them, and then, only then, will they be sent."

Straus was soon again on good terms with the Sultan. With canny diplomacy he proposed international arbitration of the American claims, knowing the Sultan would reject the proposal because it would have exposed his complicity in the Armenian massacres, thereby forcing him to settle the claims himself. By sending an open cable to the State Department that he was giving American missionaries diplomatic permission to travel, he compelled Turkey to remove the harassing restrictions which kept American citizens, as well as those of other powers, from traveling to their destinations in Asia Minor. Even more important, he succeeded in getting the Sultan to request Mohammedan tribes in the Philippines to cooperate with the American army of occupation, a step which no doubt prevented a holy war and saved many lives. He achieved this friendly act on the part of Abdul Hamid, following M. M. Noah's example, by reading to him the American Treaty with Tripoli of 1796 which stated that the United States "is not in any sense founded on the Christian religion" and was tolerant of all faiths.

Having satisfactorily settled all major problems with Turkey by the end of 1900, Straus again resigned. McKinley praised his services both officially and personally: "No one else could have done so well; you have done better than I thought it possible for any one to do." Praise from eminent Americans and honorary degrees awaited him on his return. Missionary officials were particularly enthusiastic. W. W. Howard, one of their leaders, wrote,

> Oscar S. Straus, a Jew, has done more for the Christian missions of Turkey than any United States minister ever sent out from Washington. . . . In his opinion a missionary has as much right as a merchant to the protection of the United States Government.

In Vienna on his way home Straus met Theodor Herzl and advised him to deal directly with the Sultan in his effort to obtain a charter of settlement in Palestine.

Straus was also on friendly terms with McKinley's successor, Theodore Roosevelt, and when an American vacancy occurred in 1902 on the Permanent Court of Arbitration at The Hague, Roosevelt offered him the appointment. Straus served on the Court with distinction and was reappointed in 1908, 1912, and 1920.

When persecution of Jews in Rumania intensified at the turn of the century, Straus joined Jacob Schiff in petitioning Roosevelt to issue a protest; Secretary of State Hay sent a note to the powers signatory to the Treaty of

Berlin stating that in view of Rumania's harassment of Jews the United States was unwilling to negotiate a treaty of naturalization with her. The pogrom in Kishinev in 1903 likewise aroused strong indignation and criticism. Roosevelt invited Straus and two other Jewish leaders to his home in Oyster Bay and arranged to send an open cable of protest to the American chargé d'affaires in St. Petersburg, thus giving wide publicity to the American attitude despite the Czar's refusal to accept the protest.

At this time Straus published an article in *The North American Review* demonstrating the fallacy of the "traditional friendship" between Russia and the United States. In a review of the relationship of the two nations from the time of Catherine II to Nicholas II, he offered evidence of Russia's persistent policy of self-interest and concluded, "To infer that the United States is under obligation of gratitude to Russia for any special acts of friendship shown, other than such as the laws of neutrality have imposed, is to substitute a myth and the fulsome language of ceremonial functions for historical facts."

Straus was a member of Roosevelt's "kitchen cabinet" and was in frequent consultation with him. As appreciative of Straus's good sense and practical wisdom as McKinley had been, Roosevelt declared in 1904, "I have had from Mr. Straus aid that I can not overestimate, for which I can not too much express my gratitude, in so much of the diplomatic work that has arisen in this administration—aid by suggestion, aid by actual work in helping me to carry out suggestions."

In 1906 Roosevelt offered Straus the office of Secretary of Commerce and Labor, telling him, "I want you to be a member of my Cabinet. I have a very high estimate of your character, your judgment, and your ability, and I want you for personal reasons. There is still another reason: I want to show Russia and some other countries what we think of the Jews in this country." This significant gesture was fully noticed by the world at large. Straus assumed office in December, having severed all business connection beforehand.

He was exceptionally well prepared for his new duties. His legal and merchandising activities had given him solid commercial experience, and he was equally at home in the field of labor. As a founder of the National Civic Federation in 1900 he had promoted voluntary conciliation between employers and labor unions, maintaining that "industrial peace, to be permanent, cannot rest upon force, but must rest on justice, and in essential industries especially, upon a high sense of responsibility to the public by both employers and employed." On intimate terms both with industrialists and with labor leaders, he made good use of these friendships during his tenure in office.

Immigration issues occupied much of his attention. Japanese in California were being subjected to harassment and molestation by an unfriendly populace, and legal restrictions against them aroused keen resentment in Japan. Roosevelt and Straus were opposed to these prejudicial acts by state and local officials, but were unable legally to interfere in California affairs. Their effort to mollify the Japanese with a "gentlemen's agreement" was partially successful, but the Japanese immigrants remained a thorny problem for the Roosevelt Administration.

The mass migration from Europe to the United States during the 1900's, and especially the hegira of Jews from Russia after the pogroms of 1905, also absorbed much of Straus's time and thought. The rejection of ill or illiterate immigrants on Ellis Island, often causing separation of families, preyed upon his natural sympathy. He therefore refused to delegate final decisions concerning immigrants who became deportable because they seemed "likely to become a public charge," and held up each case for his personal consideration.

During the 1908 Presidential campaign Straus worked actively for Taft's election. Roosevelt had said that Taft wanted him to remain in the Cabinet, but after the election

Taft changed his mind. Instead he offered Straus the post in Turkey, now raised to an ambassadorship, with the intimation that he would be given a more important embassy later. Straus was not eager to return to Turkey for the third time, but Taft pointed out that the Turkish revolution in 1908 had created an acute crisis for minorities in Asia Minor and that he was best equipped to handle it. Again accepting the office as a patriotic duty, Straus was fully successful in protecting American rights in Turkey. He obtained the exemption of foreign cultural institutions from Turkish supervision as well as the right of American colleges to own property. With the critical problems resolved and with the intimated promotion not forthcoming, he decided to resign late in 1910.

While still in Turkey, Straus was asked by Roosevelt to meet him in Cairo early in 1910 on Roosevelt's return from Africa. The two men discussed the unforeseen turn of events in the Taft Administration but reached no definite conclusions. Straus was certain that Roosevelt could be renominated at the Republican convention and was ready to help him, although he later opposed Roosevelt's radical stand on the recall of judicial decisions, knowing that it would split the party and deprive him of the nomination. When the "Old Guard" renominated Taft, and Roosevelt formed the Progressive party, Straus reluctantly accepted the Progressive nomination for governor of New York in the hope of helping his friend. In the campaign he concentrated his efforts on Roosevelt's election rather than on his own, but in the final vote he ran ahead of Roosevelt in New York state—393,000 to 389,000. The day after the election Roosevelt wrote to him, "Dear Oscar, I count myself fortunate in having run on the same ticket with you and in having the privilege of supporting you. You are the kind of American who makes one proud of being an American."

Now freed of official duties, Straus gave more attention to the problems of world peace and industrial arbitration. As a founder of the American Society of International Law in 1905 and as a leading member of the League to Enforce Peace he was active in the campaign to abolish war. In 1913 he took a leisurely trip through North Africa and Europe, meeting with men of eminence everywhere and discussing with them matters of peace and international amity. He was still in Europe in 1914 when war broke out, and while in London he was very helpful to many stranded Americans.

Straus chaired the Board of Railway Labor Arbitration Committee in 1912, dealt with its intricate problems, and offered rulings which were long in effect. In 1915 he was appointed chairman of the New York Public Service Commission, and he arbitrated numerous labor complaints. He was also a prominent member of the President's Industrial Conference of 1919-20.

After the war in Europe ended, Straus, as a leading member of the League to Enforce Peace, was at Versailles throughout the Peace Conference. At a critical juncture he persuaded Leon Bourgeois, who represented Clemenceau, to accept the wording of a contentious clause in the Covenant of the League of Nations. President Wilson was grateful and wrote to him on May 1, 1919 to say "how valuable in every way your own support of and enthusiasm for the League of Nations has been. It is a real pleasure to receive your unqualified approbation."

On his return to the United States in June Straus campaigned for the acceptance of the League.

While in Versailles he was in close contact with Jewish representatives and helped to safeguard Jewish minority rights in the Peace Treaty. He met with Herbert Samuel of England and expressed sympathy with the Balfour Declaration on Palestine. Always taking a positive interest in Jewish affairs and ever reacting strongly to anti-Jewish prejudice—on learning years before that a government circular countenanced Jewish discrimination, he had told Roosevelt he would resign from the Cabinet if it was not withdrawn—he fully earned Cyrus Adler's praise. "No Jew in America ever had so full and rounded out a public life as Oscar Straus, and naturally much of this was spent in the large world. But he was not of those who thought at any time that his public career demanded severance from Jewish tradition."

He spent much of his time writing, completing *Thomas Paine: Foremost Constructive Statesman of His Time* in 1921. In this study he lauded Paine's liberalism, pointing out that until Paine published *Common Sense*, Americans, even after Bunker Hill, thought only of taxation and the redress of grievances and not of independence. This little book, he stated, "stirred up the conscience of the people and won over Washington and several of the foremost leaders to the cause of Independence." Thus in the maturity of his thinking he held that Williams and Paine were the two great American libertarians:

> When I first began independently to study American history, two outstanding contributors who have made not only America, but the whole world their debtors, aroused my special interest and sympathetic admiration for their moral courage and visioned foresight because of which they were maligned and persecuted in their generation and their transcendent services obscured and belittled for years thereafter. I refer to Roger Williams, the pioneer of religious liberty, who was the first to found a political community with Church and State separated. The other was Thomas Paine, who was the first to advocate American Independence and our form of representative democracy.

In 1922 Straus published his memoirs, *Under Four Administrations*, reviewing his life activities and achievements with a simplicity and forthrightness and clarity which were hallmarks of his character. He died in 1926. Not long after, Congress passed a resolution authorizing the erection of a memorial to him in Washington, an honor seldom given to men other than Presidents.

FACTIONS IN
JUDAISM

For centuries Jews in Europe adhered to a rigidly constrained Orthodox ritual, their ghetto life enforced physically by external restrictions and persecution and spiritually by the internal strictness of rabbinical rule. Confronted by Christian hostility and oppression, fearing extinction unless they held together, they clung to their beliefs and threatened with excommunication anyone entertaining heretical views—such as Uriel Acosta and Baruch Spinoza in seventeenth-century Holland. A few, driven by doubt and riven by ambition, resorted to apostasy; but their defection served only to tighten the rabbinical reins on the Jewish community.

Cultural enlightenment in the eighteenth century, abetted by greater economic opportunity, filtered through the gates of the ghettos and attracted the more restive inhabitants. Moses Mendelssohn persuaded a number of German Jews to discard the ritual along with their ghetto gabardines and strive to live like liberal Europeans.

Most of the Central European Jews who migrated to the United States during the early nineteenth century, were tradesmen or petty merchants who had grown up in an Orthodox environment and observed the accustomed ritual unquestioningly. Conditions in America, however, militated against their habitual piety—peddlers in rural districts had neither the opportunity nor the emotional compulsion to observe the ritual and dietary laws. The religious faith of even those who settled in cities and formed congregations became flabby and passive, since there were few rabbis to prod and stimulate them.

After 1830, when more Jews began to arrive, including some trained in rabbinical lore, Jewish religious services began to simulate those of European Ashkenazic synagogues. The prevailing Sephardic ritual, also conventionally Orthodox, was replaced by the Ashkenazic ritual of their homeland, and was increasingly liberalized by rabbis imported from Germany. In time Judaic observance among the several factions in America assumed its threefold division of Orthodox, Conservative, and Reform liturgy.

Until the 1880's the Orthodox ritual was followed mostly by the small Sephardic community. The large number of immigrants from Eastern Europe, who began arriving at that time, were thoroughly Orthodox by training and habit. With them came rabbis and Talmudic scholars who helped establish synagogues and religious schools comparable to those left behind. As their numbers grew, they were able in 1896 to organize a strictly Orthodox yeshiva for rabbinical students. In 1915 it was merged with Yeshiva Etz Chaim and became Neo-Orthodox; thirteen years later it was named Yeshiva College and offered a secular liberal arts course in addition to its rabbinical seminary. The Union of Orthodox Jewish Congregations, formed in 1898, and Agudath Harabbonim, established later, are, respectively, lay and rabbinical Orthodox organizations. In time adapted to its American environment, Orthodox Judaism lost much of it medieval character but retained most of its traditional liturgy.

The more firmly the German Jews established themselves in their American milieu, the less they cared to emulate the Orthodoxy of their fathers. Many readily accepted the innovations of the Reform rabbis from Germany. Some, however, who were loath to break completely with the religion of their parents, followed the more modest reforms expounded by Rabbi Samson R. Hirsch in Germany, who attempted to revitalize Jewish traditions by adapting them to contemporary conditions. His rabbinical followers soon officiated in a number of American synagogues.

Although German-born Isaak Leeser (1806–1868) was not formally trained as a rabbi and had no connection with Rabbi Hirsch, he was the first religious leader to promote Conservative Judaism in America. In 1829 he was invited to serve as reader and rabbi in a Philadelphia synagogue. He wrote on liturgical subjects, among his publications were *The Jews and the Mosaic Law* (1833), and a Hebrew and English edition of the Pentateuch (1845). He also edited *The Occident and the American Jewish Advocate* from 1843 to his death 25 years later. Although he favored only mild reforms, he insisted on their validation by a synod of rabbis, and no such organization then existed in the United States. He was eager to establish a seminary, but Maimonides College which he started in 1867 closed after six years of struggle.

In 1851 the Italian-born Sabato Morais (1823–1897) took over Rabbi Leeser's post in the Mikvah Israel congregation. His coming marked the transfer of influence in the American congregations from the laity to the rabbinate. Morais was indeed a prophetic figure in both appearance and action. A genuine educator, he furthered schooling at all levels and joined Lesser in organizing Maimonides College. When the 1885 Reform Conference rejected the sacredness of the Old Testament and the Talmud, he and six other rabbis issued a call for the establishment of a Conservative seminary and stated that "it was imperative to make a strong effort for the perpetuation of Judaism in America." The result was the formation of the Jewish Theological Seminary in January 1887, with Morais serving as its president until his death a decade later.

The most illustrious Conservative leader was Professor Solomon Schechter (1848–1915). He was born in Rumania, and received his secular education in Vienna. Invited to England by Claude Montefiore, Schechter made important discoveries in the rich Hebraic source materials in the British Museum. He taught Semitics at Cambridge University and became the outstanding scholar in this field. In 1901 he assumed the presidency of the Jewish Theological Seminary, and in time greatly enhanced its prestige. He was not a narrow theologian, but he opposed Reform Judaism for fear that "liberal Judaism led to liberal Christianity." In 1906 he disappointed some of his wealthy contributors by joining the Zionist movement.

Cyrus Adler (1863–1940) succeeded Professor Schechter as president of the Seminary and as a leader of Conservative

Judaism. American-born and the first recipient of a doctorate in Semitics at Johns Hopkins University in 1887, he was for many years curator of Semitics and subsequently librarian of the Smithsonian Institution. He was a founder of the Jewish Publication Society (1888) and the American Jewish Historical Society (1892), and an editor of *Jewish Encyclopedia* and *American Jewish Year Book*. When Dropsie College was started in 1908, Adler became its first president. He and others met in 1931 to define their Conservative position and resolved to "stand firmly on the rock of Jewish tradition and Jewish law," but they agreed to take a "liberal view . . . and not the severe view of Jewish tradition" espoused by the Orthodox rabbis.

Even the Conservative faith was too "orthodox" for some Jews who remained Jews out of sentiment and habit, but were unwilling to adhere to dietary laws, Sabbath observance, and daily prayer with shawl and philacteries. Many of them gravitated to the Reform temple. The first congregation to do so was the Reformed Society of Israelites in Charleston, starting in 1824 with Gustav Pozanski as rabbi. Timid efforts at reform in other cities followed, but not until 1845 was Temple Emanu-El in New York, the "Cathedral of Reform," established, with Dr. Leo Merzbacher as rabbi.

The first aggressive advocate of Reform was Rabbi Isaak Mayer Wise (1819–1900), who arrived in New York in 1846. A fine scholar and skillful administrator, he introduced family pews to replace the traditional separation of women worshippers, sermons in German, and a mixed choir. When his reforms split the Albany congregation, his followers founded a separate synagogue for him, and he served them until he went to Cincinnati in 1854.

Many Jews, while observing few Judaic practices personally, wanted the synagogue service to correspond to the one they remembered from their native towns. The result was a babel of rituals. To bring order and a sense of decorum into the synagogue service, Rabbi Wise prepared *Minhag America* in 1847 and promoted it as a book of common prayer. In 1855, at the Cleveland conference of rabbis, it was, with a few changes, accepted for general use by congregations west and south of the Alleghenies and remained standard until replaced by the *Union Prayer Book* in 1894.

Wise advocated the establishment of a Reform seminary, and was instrumental in establishing Hebrew Union College in Cincinnati, which opened in 1875 and in time became the official seminary of Reform Judaism. The rabbinical meetings convened at his urging tended to widen rather than narrow the rift between his followers in the Middle West and the Reform rabbis in the East. In 1889 the Central Conference of American Rabbis elected him president, an office he held to the end of his life. All through the years he edited *The American Israelite* and *Deborah* (in German); he wrote novels as well as numerous religious works.

Other prominent Reform rabbis appeared after 1850, but their views lacked unanimity. In general they decried usages and ceremonies based upon what they considered to be erroneous conceptions. Rabbi Samuel Adler (1809–1891), who in 1857 became rabbi of Temple Emanu-El, stated most clearly the objectives of the Reform congregations:

> The first and most important step for such a congregation to take is to free its service of shocking lies, to remove from it the mention of things and wishes which we would not utter if it had to be done in an intelligible manner. Such are lamentation about oppression and persecution, the petition for the restoration of the sacrificial cult, for the return of Israel to Palestine, the hope for a personal Messiah, and for resurrection of the body. In the second place, to eliminate fustian and exaggeration, and, in the third place, to make the service clear, intelligible, instructive, and inspiring.

Here he was expressing the point of view of his affluent and influential parishioners, who were no longer suffering from persecution and were quite reconciled to forgetting the land of Israel.

Rabbi David Einhorn (1809–1879) was an even more radical reformer than Rabbi Wise. Gaining prominence as a rabbi in his native Germany and in Hungary before coming to America in 1855, he very soon came into conflict with Rabbi Wise in his advocacy of thoroughgoing reforms. He started *Sinai* (in German) to propound his views on Reform Judaism, and his suggestions were subsequently incorporated in the *Union Prayer Book*.

Probably the most effective advocate of Reform Judaism was Rabbi Kaufmann Kohler (1843–1926). A student of Rabbis S. R. Hirsch and Abraham Geiger in his native Germany, he had become too radical to obtain a rabbinate in Germany. Migrating to New York in 1869, he was welcomed by Rabbi Einhorn, whose daughter he married the following year. At first rabbi in Detroit and then in Chicago, he started services on Sunday in addition to those on Saturday, and sought to harmonize Reform Judaism with contemporary science. When his father-in-law died in 1879, he was called to his place as rabbi of Temple Beth-El in New York. In 1885 he called a rabbinical conference in Pittsburgh, where he expounded the guiding ideas of Reform. He formally rejected the dietary laws, modified the Messianic concept into that of "truth, justice, and peace among all men," and declared that Judaism had to be based on reason and social justice. The platform adopted also declared, "We consider ourselves no longer a nation, but a religious community, and therefore expect neither a return to Palestine, nor a sacrificial worship under the sons of Aaron, nor a restoration of any of the laws concerning the Jewish state."

In 1903 Kohler was elected president of Hebrew Union College. His chief work, *Jewish Theology Systematically and Historically Considered* (1910 in German, 1918 in English), is a historical analysis of the nature of Judaism.

As radical a departure as Reform Judaism was from the traditional Orthodoxy, it still failed to appeal to quite a few Americanized Jews and was completely rejected by Jews of diverse origins who had become dedicated to social justice and

Marxian socialism. Agnostics or atheists, they considered religion irrelevant or baleful. A few sought sublimation in the deed instead of creed. Of the later, Felix Adler became the guiding sage and standard bearer.

6
Felix
Adler

PHILOSOPHICAL
ETHICIST

THE SON and grandson of prominent rabbis, Felix
Adler was born in Germany in 1851 and brought to America
in 1857. Bright, serious, conscientious, he excelled as a student and was graduated from Columbia College in 1870.
The trustees of Temple Emanu-El, considered him a potential successor to his father's rabbinate, and he was sent
to Germany to complete his religious preparation. For
three years he studied Semitics and Judaism with leading
German rabbis and philosophy at the Universities of Berlin and Heidelberg. The more deeply he delved into the
nature and history of religion, the more skeptical he became of the theological concept of God, the divine origin
of the Bible, and the fundamental tenets of Judaic and
Christian creeds. Viewed in the light of science and philosophy, dogmatic religion appeared to him a combination of
hypocrisy, superstition, and fanaticism, destructive of its
prime virtue—its ethical component. He was particularly
influenced by Kant's idea of an ethical society: "So act as

to treat humanity, whether in thine own person, or in that of any other, in every case as an end withal never as a means only." Following this principle, he recognized man's inviolability and innate spirituality.

Adler was personally abstemious and idealistic, even prudish, and repelled by the carousing and sexual looseness of his German fellow students. Strongly affected by Albert Lange's *The Labor Question*, he became critical of economic inequality and determined to help workers and women achieve greater recognition from society. He was awarded a doctorate *summa cum laude* in 1873, and returned to New York.

When the trustees of Temple Emanu-El asked him to deliver a sermon, presumably to relate his experiences abroad, Adler obliged with an address in which he intimated a new type of religion, one stressing the ethical responsibilities of society without resorting to God or creed. He admitted that the only part of Judaism he sincerely admired were the ethical precepts of the Old Testament prophets; that he could not honestly repeat the rabbi's weekly statement, "And this is the Law which Moses set before the people of Israel," since he now knew that the Torah was a "mosaic . . . with hardly a single stone in it which can with certainty be traced to the authorship of Moses."

The trustees agreed with their young protégé that his views made it impossible for him to enter the rabbinate. His father, Rabbi Samuel Adler, was deeply disappointed, but respected his son's honesty of purpose. "There is a truth," he told him, "deeper than the faith you see, and that is the utmost fidelity in truth-seeking. Follow your vision, and God speed you to the end."

Felix Adler gathered a few young friends who had an equally idealistic outlook on life and formed a Union for the Higher Life based on sex purity, devotion of one's surplus means to the improvement of the poor, and continued intellectual development. Inclined to priggishness, Adler wanted even his close associates to address him as "Dr.

Adler" in the presence of others; yet such was his dignity of person that they did so without question and appreciated his otherwise reasoned humility. A colleague later remarked, "One is awed in his presence, one does him unconscious reverence."

Aware of his need to earn a living, friends established for him a three-year lectureship at Cornell University, where he gave courses in Hebrew and Oriental literatures. At the end of the period these friends offered to underwrite the lectureship for another three years, but it was refused presumably because Adler's religious views had antagonized the more conservative members of the faculty.

Adler's ethical ideals and earnestness had by this time won the admiration of a number of his New York associates. Most of them were members of Temple Emanu-El, attached to Judaism, yet reasonably skeptical of certain of its tenets. He agreed to address them on May 15, 1876. Affected by Emerson's doctrine of self-reliance yet critical of his pantheism, admiring the ethics of Jesus but objecting to the Christian creed, steeped in the ethics of the Hebrew prophets yet rejecting the irrational aspects of Judaism, Adler propounded an ethics free from creed and dedicated to the deed. He told his listeners that it was necessary to arouse the conscience of man, to stimulate his loftier purposes; not what they believed, he assured them, but what they did was important.

> We propose to entirely exclude prayer and every form of ritual. . . . Candidly do I confess that it is my dearest object to exalt the present movement above the strife of contending sects and parties, and at once to occupy that common ground where we may all meet, believers and unbelievers, for purposes in themselves lofty and unquestioned by any. . . . Believe or disbelieve as ye list—we shall at all times respect every honest conviction. But be one with us where there is nothing to divide—in action. Diversity in the creed, unanimity in the deed! This is that practical religion from which none dissents. This is that

platform broad enough and solid enough to receive the worshipper and the "infidel." This is the common ground where we may all grasp hands as brothers, united in mankind's common cause.

Short of stature and not impressive physically, appearing formal and aloof, he spoke with a calm forcefulness and firm persuasiveness which gave his words the power of authoritative utterance. His listeners, already predisposed, were deeply moved. Eager to establish their group on a permanent basis, with Adler as their leader, they formed the Ethical Culture Society "unhampered by sectarian religious dogmas" and arranged to begin their Sunday meetings in October. Joseph Seligman, one of the most prominent Jews in America and a leading member of Temple Emanu-El, agreed to serve as president.

In his first discourse that fall Adler expounded a "new religion of morality, whose God was the good, whose church was the universe, whose heaven was here on earth and not in the clouds." Later he offered his version of faith to those who felt the need of one: "I believe in the supreme excellence of righteousness; I believe that the law of righteousness will triumph in the universe over all evil; I believe that the law of righteousness is the sanctification of human life; and I believe that in furthering and fulfilling that law I also am hallowed in the service of the unknown God."

It is noteworthy that the men and women who joined the Society in its early years were no longer satisfied with the religion in which they had grown up. They wanted standards and guidance consonant with the economic, social, and other contemporary conditions they faced. In the words of "Analyticus," they were "above all afraid of the eternal Jewishness within themselves. . . . Without finally deserting the faith of their fathers for an alien faith, these Jews could escape the odium of the Jewish badge and the Jewish name. What for Felix Adler was an ethical emancipation became for his followers a racial exodus."

Ironically, their predominant membership in the Ethical Culture movement kept non-Jews from joining it in any number, so that it remained largely a Jewish organization —although most of its later leaders came from Christian denominations.

True to his ethical ideals, Adler translated his thought into deed. In 1877 he founded the first free kindergarten in the East for children of workingmen. This was followed a year later by the establishment of a free Workingman's School, with manual training one of its early features. Some years afterward, when Society members who were able to pay tuition wished to send their children to the school, the name was changed to Ethical Culture School and one third of the pupils continued to be given free scholarships. Its manual-training and dramatic programs proved so successful that they were introduced in New York public schools. When Adler and his associates planned to build the Fieldston School in Riverdale, Adler's invitation to John D. Rockefeller, Jr., to visit the classes resulted in a gift of $400,000, with a supplementary contribution later.

Adler's sense of human decency was horrified by the dank, crowded tenements in the East Side slums. He advocated improved living quarters for workers, and in 1882 was named a member of the newly established Tenement House Commission, formed "to investigate and remedy the intolerable conditions in the city's congested tenement districts." The work of this commission resulted in the erection of the model tenements on Cherry Street, with windows in every room and with an assembly hall for a kindergarten during the day and social events in the evening. Another of Adler's achievements was to send nurses into the homes of the poor.

In 1883 Adler and Edmond Kelly formed the Good Government Club, later renamed City Club, which became the spearhead of reform in New York. With child labor endemic in those years—1.7 million listed in the 1900 census—Adler joined the National Child Labor Committee in

1894 and served as its president from 1904 to 1921. In 1894 he also became a member of the Lexow Committee which exposed crime and graft within the city. After receiving a youth's complaint that his home was surrounded by brothels, he helped form the Committee of Fifteen "for cleaning the city of the cancers of vice and graft." He also participated in labor arbitration and was a member of the group that settled the garment strike of 1910.

As a social reformer Adler tended to probe the depths of social phenomena. He was critical of most efforts at human amelioration because they neglected its moral aspects. "If there be no such thing as morality, or if morality be but an epiphenomenon of economic conditions, what warrant have the hungry or disadvantaged for complaining?" And he stressed in italics, *"Social reform is the transformation of all social institutions in such a way that they may become successive phases through which the individual shall advance toward the acquisition of an ethical personality."* It was this attitude and application toward social conditions that elicited Jacob Riis's statement in *The Making of an American* that "The strongest moral force in Christian New York was and is Adler, the Jew or heretic, take it whichever way you please."

In 1903 a group of his admirers established for Adler a chair in social and political ethics at Columbia University, which he occupied to the end of his life. In 1908 he was Roosevelt Exchange Professor at the University of Berlin. In May, 1923 he was invited to Oxford to deliver a course of six Hibbert Lectures, published as *The Reconstruction of the Spiritual Ideal*. All the while, of course, he devoted himself to the expansion and improvement of the Ethical Culture movement, supervising and stimulating individual leaders, lecturing regularly in New York and other cities, attending summer schools and conferences, and furthering the Society's educational system.

Adler was in his eighty-second year when he died in 1933. President Franklin Roosevelt wrote to Mrs. Adler, "Those of us who were privileged to know him in life have lost a true friend and valued adviser. The Nation mourns the passing of a profound philosopher, a cultural leader of spiritual force, a philanthropist, and a beloved citizen." Oswald Garrison Villard, who knew Adler well but who resigned from the Society when it refused to oppose World War I, stated that he was "a man with a splendid mind, which busied itself from beginning to end with the tremendous problems of human relationships, and always from the point of view of pure ethics."

For many years Felix Adler lectured on most Sundays, applying the principles of ethics to current events, clarifying his moralistic philosophy, expounding ideals of behavior, extolling the idea of the good life. He preached a religion without the myths, rituals, and dogmas of established theologies, stressing the duty of man to men and the goal of ethical grandeur. In one of his early addresses he stated:

> The dogmatic assertion of religious teaching we hold to be a serious evil, and dogma as such we cannot accept. On the other hand we behold in conscience the root of whatever good religion has achieved, and the law of conscience must suffice to guide and elevate our lives. To refresh our moral sentiment is the one thing needful in our time, and indeed presents a task on whose accomplishment the highest interests of society depends.

In the exposition of his philosophy he stated that ethics is "the idealism of character"; that moral law, which can neither be proven nor denied, "is the root from which springs every value, every grace, all wisdom and all achievement." Interpreted in the light of current conditions, morality demands three things from every human being: "greater simplicity in manners, greater purity in the passions, greater charity . . . charity that prevents rather than cures." In a discourse on general religion, he maintained that although it ought to stand for the highest truth, it no longer does. Indeed, it is at war with "the highest intelligence of the day," is no longer inseparably connected with conscience. The exigencies of modern times, he emphasized, demand "a new movement for the moral elevation of the race. . . . While all men may not be capable of the highest order of intellectual action, all men are capable of heart goodness, and goodness is the better part of religion." In sum, the supreme ethical rule must be "act so as to elicit the best in others and thereby in thyself."

The preface to *Life and Destiny* (1903) explains that Adler used the word "spiritual" as a shorthand expression for the entire nature of man in which morality is supreme. Employing the Hebrew legend that the world exists by virtue of its thirty-six saintly men who in their functioning keep it from destruction, he stated his cardinal principle that "every man, however humble, is worthy of reverence because, in his limited sphere, he can be a beneficent, forward-working agent, he can help a little to create the perfect man." The basis for this reverence was not a matter of reason but of inner experience—a sense of "longing for companionship with the best in every nature." Believing that every man is capable of this inner ethical experience, he urged the cultivation of patience and a humble spirit. He further stated that because Judaism is essentially an ethical religion, "all of us are spiritually the heirs of the Hebrew prophets, including among them Jesus, the greatest of their number."

He insisted repeatedly that not happiness but worthiness is the purpose of life, that happiness may come as an accessory but must never be made an end in itself. The tokens of the higher life, he stated, are purity, serenity, objectivity, wisdom, and humility. "The higher life cannot be attained without rigorous self-discipline, and self-discipline always involves pain, but the end in view is worthy of the sufferings we are called upon to endure, the prize is worthy of the price exacted of us." And he reiterated, "Let us found a religion upon a basis of perfect intellectual honesty. Religion, if it is to mean anything at all, must stand for the highest truth . . . based not upon legend and tradition, not upon the authority of any book, but upon the moral nature of man."

Adler was not unaware of man's evil impulses. In 1911 he helped organize and attended the International Races Congress, at which discussion centered on the serious world problems arising from racial rivalries. He saw World War I as the result of greed and lust for power as well as of the modern worship of technology. "The machine obsesses and controls mankind." In a number of discourses, appearing in 1915 as *The World Crisis and Its Meaning*, he wrote prophetically that unless men modified their aims and ambitions the current war would not be the last.

> No, I see no hope of peace, no promise of anything better than a temporary truce, to be followed by new struggles for the chastisement of the offender. Perhaps for centuries to come the nails of war must still be driven through the hands and feet of humanity. But out of the crucifixion shall come transfiguration. . . . The great ethical error of the world till now has been that in the rightness of self-defense men have become most unrighteous, because in self-defense they have thought of their right as sundered from the right of others. Yet my right is but one blade of the shears, and the right of my fellow, even though he be the oppressor, is the other blade.

The remedy, he maintained, lay in each man making an effort to see the fair and friendly aspect of others. By a gradual approximation to this moral ideal one makes progress, furthered, among individuals as well as nations, by "self-limitation in regard to wealth." *"The key to social reform,"* he emphasized, *"is to bring about the right way of looking upon fellowmen. . . . To work that the work of the world shall be better done because you have worked on it."* Since this ethical progress can be achieved only gradually, he suggested that one view life as a series of ascending terraces, each one rising above its predecessors.

In the Hibbert Lectures he was critical of both capitalism and socialism, which he considered as "unreligious," debasing man by making service subordinate to income instead of the contrary.

Work must be considered as an opportunity for the perfecting of the personal relations involved therein. . . . These personal relations must be spiritual, that is, exemplifying the ideally organic relations. . . . The supreme task is that of personalizing the depersonalized masses of mankind, and their present depersonalized masters as well.

He considered himself an idealist who was fully aware of the evils perpetrated by mankind in historic times. "There is not a so-called civilized people," he asserted, "whose record does not contain the stain of actual crimes such as must bring the blush of shame to the lover of his country." Yet he was certain that men, and their social groupings, are potentially capable of ethical aspiration. Applying his ethical principles to current problems of international relations, he urged the resort to the spiritual rule.

Help to elicit the best in other nations, and thereby in thine own. This practically means to study the types of the sister nations, to seek as far as possible to assimilate these, and thus to put oneself in the position of being able to correct their faults, to strengthen them where they are weak, while in the process of so doing, the evil traits in one's own type will gradually diminish and tend to disappear.

He was critical of the League of Nations because he thought it a league to enforce peace, and force and peace are antithetical. What such an incipient society of mankind must strive for, he pointed out, was "to devise methods by which the formation of a world conscience be accelerated." As a beginning he proposed international conferences on single topics. He assumed that progress ought to be, and therefore would be, achieved.

Progress means advance toward a society which shall more adequately reflect in all its relations the pattern of the spiritual world. God as reflected in the face of Christ is the theological way of putting this idea; to see the world of spiritual perfection as reflected in the face of humanity is the turn I give to the same thought.

A sexual purist from early young manhood, Adler devoted numerous discourses to the problems of marriage and divorce. Marriage was to him a sacred union for the perpetuation of the race, subserving "a vast and wonderful social end. . . . Permanence in marriage relations is the spiritual *sine qua non.*" He opposed divorce as selfish and immoral—"one can no more disown a spouse than he can disown a child."

Marriage, he insisted, confers benefits of the highest kind by ministering to moral growth. Aware that there is no perfect compatibility even in the best of marriages, he advised that harmony be secured by an effort at accommodation. In cases where incompatibility was not remediable he suggested separation—but not divorce. "Do not seek to cast from you the being to whom at the altar you vowed your troth, for better or for worse. Accept the bond which in one sense limits your liberty, but in another sense, by the very fact of your accepting it voluntarily, gives you a far nobler liberty."

Adler was not only an ethical prophet but an efficient administrator. His supervision of the schools he founded was direct and detailed. He took great pains to encourage and further the training of prospective leaders for the Ethical Culture Societies established in the United States and abroad. He attracted a number of able and dedicated young men, most of them graduates of Christian seminaries, who devoted themselves to their work with the fervor of converts. Adler expected his associates not only to follow his teachings but to emulate him in personal neatness and social manner. As a young man, Morris R. Cohen, the eminent philosopher, was helped by Adler to do graduate work at Harvard, but discouraged by him from becoming an

Ethical leader because his "physical appearance and care-
less dress would be a handicap."

Felix Adler was a serious moral philosopher who lived
his life in accord with his ideals. He expounded the ethical
ideals which aimed at man's highest morality and which
he regarded as essentially the only religion applicable to
contemporary society. In abandoning Judaism he retained
the Hebrew tradition of ethics and related it to conditions
of his time. To the exhortations of Isaiah he added the
moral imperatives of Kant, and portraits of both adorned
his study. "Analyticus" depicted him well.

> Basically he is the ancient Hebrew prophet, inheritor of
> the moral fervor and ethical passion of Amos, of Isaiah.
> Hater of injustice and oppression, pleader for righteous-
> ness and the supremacy of the moral law in every relation-
> ship of life, believer in the innate human worth of man,
> and in man's potential spiritual grandeur, he has caught
> not only the accents but the impulse of his prophetic fore-
> bears, and translated them into the language and fitted
> them to the mood of modern times.

Although he rejected traditional Judaism, he did not
cease to be a Jew in spirit, and was accepted as such by
his contemporaries. Like most Reform Jews he responded
negatively to the concept of Zionism; as late as 1919, when
the Balfour Declaration had excited the enthusiasm of
Jews all over the world, he continued to regard it as "a
delusive ideal," questioning the right of Jews to Palestine
and pointing out that they had no common speech, no
common types, no homogeneity.

The ethical imperative he preached Sunday after Sunday was intellectually persuasive—but not impelling—
having a rarified essence more readily appreciated than
translatable into action. His message had "light but not
heat," and lacked the passion to move men powerfully.
Consequently Adler the man was in the end greater than

his work. He aroused reverence in the small company of his followers but not in the mass of mankind. But to the few thousands who sat at his feet he gave life a new meaning and a new purpose: "the experience of a unique personal worth, of indefeasible selfhood recoiling from twisted relations with others as from an injury and longing for companionship with the best in every nature."

Although the Ethical Culture movement has remained rather small in membership the world over, its high moral standards have gained it the respect of most men of liberal intelligence. Its educational pioneering has influenced both public and private schools. And its Sunday lectures in printed form have been read with interest by many who have not joined the Society.

THE PASSION FOR
SOCIAL JUSTICE

A passion for the public good and legal justice has been a notable Jewish characteristic from Biblical times to the present. Isaiah was only the most exalted of many Hebrew prophets who denounced the selfish rich and expounded the rights of the poor and oppressed. And in every generation since then men of social conscience have sought to succor the needy and defend the exploited. The Talmud is indeed a vast repository of rules and regulations for the protection of the people from injustice and inequity.

When the Enlightenment in Europe enabled individual Jews to leave the ghetto and acquire the rights of citizenship, not a few soon distinguished themselves as advocates of personal liberty and social justice. In each country a number entered the legal profession and devoted themselves to the defense of the weak and the abused; some rose to high positions as jurists and judges. In countries of the British Commonwealth, Jews were admitted to the bar around the middle of the nineteenth century, and several quickly achieved top rank; among them were George Jessel, Rufus Isaacs (the Marquess of Reading), and Arthur Cohen in England; Chief Justice Isaacs in Austrialia, and Chief Justices Sir Arthur and Sir Michael Meyers in New Zealand.

In the United States, where Jews early gained prominence as lawyers devoted to the public good, the following sampling is illustrative of the various ways in which Jewish lawyers employed their talents to serve their fellow men.

Lewis N. Dembitz (1833–1907), a dedicated lawyer, was born in Posen and educated in Germany. He migrated to the United States following the defeat of the 1848 revolution in Austria-Hungary. In 1853 he was admitted to the bar in Kentucky, where he became active in the antislavery movement and in 1860 was one of the three delegates to nominate Lincoln for the Presidency. More the scholar than the practitioner, he wrote on legal subjects, became proficient in Jewish history and literature, and was an early exponent of Zionism. In 1926 Justice Brandeis thus characterized this good man who had early influenced his thinking,

> The deepest of his studies were those allied to the Jewish religion. He was Orthodox. He observed the law. But, he was not satisfied with merely observing it. He sought to understand the law in order to find its reason; he studied deeply into the history of the Jewish people. . . . It was natural that he should have been among the first in America to support Herzl in his effort to build a new Palestine.

Simon Wolf (1836–1923) was a superlative example of the Jewish lawyer who dedicated himself to the public good. Born in Bavaria and brought to the United States in 1848, he was admitted to the bar in 1861. He was rejected by the army at the start of the Civil War, and went to Washington to practice law. He was one of several men who persuaded Lincoln to rescind General Grant's Order No. 11, which excluded civilian Jews from army lines. Wolf was active in the American Union of Hebrew Congregations, and as chairman of its standing committee for thirty-three years made himself "the spokesman of the Jews in the United States." Persuading immigration authorities that persons dependent on private charity were not necessarily public charges, he helped save a large number of Jewish immigrants from deportation. When an article in an 1891 issue of *The North American Review* slandered Jews as army shirkers during the Civil War, Wolf, as stated earlier, went to great trouble to offer documentary evidence that more than 6,000 Jews had served in the federal forces and over 1,000 in the confederate army—actually a relatively high percentage of the Jews then in the United States. Max J. Kohler succinctly summarized his career:

No subject arose from 1870 to 1923 affecting the interest of American Jews, in which he was not active; and if, in a rare instance, he was not directly appealed to by those immediately concerned, the Government itself would call him into council, so well known was his devotion to Jewish interests, good judgment, and sterling American patriotism.

Louis Marshall (1850–1929) was the most prestigious Jewish leader of his time. Born in Syracuse, and with a degree from Columbia Law School, he specialized in constitutional law. In 1894 he became a partner in the New York firm of Guggenheimer, Untermyer and Marshall, with which he remained associated to the end of his life. He was engaged in numerous cases involving principles of constitutional and corporation law. He also argued various cases affecting the public interest before the highest courts in the land.

In 1902 Marshall served on a commission to investigate slum conditions on New York's Lower East Side. Later he acted as chairman of a New York state commission on immigration. In 1910 he and Jacob Schiff forced a settlement of the garment strike in New York—his word "protocol" becoming the persuasive term to the wary labor leaders. Although he was a Republican and opposed to socialism, he joined other eminent lawyers in asserting the legal right to be seated of the five Socialists elected to the New York legislature in 1920.

When Jews in Eastern Europe became the hapless victims of war in 1914 and later, Marshall assumed the presidency of the American Joint Relief Committee. As president of the influential American Jewish Committee (1912–1929) he was opposed to the idea of a Jewish Congress, but accepted it to keep harmony within the Jewish community. In 1919 he went to Versailles as head of the American Jewish Committee and acted as conciliator among the several factions, offering a formula which enabled the various representatives to work together to obtain for Jews "the rights of the most favored minority" at the Peace Conference. In the 1920s, he helped expose the forged and slanderous nature of *Protocols of the Elders of Zion*, and, with others, pressured Henry Ford to admit his error in publishing them and to make a public apology for his anti-Semitic agitation in *The Dearborn Independent*.

For years Marshall was president of Temple Emanu-El. Concurrently he also presided at the conservative Jewish Theological Seminary, and took a leading part in the operation of YMHA and other Jewish organizations. Summing up his career Justice Benjamin Cardozo said, "He was a great lawyer, a great champion of ordered liberty, a great leader of his people, and a great lover of mankind."

Samuel Untermyer (1858–1940), Marshall's partner, was also involved in civic reform and Jewish affairs. Born in Virginia and graduated from Columbia Law School, he settled in New York and quickly developed an extremely lucrative practice in civil, criminal, corporate, and international law. In 1913 he served as counsel for the Pujo Committee, which brought about the enactment of the Federal Reserve Act, legislation establishing the Federal Trade Commission, and other reform measures. For years he urged the regulation of public utilities. Although he was an influential Democrat, he never sought public office.

In spite of his membership in the American Jewish Committee, Untermyer favored Zionism as a means of helping persecuted Jews settle in Palestine, and for several years he served as president of the Palestine Foundation Fund. In 1923 he acted as attorney for the journalist Herman Bernstein who sued Henry Ford for slander in articles published in *The Dearborn Independent*; the case ended in 1927 with Ford's apology to Bernstein.

Julian W. Mack (1866–1943) was born in San Francisco, attended Harvard Law School and then made his home in Chicago, where he taught at Northwestern and Chicago Law Schools. In 1903 he was elected judge of the circuit court of Cook County. In 1919 he was appointed judge of the United States Circuit Court of Appeals, and served on it with distinction.

His involvement in Jewish affairs was strongly stimulated

by the plight of East European Jews during World War I, and he devoted himself to collecting funds for their relief. He became an associate of the Brandeis group of Zionists and was president of the Zionist Organization of America from 1918 to 1921. He was an outspoken supporter of the proposal for a Jewish congress, and was elected its first president in 1919. During the Versailles Peace Conference he worked with Marshall and exercised great influence as chairman of the Committee of Jewish Delegates. As a close friend of Julius Rosenwald and other well-known Jewish philanthropists, he aroused their benevolent interest in the work of various Jewish institutions.

Hugo Pam (1870–1930) was congenially associated with Mack in various Jewish causes. He was born in Chicago and began his legal career in 1893. In 1911 he was elected to the superior court of Cook County and re-elected three times. He took a positive part in communal affairs and paid particular attention to the advancement of mental hygiene. He also joined numerous Jewish organizations and became a Zionist in 1912. When the project for the Jewish Congress was being considered in 1915, he served as chairman of the preliminary conference in Philadelphia.

The foregoing sampling, men of Germanic or American birth, were both conscious of their Jewish heritage and intensely devoted Americans. Their interest in human welfare was a natural concomitant of their Jewish upbringing: their leadership in Jewish affairs was to them a privileged obligation to—primarily—their fellow Jews. This was not the case with a good many Russian Jews who began to reach the United States in the 1880's. While the majority of the East European immigrants were poor, pious, and relatively ignorant provincials, a number were educated and class-conscious rebels who had left Russia to avoid arrest and exile and who came to New York with hopes of an ideal society. Along with other newcomers they worked in sweatshops, but in their free time they gathered to exchange ideas about socialism and anarchism, free love and frank atheism. The more ambitious devoted their evenings to study for the various professions, and not a few became leaders of labor unions and the radical movement. Among them the following three, all lawyers, are both typical and significant.

Morris Hillquit (1870–1933) came to New York in 1887 and worked for a time in shirt and waist sweatshops. He was a founder of the United Hebrew Trades in 1888 and a member of the Socialist Labor party. Taking evening course in law, he was admitted to the bar in 1893. In 1897 Hillquit was one of the leaders in the revolt against Daniel De Leon's domination of the Socialist Labor party and in the formation of the Socialist party two years later. He frequently ran for office on the Scoialist ticket, and made an especially good showing as a mayoralty candidate in 1917. In 1920 he was one of the chief defenders of the ousted Socialist legislators. Shortly before his death he helped frame the National Recovery Act labor code for the garment industry. Respected by friends and adversaries alike, he remained true to his Marxian ideals; his books on American socialist history and theory are works of sound scholarship.

Louis B. Boudin (1874–1951) was among the first of the Russian-born Jewish immigrants to gain prominence as a socialist and legal scholar. On reaching the United States in his teens, he worked his way through law school and became active in the socialist and labor movements. He wrote on Marxist theory and on American legal history, and his two-volume work, *Government by Judiciary* (1932), is generally regarded as erudite and authoritative.

Jacob Panken (1879–   ), who came to this country in 1890, lived for a time on a farm in Connecticut, then went to New York where he worked in a garment factory during the day and studied law in the evening. Admitted to the bar in 1905, he became involved in radical and labor organizations, gained wide popularity on the East Side, and was president of the Jewish Forward Association from 1917 to 1921. In 1918 he was appointed a justice of the municipal court and served for ten years. When the domestic relations court was established in 1934, he became its first judge. During World War I he joined Jewish relief committees and was a founder and president of the Organization for Rehabilitation Training (ORT), which helped to re-establish European Jews.

Joseph M. Proskauer (1877–1955) exemplifies the successful jurist and civic leader who devoted himself to Jewish causes. Born in Mobile, and graduated from Columbia Law School in 1899, he practiced law in New York. In 1923 he was elected to the New York supreme court, and four years later he was appointed associate justice of the appellate division, but he resigned in 1930. Long associated with communal and philanthropic organizations, he was president of YMHA, the Federation for the Support of Jewish Philanthropic Societies, and the American Jewish Committee. An opponent of Zionism, he defended Jewish rights in various parts of the world. In his autobiography, *A Segment of My Times* (1951), he described his painful reaction to anti-Semitism,

> There have been compensations in the comradeship of many Christian friends. But none of them ever can know, I believe, the poignant grief, the self-consciousness, the hindrance to free intercourse that stems from the cancer and from their failure, inexplicable to me, to excise it ruthlessly by action, instead of condoning it, at least in part, by inaction.

Arthur Garfield Hays (1881–1954) revealed his Jewish heritage through his devotion to the ideal of civil liberty rather than to specific Jewish interests. Born in Rochester and a graduate of Columbia Law School, he became the first of a considerable number of Jewish lawyers who gave their services to the American Civil Liberties Union of which he was a founder. Hays took a leading part in the ACLU's defense of radicals and conscientious objectors during World War I and for decades thereafter. In 1933 he went to Germany to defend the Communists on trial for the alleged burning of the Reichstag. His book, *Let Freedom Ring* (1928, 1937), is an engaging and persuasive exposition of civil liberty. Stuart Chase called him "a soldier in the eternal warfare against tyranny and intolerance."

Monte M. Lemann (1884–1959), born in Louisiana, was

graduated from Harvard Law School in 1906. He entered private practice in New Orleans, and for twenty years was a member of the Tulane Law Faculty. Deeply concerned with the problem of legal aid, he became a leading promoter of the New Orleans and the National Legal Aid Societies, receiving the Reginald Heber Smith Award in recognition of his services. His eminence as a practicing lawyer gained him the presidency of both the New Orleans and the Louisiana State Bar Associations.

Walter H. Pollock (1887–1940) was, like his father Gustav Pollock, actively identified with the cause of liberalism. A graduate of Harvard Law School, he became associated with various state and federal investigating committees. When nine Negro boys were convicted on the charge of rape in Scottsboro, Alabama, Pollack carried their appeal to the Supreme Court and obtained a new trial.

Jerome N. Frank (1889–1957) was brought up in Chicago, where his father was a lawyer. Graduating in 1912 from the University of Chicago Law School, he practiced law until 1929. Notably liberal in his views, he in the 1920's served as a consultant to W. E. Dever, the reform mayor. With the advent of the New Deal he was engaged as counsel to the Agricultural Adjustment Act and the Federal Surplus Relief Corporation, as special counsel to the Reconstruction Finance Corporation in its organization of the railroads, and as litigation counsel to the Works Project Administration. He returned to private practice in 1936, but the following year he was appointed a member of the Securities Exchange Commission, of which he became chairman in 1939. Two years later he was appointed a judge in the Federal Circuit Court of Appeals. Co-author with Judge Mack of the meritorious work, *Law and the Modern Mind* (1930), he also wrote *Save America First* (1938) and numerous scholarly books and articles.

Few Americans have achieved the legal eminence of Benjamin N. Cardozo (1870–1938). He came of an old and distinguished Sephardic family, a branch of which settled in

America in the eighteenth century. Yet he grew up under the cloud that stigmatized his father's career. The elder Cardozo (1828–1885), a prominent lawyer, was in 1863 elected to the court of common pleas and in 1867 to the New York supreme court. During the latter campaign a circular distributed to Jewish voters read, "Brethren, exercise your suffrage wisely and re-elect this honored man to the office for which he is so eminently fitted." As a sachem of Tammany, however, he was obligated to Boss Tweed and granted him various favors, among them the appointment of a receiver for the Erie Railroad, which led to an investigation by the state assembly. To avoid the embarrassment of a public trial, Judge Cardozo resigned his office in 1874. This was generally regarded as an admission of guilt, and caused him to lead a subdued and stigmatized existence to the end of his life.

Benjamin, a highly sensitive boy, was keenly affected by his father's political disgrace and resolved to redeem the family name from obloquy. Entering Columbia College in his sixteenth year, he made a brilliant record and graduated in two years. Too philosophical for success in the hurly-burly of daily practice, he trained himself to become a "lawyer's lawyer." In 1912 he was recommended for appointment to the New York supreme court, the next year he was elected to the same office, but in 1914 he was elevated to the New York State Court of Appeals at the request of the other judges on the court. Ten years later he became chief justice. In the interim he had become the influential liberal interpreter of common law. Thus when the Buick Motor Company argued that its duty was to the dealer and not to the purchaser of a car, Cardozo held that this was nonsense since the customer needed full protection. In another case he maintained that "danger invites rescue" and ruled that the person who was hurt in the effort to help an injured train passenger was also entitled to compensation. In the Benjamin Gitlow case he asserted that since no actual violence resulted from Gitlow's "Left Wing Manifesto," he had the protection of free speech. When the case was taken to the Supreme Court, he was overruled by the conservative majority, but had the satisfaction of having Holmes and Brandeis uphold him in their dissent.

In 1920 Cardozo published *That Nature of the Judical Process*, an analysis of the judicial process unequaled in legal literature. In *The Growth of the Law* (1923) he demonstrated that no simple approach to legal problems is adequate. *The Paradoxes of Legal Science* (1928) discussed the relation between justice and the law and stressed that the legal process must be one of compromise and concordance.

When Justice Holmes retired from the Supreme Court in 1932, there was general agreement among leading lawyers, judges, and politicians that Cardozo was his logical successor. President Hoover hesitated ostensibly because New York already had two Justices on the Court. Senator William Borah assured him, however, that "Cardozo belongs as much to Idaho as to New York. If there were two Virginians on the Court and John Marshall was a candidate for the vacancy, I don't think there would be any hesitation in appointing him." Nomination and confirmation thus became a matter of course.

Cardozo accepted the honor reluctantly. Nor was he content after he joined the Court. He was sensitive to insinuations that one Jew was enough on the Court, and Justice J. G. McReynolds' open anti-Semitism grieved him acutely.

During his six years on the Court he contributed to the liberal thesis of Justice Brandeis that the Constitution must not be construed as a rigid document but as a living organism growing and broadening to meet the needs of the nation. "Justice," he stated, "is a concept far more subtle and indefinite than any that is yielded by mere obedience to rule. It remains, to some extent, when all is said and done, the synonym of an aspiration, a mood of exaltation, a yearning for what is fine and high."

Cardozo was keenly aware of his Jewishness. He had gone through the rite of Bar Mitzvah and remained a lifelong member of the Sephardic Synagogue. A confirmed bachelor—he was said to be married to the law but more truly in bondage to fraternal fealty—he was most intimate with members of his immediate family. He went out of his way to help the oppressed Jews in Europe. When the Nazi atrocities became known, he was deeply distressed and turned to Zionism as a possible solution. His health became impaired some time before he died in 1938.

7

Louis D. Brandeis

COUNSEL
FOR THE
PEOPLE

LOUIS DAVID BRANDEIS'S immediate kin were enlightened Bohemian Jews who venerated learning and enjoyed the amenities of European culture. Adolph Brandeis, Louis's father, reached this country in 1849, and he was soon followed by the Wehle and Dembitz families—all hopeful of finding personal freedom and material comfort. Most of them settled in Louisville. Adolph became a grain and produce merchant and married Frederika Dembitz, to whom he had been engaged in Prague.

Louis David Brandeis was born on November 13, 1856, the youngest of four children. A precocious child and an excellent student, he was influenced at an early age by his uncle Lewis Dembitz, a gentle and scholarly liberal lawyer. At sixteen Louis was awarded a gold medal "for preeminence in all his studies." In 1872 his father, who had suffered reverses in the economic depression, took the family to Europe. There Louis was at first tutored privately and then attended the Dresden Annen-Realschule for three terms. As in Louisville, he was again an honor student and prize-winner. Yet he was irritated by the Prussian school discipline. "I was a terrible little individualist in those days," he stated years later, "and the German paternalism got on my nerves."

Admiration for his uncle influenced him to change his middle name to Dembitz, and, in further emulation of him he decided to study law. In May, 1875 he was back in Louisville, and the following September he was enrolled in Harvard Law School. He graduated with the highest rating in his class; his record has remained unequaled in the history of Harvard Law School. Brandeis was no longer satisfied to live in the West, and within a year left a job in St. Louis to join his classmate Samuel D. Warren in a partnership in Boston. Since Warren was also very able and highly placed socially, the partnership prospered. To gain additional experience Brandeis also served as law clerk to chief justice Horace Gray of the supreme judicial court of Massachusetts until 1881, when the latter was elevated to the Supreme Court of the United States.

Brandeis worked hard, but also enjoyed himself socially. Fully assimilated to his gentile environment, he was a welcome guest in Brahmin homes and developed a congenial group of friends. It was at this early period that he met and was befriended by Oliver Wendell Holmes, Jr.

In March, 1882, when Brandeis was twenty-five, Harvard's president, Charles W. Eliot, invited him to give a course on evidence at the Law School. Since he was toying with the idea of an academic career, he gladly accepted the offer. Subsequently, however, he refused an assistant professorship. He had become attracted to trial cases and enjoyed familiarizing himself with the social background of the law. What primarily interested him, then and later, were human motivation and the quality of justice.

In 1889, Warren gave up law to succeed his father as head of the family paper business. Although the partnership was dissolved, the two friends collaborated on a paper, "The Right to Privacy," which Roscoe Pound praised as doing "nothing less than add a chapter to our law."

Brandeis had by then established himself as one of Boston's leading corporation lawyers, with a lucrative practice. He strongly disapproved, however, of the tendency of lawyers to become *de facto* employees of corporations. "I would rather have clients," he stated pointedly, "than be somebody's lawyer." His office became one of the busiest in New England and his reputation spread to New York and other industrial centers.

He married his second cousin Alice Goldmark on March 23, 1891. She too was quick of mind, cultivated, and imbued with broad social sympathies. She shared her husband's aims and ideals, and fully agreed with him on a modest mode of living in order to be free of financial pressure. For on this point his mind was fixed: he dreaded the thought of financial insecurity, believing that "the man without some capital can only continue to slave and toil for others to the end of his days." To assure his independence he saved his surplus earnings and in time accumulated a considerable fortune.

Brandeis worked strenuously, but he knew how to relax. He enjoyed social conversation, tramping through the woods, sailing, riding horseback over country roads. His wife and he, close companions, took delight in bringing up their two daughters and in spending much of their leisure together.

Brandeis's career as a social crusader began slowly. As a young lawyer in the 1880's he had taken a mild interest in public affairs and joined others occasionally in furthering civic reforms. In 1890 his attention was attracted to the shady political aspects of the liquor business, and he advocated remedial legislation. Four years later he was engaged as counsel by a wealthy woman who was distressed by the abysmal condition of the Boston pauper institutions. He presented evidence of mismanagement and faulty organi-

zation before the board of aldermen and succeeded in re-
forming the department in charge of public institutions.
His fee of $3,000 he donated to charitable and civic or-
ganizations. Thereafter he refused payment for work of a
public nature and soon became known as "counsel for the
people."

Franchises to traction companies next aroused his
interest. It seemed to him wrong for the city to grant valuable monopoly rights to private corporations without adequate return to the people. When metropolitan Boston
decided in the late 1890's to build subways, the traction company requested a long-term franchise that would place all
transportation facilities under its sole control. Edward A.
Filene, the wealthy and public-spirited merchant, engaged
Brandeis to help him fight it. They formed the Public Franchise League and enlisted a group of civic leaders in a successful campaign to reduce the term of the lease and to
obtain proper compensation for the city. When Filene
insisted on paying Brandeis for his months of effort, the
latter countered, "I'll take half of what you get out of it."

More than ever he now believed that it was wrong for
a corporation lawyer to serve his clients at the expense of
the public. He maintained that such a lawyer, not having
"studied economics and sociology [was] very apt to become a public enemy." Moreover, it was his view that a
lawyer was duty-bound to instruct and lead public opinion.
"All law is a dead letter without public opinion behind it,
but law and public opinion interact and they are both capable of being made." In the fight against the traction company, he had incurred the sharp hostility of the wealthy
men connected with it. Some of these bankers and industrialists were prominent Brahmins with whom he had long
been very friendly, but as the campaign continued, they
openly impugned his motives.

In the process of investigating the transportation franchise, he discovered that graft and corruption were per-
verting the city and state legislators. Certain of them, in
the habit of exchanging favors with public corporations,

had as many as 200 friends and henchmen on company payrolls. With the aid of other prominent citizens he formed the Good Government Association and began a publicity campaign against corrupt office holders. "The politician can stand any amount of attack," he explained, "but he cannot stand the opposition of public opinion."

Ironically, in his effort to be fair to both the public and corporations, he also incurred the hostility of certain reformers. The Consolidated Gas Company, organized in 1904, followed the current practice of other industrial combinations by attempting to water its stock and raise prices. A few public-spirited citizens called on Brandeis to help them stop this practice. His first move was to study the manufacture and sale of gas. When he discovered that it would be possible for Consolidated to lower the price to consumers and still make a fair profit, he thought it best to come to an understanding with the company on this basis rather than to fight for public ownership. He managed to persuade the head of Consolidated to use a sliding scale of prices but the plan failed to satisfy the zealous reformers.

He was still involved in the fight for cheaper gas when he was drawn into the investigation of life insurance companies. In 1905 the struggle for control of the Equitable Life Assurance Company threatened its disruption. Certain of Boston's large policy holders became alarmed, formed the New England Policy Holders Protective Committee, and persuaded Brandeis to serve as counsel. Sensing an involvement of the public good, he insisted on functioning without a fee. A summer's study of the life insurance business convinced him of the need of "radical changes in the system." At his recommendation the legislature created the Armstrong Committee with Charles Evans Hughes as counsel. Soon the egregious practices of high insurance officials became front-page news, and the legislature enacted some of the committee's recommendations into law.

Brandeis considered the measures quite inadequate. What perturbed him particularly was the realization that the large insurance companies, collecting many millions in premiums, were in a position to dominate the money market and to manipulate the nation's economy to their own ends. He was also disturbed by the shocking revelations in the field of industrial insurance: the companies spent as overhead forty cents of every dollar paid by workers, two thirds of these industrial policies lapsed or became forfeit within three years of issue, and workers were paid back only one third of their actual premiums.

Searching for a remedy, he studied annual reports of life insurance companies, savings banks, and state insurance commissions. He found life insurance to be essentially a very simple business, requiring primarily "honesty, accuracy, persistence, and economy." From a study of 188 savings banks he learned that their overhead costs were 17 times lower than those of insurance companies. He thereupon concluded that savings banks could add insurance departments and operate them as economically as their other divisions. He published a detailed exposition of the plan in *Collier's*; presented with the zest of a muckraker, the project received wide national publicity.

With the cooperation of a few key bankers, Brandeis organized the Massachusetts Savings-Bank Insurance League and campaigned for the necessary legislation. When the plan was legalized, such men as William L. Douglas, a former governor and large shoe manufacturer, helped Brandeis persuade certain bank officials to give the scheme a trial. Labor leaders also helped to promote it within their unions. Brandeis considered the reform his "greatest achievement," and his active interest in it continued to the end of his life. Although savings banks did not compete with insurance companies, their mere presence in the field forced the companies to lower their rates by twenty percent and to provide policy holders with additional advantages.

Experience and reflection intensified Brandeis's belief that monopoly was an evil tendency in American business; that bigness was not necessarily an advantage and was often a handicap to efficiency. "Human nature is such," he maintained, "that monopolies, however well intentioned, and however well regulated, inevitably become, in the course of time, oppressive, arbitrary, unprogressive, and inefficient."

When General Samuel C. Lawrence and his son William, large stockholders in the Boston and Maine Railroad Company, asked Brandeis in 1905 to serve as counsel in their effort to prevent the projected merger of that railroad with the New Haven Railroad Company, he readily agreed—refusing a fee on the ground that the case was affected with a public interest. (Subsequently he paid his partners over $25,000 of his own money as their share of his entitled remuneration.) His initial efforts to stop the merger were frustrated by backers of the New Haven, and he was abused as a "chronic howler."

Brandeis began to familiarize himself with the New Haven's financial operations. When President Charles S. Mellen refused him the information he requested, he dug it out of state, federal, and stock-exchange reports, spending $6,000 of his own money to do so. Persuaded of the unsoundness of the company, he was appalled to find that it was paying its customary 8-percent dividend in 1907 when its earnings that year in no way justified it.

He wrote a critical pamphlet on the subject of the railroad's finances, and large stockholders and the company's paid publicists attacked him as a vicious and irresponsible trouble maker. Yet a number of civic-minded citizens, alarmed by his findings, came to his defense and helped him form the Massachusetts Anti-Merger League to oppose the New Haven bills in the legislature.

Brandeis continued his study of the railroad's financial condition and publicized the fact that it paid its 8-percent dividend in 1908 in the face of an actual deficit. When the state committee headed by Charles Francis Adams approved the merger, Brandeis was quick to point out that members of the committee were New Haven stockholders. He also made known the facts that the New Haven's obligations were three times the value of its capital, that its funded indebtedness had increased more than elevenfold in fifteen years and amounted to two and a half times the market value of its outstanding stock. By 1912 Mellen could no longer conceal the railroad's plight.

The election of Woodrow Wilson made possible an impartial investigation of the New Haven by the Interstate Commerce Commission. The hearings uncovered various false bookkeeping entries as well as phony sales and repurchases of stock. The company accused Brandeis of unethical practices and intimated that he was in the employ of "the man higher up." It also employed C. W. Barron, at a cost of $133,000, to publish a number of articles favorable to itself and damnatory of Brandeis. In the end, the federal report placed the blame where it belonged: "Had the stockholders of the New Haven, instead of vilifying the road's critics, given some attention to the charges made, their property would today be of greater value and the problem an easier one."

Although dividends were reduced and Mellen resigned, Brandeis maintained that the roots of the company's difficulties remained untouched. A second investigation undertaken at his urging, made clear that the financial operations of the board of directors, controlled by the late J. P. Morgan, were both "reckless and profligate." Eventually the Attorney General started a suit for the dissolution of the New Haven system. Not until 1927 were dividends resumed, so damaging had been the interference by bankers in railroad management.

Brandeis further antagonized New England's wealthy conservatives when he opposed the tie-in clause in the sales contracts of the United Shoe Machinery Company. They accused him of a rank betrayal of trust, since he had previously served as a director of the company in the interests of one of his clients. He had, moreover, invested $10,000 of his own money in the firm's preferred stock, and in 1906 as its counsel, had defended the tie-in policy. At the time, Brandeis explained subsequently, he had believed that the company's efficiency favored the interests of shoe manufacturers. He changed his mind when some of his clients complained that the tie-in clause restricted their operations. When he failed to persuade Sidney Winslow, the United president, to delete the objectionable clause, he resigned as director and counsel and sold his stock.

For the ensuing three and a half years he refused to act in cases pertaining to the United. In 1910 he advised a client that the tie-in clause, in the light of recent court decisions, was probably illegal and that he might buy the superior machines of T. J. Plant, a new manufacturer. The United exerted pressure upon friendly bankers not to renew a loan to Plant, thereby forcing him to sell his business to United. Brandeis told Senator Robert M. LaFollette, "The United Company's purchase of Plant's business, particularly the only competitor in shoe machinery, was the most flagrant instance of violating the antitrust law that I have known."

When the Shoe Manufacturers Alliance asked Brandeis to serve as counsel against the United, he agreed—again without a fee. At the antitrust hearings of a Congressional committee his testimony was condemned by Winslow as "grossly inaccurate and wilfully untrue." Winslow also issued a pamphlet entitled "The Reversible Mind of Louis D. Brandeis," in which he sought to discredit him by means of cleverly juxtaposed statements taken out of context. This attack notwithstanding, the government proceeded to act against the United in 1915 under the Clayton Antitrust Act.

Although Brandeis was primarily a corporation lawyer, the brutal Homestead strike in 1892 aroused his interest in industrial labor relations. He observed the conditions of employment, read books on labor economics, and discussed the subject with men specializing in the field of social problems. He was soon convinced of the necessity of labor unions. In 1902 he stated, "If unions are lawless, restrain and punish their lawlessness; if they are arbitrary, repress their arbitrariness; if their demands are unreasonable or unjust, resist them; but do not oppose unions as such." He favored the incorporation of unions to make them more responsible and consequently more acceptable to employers, thereby antagonizing leading labor leaders. In 1902 he helped to prepare the case of the striking coal miners for consideration by a Presidential committee.

Certain that the root of labor unrest lay not so much in low wages as in irregular employment, he was surprised to find that both employers and workers accepted unemployment as inevitable. In a number of instances he demonstrated to employer clients the advantage of steady employment and ways of eliminating seasonal peaks and depressions. He also sought to persuade them of the desirability of trade unions. "In a democracy," he maintained, "we must avoid industrial absolutism, even though it be benevolent despotism." At the time, however, most employers subscribed to the views of George E. Baer, a wealthy coal-mine operator, who asserted that employers were "Christian men to whom God in his infinite wisdom has given the control of the property interests of the country." Brandeis recoiled from such arrogance. After settling a strike in 1907, he wrote to his brother Alfred, "I am experiencing a growing conviction that the labor men are the most congenial company. The intense materialism and luxuriousness of most of our other people makes their company quite irksome."

He was increasingly perturbed by the social insensibility of those judges who clung to the letter of superannuated laws and ignored aspects of modern industrial society. When the Supreme Court in 1905 invalidated a New York ten-hour law for bakers—the majority calling the law in question a "mere meddlesome interference with the rights of individuals"—Brandeis became eager to demonstrate the fallacy of this ruling.

The opportunity came two years later when he was asked to defend the Oregon ten-hour law for women workers. He engaged his sister-in-law Josephine Goldmark of the National Consumer League to gather reports and statistics on the effects of overwork on the health of women. These social and medical data, obtained from all parts of the world, he studied and sifted. In his long brief he devoted almost the entire argument to the pertinent facts, rather than to legal precedent. Sweeping aside the abstraction of freedom of contract, he shocked the Justices into an acknowledgment of the realities of modern industrialism.

The unexpected success of his novel brief gave a sudden turn to the course of American social legislation. The facts of industrial life had established their pertinence in the nation's highest court, now and then ignored or disdained, but generally taken into account. Despite his failure in 1914 to validate the Oregon minimum-wage law, many competent observers felt that, in the words of Judge William Hitz, "he not only *reached* the Court, but he *dwarfed* the Court, because it was clear that here stood a man who knew infinitely more, and who care infinitely more for the vital daily rights of the people than the men who sat there sworn to protect them."

His reputation as a successful mediator and friend of labor brought him into the 1910 deadlocked cloakmakers' strike in New York. The suffering of tens of thousands of strikers and their families gained the attention of public-spirited citizens, who perceived that the strike was the desperate reaction to years of exploitation and abuse.

Meyer Bloomfield, a prominent Boston social worker, interested A. Lincoln Filene in an attempt to settle the strike, but a visit to New York revealed that both sides were adamant on the issue of the closed shop—the radical union leaders insisting on it and the employers refusing to consider it. When Filene realized that only "a big man" might manage to break the deadlock, he persuaded Brandeis to make the attempt.

Arriving in New York, Brandeis chaired a conference between representatives of the union and of the manufacturers. Placing the issue of the closed shop, to which he

himself was opposed, last on the agenda, he dealt first
with the simpler problems. To keep the sessions from breaking up he used "flattery, cajolery, and diplomacy." When he
finally brought the representatives to the pivotal topic of
the closed shop, he offered a compromise solution which
became a milestone in the history of industrial relations:
the preferential union shop, in which "the manufacturers
should, in the employment of labor hereafter, give the pref-
erance to union men, where the union men are equal in
efficiency to any non-union applicants." The manufacturers,
were soon persuaded; the radical union leaders, fearing
the danger of compromise, balked. *The Jewish Daily Forward*, read by most strikers, called the idea "a scab shop
with honey." It took much discussion and the persuasive
talents of Brandeis and his two fellow mediators, Morris
Hillquit and Hamilton Holt, as well as the intercession of
Louis Marshall and Jacob Schiff, to induce the union leaders to accept the settlement, called by Marshall "a protocol
of peace" to make it sound more impressive.

The settlement resulted in the establishment of machinery for the settlement of future disputes and grievances. Brandeis agreed to serve as chairman of the board
of arbitration, but limited his role to matters of basic policy.
During the ensuing five years he sought to keep the protocol from breaking down despite the sniping from both
sides. When it finally collapsed in 1916—it had by then
become "a mechanism of joint frustration"—there was
general relief. But Brandeis had had the satisfaction of
keeping a major part of the unstable garment industry
free from strikes for six years.

The political insurgency which culminated in the election of Woodrow Wilson to the Presidency brought Brandeis
into the national scene. His reputation as "counsel for the
people" led to his choice as lawyer for the conservationists
in the Congressional hearings of charges made against
Secretary of the Interior Richard A. Ballinger in connection with the dismissal of Louis R. Glavis, an advocate of

conservation. Norman Hapgood, editor of *Collier's*, who had published Glavis's anti-Ballinger article and feared a libel suit if the Secretary were exonerated, engaged Brandeis as counsel for Glavis.

Brandeis immediately made a careful study of the scope and functions of the Department of Interior, and became so familiar with the details of its activities that he was able to prompt Department witnesses concerning their official duties. He soon perceived discrepancies in the government evidence, but the Committee majority refused to aid in the procurement of significant documents and hampered his interrogation of witnesses. Fortunately for him, the three liberals on the Committee blocked the majority efforts at a "whitewash."

Although Brandeis suspected collusion between two high government officials in connection with Ballinger's official exoneration, he was unable to prove it—until a young stenographer came to his assistance. The stenographer revealed that President Taft's letter approving Glavis's dismissal was written by Assistant-Attorney General Oscar Lawlor in Ballinger's office. The White House, unaware of Attorney General George W. Wickersham's delivery of the letter, issued a quick denial, only to admit the truth the next day. The Committee's majority, enraged that Brandeis had caught President Taft in an untruth, delayed its report for months and then cleared Ballinger by a vote of seven to five, but bitter criticism by the minority and by liberals the country over forced Ballinger to resign.

If Brandeis added to his enemies among the privileged and the conservatives, he gained numerous admirers among influential insurgents. Senator LaFollette, Representative Norris, and other progressive government officials became his close friends and began to depend upon him for advice. As the country's outstanding liberal lawyer he was asked to serve on many important cases affecting the public interest. Thus, when the railroads north of the Ohio and east of the Mississippi rivers applied for a rate increase, he was asked to serve as counsel to the Interstate

Commerce Commission. Revealing inefficiency and incompetence in the operation of the railroads, he demonstrated to their executives on the witness stand that if they were as interested in reducing costs as they were in raising rates and dividends they could save a million dollars a day and make a rate increase unnecessary. He pointed out specifically how to effect this saving and was corroborated by efficiency experts and western railroad officers. The I.C.C. thereupon denied the increase.

Three years later the same railroads again asked for a rate increase, and once more the I.C.C. called on Brandeis. He brought himself up to date, and his questions, as they elicited information about dubious ethics and obvious inefficiency, proved embarrassing to both large shippers and railroad spokesmen. Some of the opponents of the rate increase resented the revelation of favors to large shippers, claiming that Brandeis was unfair. Brandeis's final finding was that the net income of the railroads was "smaller than is consistent with their assured prosperity and the welfare of the community," but that there were other means of remedying the situation than by horizontal increase. Thereupon Clifford Thorne, representing Midwestern shippers, criticized him for favoring the railroads. The Commission, however, favored Brandeis's recommendation.

A firm believer in the advantages of competition, Brandeis found that large railroads and gigantic corporations "far exceeded the limit of greatest efficiency." Testifying before the Senate Committee on Interstate Commerce in 1911 he was particularly critical of the heads of the money trust who dominated the policies of large corporations. He also maintained that monopoly was not only undemocratic but tended to become "inefficient both economically and socially," since it "develops a centrifugal force greater than the centripetal forces." He further deprecated the relation of trusts to their employees, declaring that democracy thrives only when men are free and that men are not free without industrial liberty. "Without the right to organize, short hours, high wages, and the best of working conditions, whether introduced by legislation or by welfare departments of great corporations, can do no more than to make slavery luxurious."

Some months later he assisted another Congressional committee in an investigation of the United States Steel Corporation whose chairman, Judge E. H. Gary, had boastfully testified that his labor policy "compares favorably with that of any line of industry in this country or any other country at the present time or any period in the history of the world." Brandeis countered by asserting that the company employed tens of thousands of men twelve hours a day and seven days a week at bare subsistence wages. Such industrial oppression, he insisted, was "alien to American conditions."

The election of 1912 enabled him to inject his antitrust views into the political campaign. He admired Senator LaFollette and he joined the National Progressive Republican League to promote his candidacy for the Presidency. But LaFollette was sidetracked in favor of Roosevelt, and Brandeis, who did not consider the former President a true progressive and who disagreed with his trust policy, offered his assistance to Woodrow Wilson. He visited the Democratic nominee in August to explain his views on trusts, and several weeks later, when Wilson came to Boston, the two discussed campaign issues. Shortly thereafter Wilson telegraphed Brandeis: "Please set forth as explicitly as possible the actual measures by which competition can be efficiently regulated. The more explicit we are on this point, the more completely the enemy's guns will be spiked." In compliance, Brandeis wrote a series of editorials and signed articles for *Collier's* defining and highlighting the basic issues of the campaign. He was especially critical of Roosevelt's acquiescence in the weak monopoly plank and his acceptance of George Perkins, a Morgan partner, as his treasurer and campaign manager.

President-elect Wilson thought highly of Brandeis— "a talk with Brandeis always sweeps the cobwebs out of one's mind"—and was prepared to offer him a Cabinet post. On learning of this possibility, highly placed Bostonians and a number of influential politicians accused Brandeis of unfitness for the high office. This was early disproved by Norman Hapgood, who investigated the incriminating charges and insinuations at Wilson's request, but the President yielded to keep party harmony at the outset of his Administration. He did offer him the chairmanship of the new Commission on Industrial Relations, but Brandeis preferred to serve as an informal adviser to Wilson and the several members of the Cabinet. During the fight for the currency bill he sided with Secretary of State Bryan in his insistence on governmental control of the currency. In the furtherance of antitrust legislation he told Wilson that "the fearless course is the wise one," and his ideas prevailed both in the Clayton Act and in the measure creating the Federal Trade Commission.

In 1914 Brandeis's views on banking and business appeared in two books. *Other People's Money and How Bankers Use It* consists of a series of articles originally published in *Harper's Weekly*; and *Business—A Profession*, a collection of papers and speeches reflecting his activities as a business analyst and social critic. In these books he made effective use of the Pujo Committee Report on Wall Street financial manipulations. Explaining that the "banker-barons levied . . . a heavy toll upon the whole community," he maintained that even more serious was "the effect of the Money Trust in directly suppressing competition. . . . Monopoly arrests development, and through arresting development prevents that lessening of the cost of production and of distribution which would otherwise take place."

His criticism of interlocking directorates was particularly stringent. Nor did he favor the spread of stock-ownership, then coming into favor. It was his view that instead of democratizing business, it was in fact encouraging "absentee ownership of the worst kind," since it permitted the management of a company to exercise absolute control without any corresponding responsibility except to provide dividends to stockholders. He also advocated compulsory and complete publicity regarding new issues of stock to minimize fraud and unsound speculation. He further proposed—in 1914 a revolutionary concept—that "the State must in some way come to the aid of workingmen if democratization [of business] is to be secured." His position within the Wilson Administration enabled him to incorporate a number of his proposed reforms into law.

Brought up in a liberal, agnostic environment, Brandeis grew up knowing little of Judaism. Although he felt a strong attachment to his family and admired his uncle Lewis Dembitz, he made no effort to join the Jewish community in Boston. Although he did not deny his Jewish origin or refuse to contribute to Jewish philanthropy, his interests and predilections centered in his Boston milieu.

He became conscious of his Jewishness when his attacks upon franchises made him unwelcome in the homes where he had previously been courted. It hurt him to learn that more than one Brahmin had begun to refer sneeringly to his "oriental" mind, and the thrust cut deep. Probing the nature of the slur, he became increasingly aware of the prevailing anti-Semitism. Always ready to combat injustice and prejudice, ever inclined to explore a problem to its source, he soon familiarized himself with the history of the Jewish people. This knowledge was given concrete content by his association with the New York garment workers after 1910. Thinking of their poverty and idealism, he began to feel a sympathetic kinship with them.

When the idea of a Jewish homeland came to his attention about that time, he considered it a desirable solution to the problem of finding a new abode for the oppressed European Jews. In March, 1913 he made his first public avowal of Zionism by serving as chairman at a meeting honoring Nahum Sokolow, a leading European Zionist.

The plight of East-European Jews at the war front impelled him to accept the chairmanship of the Provisional Executive Committee for Zionist Affairs, which was to replace the disrupted Zionist organization in Europe. He was the first to donate a thousand dollars to the emergency fund and traveled to a number of cities to address Jewish communities and collect funds for the support of the war victims as well as the stranded Palestine colonies. In his speeches he expounded the nature of anti-Semitism, overt and covert, and stressed the need of Jews to exercise the rights common to others, the consistency of Zionism with Americanism, the duty of Jews to further Palestinian settlement of those not wanted in the lands of their birth. To the cry of "hyphenated Americanism," he countered, "Every American Jew who aids in advancing the Jewish settlement in Palestine, though he feels that neither he nor his descendants will ever live there, will likewise be a better man and a better American for doing so. . . . There is no inconsistency between loyalty to America and loyalty to Jewry."

For the next two years he devoted a large part of his time to Jewish affairs. Always the democrat, he fought for the establishment of a Congress that would represent every faction within the Jewish community, opposing the wealthy leaders of the American Jewish Committee who considered themselves adequate representatives of American Jewry. When a plebiscite was taken and the Congress was favored by a large majority, Brandeis's reaction was typical: "Among a free people the body which makes a decision must necessarily be democratic, since among the free people there can be no self-constituted body of men possessing the power to decide what the action of the people will be. . . . The Congress is indisputable if the end sought is to be obtained."

Brandeis exercised leadership at considerable cost to his popularity among certain Zionist functionaries. For all his sympathy and insight, he had difficulty tolerating those bent on presenting their views rather than doing their assigned work. His insistence on careful attention to detail, on regular and full reports from committees and subordinates, and on the prompt payment of pledges gave his leadership a semblance of "autocratic" strictness.

Although he resigned his Zionist office on joining the Supreme Court, he remained an active, if informal participant. When the question of a Jewish homeland in Palestine became a live issue among Allied diplomats in 1917, he took the initiative in discussing it with President Wilson and British Foreign Secretary Arthur Balfour. He also helped in the formulation and general acceptance of the Balfour Declaration on Palestine, announced in November, 1917. Two months later, when Chaim Weizmann headed a commission sent to Palestine, Brandeis admonished him to stress socio-economic objectives, stating that "The utmost vigilance should be exercised to prevent the acquisition by private persons of land, water rights or other natural resources, or any concessions for public utilities. These must all be secured for the whole Jewish people. In other ways, as well as in this, the possibility of capitalistic exploitation must be guarded against." These proposals for a democratic Palestine were enthusiastically adopted by the American Zionists at their 1918 convention.

In June, 1919, Brandeis visited England and France to consult with leading Zionists and peace delegates. On meeting Weizmann, he wrote to his wife that the man is "neither as great nor as objectionable as he has been painted. But he is very much of a man and much bigger than most of his fellows." He then proceeded to Palestine and his tour of the ancient Jewish homeland strenghened his belief in Zionism. The potential development of the eroded and arid land excited his optimism and he envisioned it as "a miniature California." To his wife he wrote, "The problems and difficulties are serious and numerous—even more so than I had anticipated; but there is none which will not be solved and overcome by the indomitable spirit of the Jews here and elsewhere." To this end he urged the 1919 Zionist convention to concentrate on the economic and agricultural rehabilitation of the neglected land. He also exerted his influence to modify the terms of the secret Sykes-Pecot Treaty, which gave part of Palestine to Syria. This was done at the San Remo Conference.

In July, 1920, as a leading participant in the world Zionist Convention in London, he insisted on practical action to strengthen the Jewish position in Palestine and clashed with those who were concerned primarily with its political problems. "We have come," he declared, "to the time when there are no politics that are valuable except the politics of action. We have got to be able to act in Palestine, and we have got to be strong outside of Palestine." This strength, he asserted, must come from an organized Jewry ready to provide the money to build up a Jewish Palestine toward its economic independence. "We are to bring into Palestine, as rapidly as we can, as many persons as we can; that really comprises the whole thing."

Weizmann strongly opposed this policy and maintained that Brandeis lacked a real knowledge of the Jews who were expected to migrate to Palestine; that he based his program on ideals of efficiency which did not square with reality. A much more practical politician, he defeated Brandeis's plan and forced him to withdraw from further participation in the convention. Subsequent developments widened the rift between the two leaders. Weizmann attended the Cleveland Zionist convention in 1921 and again won the majority of the delegates to his program. Thereupon Brandeis and his associates resigned their leadership and took their places as "humble soldiers in the ranks"— certain that their views would sooner or later "be recognized as the only ones through which our great ends may be achieved." In the years that followed Brandeis kept himself relatively aloof from formal Zionist activities, but his dream of a flourishing Jewish homeland in Palestine remained precious to him to the end.

On January 28, 1916, without consulting any Senator or party leader, President Wilson nominated Brandeis to the Supreme Court. Outcries of shock and dismay were immediate and emphatic. Eminent lawyers, prominent bankers, powerful businessmen, and leading college presidents considered the appointment an insult to the nation and joined in opposing it. Former President Taft, whom Brandeis had caught in an untruth and who had himself expected the Justiceship, called it "one of the deepest wounds that I have had as an American and lover of the Constitution and a believer in progressive conservatism that such a man as Brandeis could be put on the Court. . . . He is a muckraker, an emotionalist for his own purpose, a socialist." (Less than a decade later Taft, as Chief Justice, said of Brandeis, "I do not see how we could get along without him.") He and six other former presidents of the American Bar Association protested to the Senate Committee on the Judiciary: "The undersigned feel under the painful duty to say to you that in their opinion, taking into view the reputation, character, and professional career of Mr. Louis D. Brandeis, he is not a fit person to be a member of the Supreme Court of the United States." Fifty-five leading Bostonians, including President A. Lawrence Lowell of Harvard and a number of Brandeis's former friends, sent a similar joint objection to the nomination.

At the Senate subcommittee hearings, witness after witness sought to besmirch Brandeis's reputation and character. Louis A. Coolidge, treasurer of the United Shoe Machinery Company, remarked curtly, "It is customary to consign crooks to jail and not to the bench." Thorne, of the shipping interests, asserted that Brandeis was "guilty of infidelity, breach of faith and unprofessional conduct in connection with one of the greatest cases of this generation." C. W. Barron, the highly paid publicist for the New Haven, was especially vicious: "Brandeis at the bar may represent individual wrongs, but Brandeis on the bench puts the United States before the world below even the present standards of his Teutonic ancestors." *The Outlook* remarked editorially of these witnesses, "Hearsay, opinions, prejudice, gossip, and rumors unrelated to any fact have been put before the Committee as if they were evidence of value."

Friends of Brandeis, mostly loyal liberals, came to his defense. They wanted to expose the motives and corporate associations of the hostile witnesses, but Administration advisers insisted that subcommittee approval could be obtained only on a strict party basis and that the injection of the liberal issue would alienate the conservative Democratic Senators. Brandeis agreed to this strategy and countered every charge and insinuation with documents that often proved almost the exact contrary.

A number of prominent men spoke up in his favor. Nine of the eleven professors at Harvard Law School, including Roscoe Pound, urged confirmation. Nationally known social workers, teachers, labor leaders, and various others joined in supporting him. LaFollette asked Brandeis to prepare a brief of the testimony to use in a Senate speech, adding. "There will be some hot work before the vote comes, and the hell hounds must get what is coming to them—I mean the Bar Association presidents, University presidents —these sleek respectable crooks—whose opinions have always been for sale." Conscious of an anti-Semitic undercurrent in the attack, Brandeis wrote to his brother, "I suppose eighteen centuries of Jewish persecution must have inured me to such hardships and developed the like of a duck's back."

On April 1 the subcommittee of five Senators recommended confirmation by a party vote of three to two, but the Committee as a whole, took no action for weeks thereafter. President Wilson exerted political pressure by making public his complete confidence in Brandeis; at the same time he went out of his way to be pleasant to doubtful Democratic Senators on the Committee.

At this juncture Charles W. Eliot, former president of Harvard and probably the most distinguished living American, issued a statement that effectively nullified the criticisms of his successor and other Bostonians:

I have known Mr. Louis D. Brandeis for forty years and believe that I understand his capacities and his character. . . . His professional career has exhibited . . . much practical altruism and public spirit. He has sometimes advocated measures or policies which did not commend themselves to me, but I have never questioned his honesty and sincerity, or his desire for justice.

On May 24 the Committee recommended confirmation by a strict party vote of ten to eight. A week later the Senate affirmed the nomination by a vote of 47 to 22, and on June 5 Brandeis took the oath of office. Evaluating the fight against him, the bitterest in the history of the Supreme Court, he could not restrain his anger at those who had sought to denigrate him by slander and innuendo—and even more the fact that "the community permitted them to do so almost without a protest. This seems to me the fundamental defect."

Justice Brandeis was the first member of the Supreme Court with insight into the workings of modern business enterprise, fulfilling Justice Holmes's prediction that "the man of the future is the man of statistics and the master of economics." Simultaneously he was a warm-hearted liberal, so that he approached every case with a humane realism that frequently antagonized his conservative colleagues. Yet his dissents, often supported by Holmes, were destined to become guideposts for later majority decisions. For he was aware, according to Professor Edmond Cahn, "that the one most important cosmic fact of the twentieth century is the acceleration in the rate of social change."

He was endowed with an enormous capacity for work and scrupulously conscious of the ambiguity of language. When preparing an opinion, he first made a study of the practical aspects of the statute under consideration, then familiarized himself with the legal precedents cited in the briefs, and finally wrote and revised his opinion until every word gave its clear meaning—in one instance rewriting it twenty-six times before he was satisfied. During his first Court term he wrote more than a score of opinions and five dissents. Typical of the latter was the one pertaining to a Washington state law prohibiting employment agencies from taking fees from workers. The majority, considering only the legal aspects, invalidated it as a violation of the due-process clause of the Fourteenth Amendment. Brandeis was more interested in the abuses of the employment agencies—extortionate fees, discrimination, and collusion with foremen—and therefore stressed the more positive element of the law, which was the elimination of unemployment. "The problem," he insisted, "which confronted the people of Washington was far more comprehensive and fundamental than that of protecting workers applying to the private agencies. It was the chronic problem of unemployment—perhaps the gravest and most difficult problem of modern industry." This and other of his dissents prepared the way for the eventual acceptance of his advanced social views.

A number of his majority and minority opinions dealt with questions of organized labor and civil liberty. Unintimidated by existing ideas on natural rights and freedom of contract, he insisted on relating them to twentieth-century social realities. He maintained that legislators had the right to experiment in the areas of labor and industry. "The divergence of opinion in this difficult field of governmental action should admonish us not to declare a rule arbitrary and unreasonable merely because we are convinced that it is fraught with danger to the public weal, and thus close the door to experiment within the law." In vigorous dissents he opposed the "yellow dog" contract, the labor injunction, and the interpretation of the Sherman and Clayton Acts as repressive of union activities and thus imposing "restraints upon labor which remind of involuntary servitude." Yet sympathetic as he was to the legitimate needs of labor, he was as opposed as any of the conservative Justices to union abuses. Having long held that unions must be responsible and law-abiding organizations, he stated that "individual liberty, like civil liberty, must rest upon the solid foundation of law." He joined the majority in ruling that a trade union was suable under the Sherman Act.

Ever concerned for the protection of the individual, Brandeis was most incisive and eloquent in his defense of civil liberties. Together with Justice Holmes, who had very soon become his partner in dissent, he struck forcefully against bureaucratic arbitrariness and majority arrogance. In opposing the antilibertarian laws passed during World

War I, the two worked mind to mind in the effort to preserve civil liberties from unwarranted abuse. The touchstone of "clear and present danger," first enunciated by Holmes in the Schenck case, was used by them in a number of influential dissents. "Men may differ widely," Brandeis cautioned in the Schafer case, "as to what loyalty to our country demands; and an intolerant majority, swayed by passion or by fear, may be prone in the future, as it has often been in the past, to stamp as disloyal opinions with which it disagrees." In his dissenting opinion on the deprivation of second-class mailing privileges from *The Milwaukee Leader*, a socialist newspaper, he argued that the order was a punitive rather than preventive measure. And although he concurred in the conviction of Anita Whitney, a California communist [who failed to question the "clear and present danger" aspect of her case], he took the opportunity to restate what he considered the fundamental philosophy underlying American democracy and his objection to the arbitrary suppression of free speech.

> Those who won our independence by revolution were not cowards. They did not fear political change. They did not exalt order at the cost of liberty. To courageous, self-reliant men, with confidence in the power of free and fearless reasoning applied through the process of popular government, no danger flowing from speech can be deemed clear and present, unless the incidence of the evil apprehended is so imminent that it may befall before there is opportunity for full discussion. If there be time to expose through discussion the falsehood and fallacies, to avert the evil by the process of education, the remedy to be applied is more speech, not enforced silence. Only an emergency can justify repression. Such must be the rule if authority is to be reconciled with freedom. Such, in my opinion, is the command of the Constitution.

Late in 1931 the nation's most eminent citizens paid homage to Justice Brandeis on his seventy-fifth birthday. Fifteen years on the Supreme Court had established him as one of the great American jurists. A number of writers recalled with an air of incredulity the fear and animosity aroused by his appointment.

Age had hardly slackened his intense pace. He continued to rise early and work steadily through the day. His interest in the world remained as strong as ever. The Sacco-Vanzetti case had greatly perturbed him for he could not, despite his sympathy for them, legally grant the petition in their behalf. He was also troubled by the hectic prosperity of the 1920s, and in 1926 he declared, "I wish to record my utter inability to understand why a lot of folks don't go broke. These consolidations and security flotations, plus the building boom, beat my comprehension— unless there is a breakdown within a year."

When the crash came three years later, he was less concerned for the shorn lambs in the stock market than for the victims of forced unemployment. He despaired of any solution under President Hoover—for whom he had had great respect a decade earlier—and hoped that the crisis would bring forth a leader of vision and courage. He was of this state of mind when he wrote his dissent in the Oklahoma ice company case, maintaining that under certain conditions the production of ice assumed the attributes of a public utility. Presaging the advent of the New Deal, he declared,

> There must be power in the States and the Nation to remold, through experimentation, our economic practices and institutions to meet changing social and economic needs. . . . It is one of the happy incidents of the federal system that a single courageous State may, if its citizens choose, serve as a laboratory, and try novel social and economic experiments without risk to the rest of the country. . . . If we should be guided by the light of reason, we must let our minds be bold.

His dissent a year later in connection with the Florida tax on chain stores struck against bigness in business and asserted "that size alone gives the giant corporations a social significance not attached ordinarily to smaller units of private enterprise." Restating his long-held belief, he said that the large number of small stockholders "are subjected, through the corporate mechanism, to the control of a few men." Ownership separated from control removes the checks curbing "the misuse of wealth and power." This separation, he contended, was in large part responsible for widespread unemployment and suffering. "Only through participation by the many in the responsibilities and determinations of business," he concluded, "can Americans secure the moral and intellectual development which is essential to the maintenance of liberty."

Appearing, as they did, in a period of economic depression, these dissents served to prepare the way for the New Deal. Indeed many who gave impetus and direction to New Deal legislation were largely influenced by Brandeis's social and economic views. He became their "Isaiah," and they sought his advice with a respect that bordered on adulation. Yet he was only a partial New Dealer, for he never lost his distrust of bigness or his fear of monopoly. Thus he joined the conservatives in striking down the National Industrial Recovery Act because it encouraged monopoly. Nor did he approve of the government's effort to raise prices by limiting production or of its fumbling of the unemployment problem. Although he was fond of President Roosevelt and favored his social and economic reforms, he was critical of his "court-packing" scheme and was largely instrumental in bringing about its defeat.

Following a mild heart attack in his eighty-third year, he retired from the Court in February, 1939. He continued to take an active interest in Zionism and called on Roosevelt to solicit his help for refugees from Nazi barbarism. Nor did he slacken his attention to national and international affairs until his death on October 5, 1941.

Louis D. Brandeis combined in himself an exceptionally keen and logical mind with a surging impetus toward social justice. He could not close his mind to vested wrongs or industrial malpractices. Despite alluring offers from in-

terested companies, he held his social obligations as a lawyer above the emoluments flowing to the corporate counse-
lor. He devoted his remarkable talents to protecting the
people from the aggrandizement of large corporations.

Dedicated to the ideal of social service, he tended to
assume the role of crusader. He fought privilege and inequity wherever he felt they interfered with the public interest, thereby earning the enmity of many men of wealth.
In the end triumph was his: he gained much for the people and thrived on the enemies he made.

A true democrat and social liberal, he was no theorist.
"I have no general philosophy," he told Hapgood, the editor of *Collier's*, in 1912. "All my life I have thought only
in connection with the facts that came before me. It is true,
however, in order to work intelligently with the facts, one
must see the general direction." In fighting the abuses of
various corporations he sought primarily to remove the
anti-social excrescences of capitalism, fearful that rampant
industrialism would prepare the way for fascism or communism. Consequently he exerted himself to improve the
conditions of labor, to keep business from getting too big,
to stop bankers from using "other people's money" to control the country's economy, to help small businessmen
function independently and profitably, to preserve civil
liberties and democratic ideals, and to imbue all Americans
with his own great love of freedom and justice. These aims
and ideals he incorporated in nearly 600 opinions and dissents during his 23 years on the Court. That this effort
became a lasting monument to his eminence as a jurist
and American, was affirmed by his brother Justices on
the occasion of his retirement:

> Your long practical experience and intimate knowledge
> of affairs, the wide range of your researches and your
> grasp of the most difficult problems, together with your
> power of analysis and your thoroughness in exposition,
> have made your judicial career one of extraordinary dis-
> tinction and far-reaching influence.

JEWS IN
JOURNALISM

Few Jews were to be found in American journalism before the last decades of the nineteenth century. Among these early practitioners Mordecai M. Noah and Benjamin Franklin Peixoto (1834–1890), who made his career with the Cleveland *Plain Dealer*, were noteworthy.

One explanation for this circumstance is that before the Civil War most Jews in the United States were of Central European origin, without an adequate knowledge of English. They were mostly poor tradesmen, more concerned in establishing themselves economically than in furthering themselves culturally. It was their sons and grandsons, growing up in economic security, and even more frequently the newcomers who arrived after 1848, relatively well-educated and idealistic, driven out of Europe by political persecution, who made their mark in journalism and other intellectual pursuits.

Jewish parochial and civic journalism, initiated by enterprising newcomers, became fairly widespread after the middle of the nineteenth century. The first such specialized publication was Solomon H. Jackson's *The Jew*, started in 1823. Twenty years later Isaak Leeser founded *The Occident and Jewish Advocate*, and in 1849 Robert Lyon began to issue *The Asmodean*. In 1854 Rabbi Isaak M. Wise launched *The Israelite*. A year later M. S. Levy began to publish *The Jewish Times and Observer* in San Francisco. Samuel M. Isaaks started *The Jewish Messenger* in 1857 and merged it with *The American Hebrew* in 1902. Raphael d'C. Lewin founded *The New Era* in 1874, Max Lilienthal started *The Jewish Review* in 1880, and the B'nai B'rith established *The Menorah* in 1886. Local periodicals began to appear in every part of the country in which a Jewish community took root. Some of the weeklies, catering to the particular interests of their readers, were fairly

well edited and exerted considerable cultural influence—one of
the most prominent being the *Detroit Jewish News*, edited by
Philip Slomovitz. Scores of them are currently served by a
Jewish news organization.

East-European Jews, beginning to arrive in the latter decades of the nineteenth century, were not long in establishing
Yiddish newspapers and magazines. The first to publish a periodical on a regular basis was Kasriel H. Sarasohn, whose
Tageblatt was founded in 1881. After several abortive efforts,
the radicals began to issue *The Jewish Daily Forward*
(*Forverts*) in 1897. Edited by Abraham Cahan (1860–1951),
at its height it achieved a circulation in excess of 200,000, becoming the most widely read foreign-language daily in the
United states. In 1901 Jacob Saphirstein started *The Morning
Journal*. Four years later Louis Miller left the *Forward* to
launch *Die Wahrheit*, which was merged in 1914 with the
newly established *The Day*, edited by Herman Bernstein. In
1922 Moisseye Olgin started *Die Freiheit*, a communist daily.
Die Freie Arbeiter Shtimme, originally an anarchist weekly,
began to appear in 1890 and achieved distinction for its literary
material. Even more important was *Die Zukunft*, which has
been published monthly since 1894 as a socialist and cultural
periodical. Although the use of Yiddish has declined considerably since World War II, the *Forward* and the *Day* continue
to be read by tens of thousands.

In the late nineteenth century Joseph Pulitzer became a
leading newspaper publisher. Born in Hungary in 1847, the son
of a Jewish father and Catholic mother, and all his life estranged from Jewish sodality, he was nevertheless generally
considered a Jew. Charles A. Dana of the New York *Sun* frequently referred to him disparagingly as "Jew Pulitzer," and
The Hebrew Standard stated that "he is a Jew who does not
want to be a Jew."

At the age of seventeen, unhappy at home, he tried to enlist in the Hungarian army, but his defective vision and poor
physique caused his rejection. A recruiting agent for the American Federal army then sent him to the United States, where
he joined the regiment led by Carl Schurz. Mustered out in

July 1865, he went to St. Louis and worked at menial jobs until 1868, when he became a reporter for a German daily edited by Schurz. He soon became adept at ferreting out news ahead of other reporters. Naturalized in 1867, he involved himself in politics and was elected to the Missouri legislature in 1869.

In 1874 he acquired the bankrupt St. Louis *Staats-Zeitung*, sold its membership in the Associated Press to the *Daily Globe* for $20,000, and used the money to study law. He continued political activity, and in 1876 he made speeches for Samuel Tilden. By that time he had mastered English and developed a vigorous journalistic style. Although Pulitzer was admitted to the bar, he found that for him legal practice was neither lucrative nor congenial.

After marrying Kate Davis in 1878, he returned to St. Louis and bought the *Dispatch*. Since the *Dispatch* had Associated Press membership and the struggling *Post* did not, he merged the two into the *Post-Dispatch* and soon made the new newspaper financially profitable, doubling the previous circulation of the two within a year. A political and civic crusader, he made many enemies. When his editor killed a lawyer in an altercation resulting from an editorial criticism, the peppery publisher left St. Louis.

Moving to New York in 1883, he bought the slowly decaying *World* from Jay Gould for $346,000, which he paid in installments. He revitalized and popularized the paper by the introduction of special features, stunts, cartoons, stories, and sensational crime news, and he inaugurated reform crusades as well as appeals to the underprivileged. In 1887 he launched the *Evening World* and gave it an even more sensational emphasis. Editorially a social reformer, he exposed and criticized what he termed "the aristocracy of money," and made himself the spokesman for "the aristocracy of labor"—to his great personal enrichment.

When William Randolph Hearst came to New York in 1895, bought the *Morning Journal* from Pulitzer's brother, and then soon outrivaled the *World* papers in vulgar sensationalism, the two publishers began a struggle for readers by means of what came to be called "yellow journalism" (because of the yellow paper used). The circulation battle continued until 1900, to the financial loss of both publishers. About that time Pulitzer was a nervous invalid and frequently sought relief abroad. On his return to New York after one of these trips, he employed Frank I. Cobb and made the *World* one of the most prestigious newspapers in the country. Although as the years advanced Pulitzer became blind as well as so nervous that he could not bear the least noise, he retained his journalistic brilliance, and his newspapers made him wealthy. Among his later crusades were the agitation for an investigation of the insurance companies in 1905 and the defiance of President Theodore Roosevelt in connection with financial irregularities in the Panama Canal project.

As early as 1903 he had announced his intention to establish a school of journalism at Columbia University. When he died in 1911, he left two million dollars for the school, of which the income from a quarter of it was designated for "prizes or scholarships for the encouragement of public service, public morals, American literature, and the advancement of education." He further provided that his newspapers be continued unchanged and independent, but in 1931 his sons obtained legal approval to sell the *World* properties to the Scripps-Howard organization, which merged the *Evening World* with the *Telegram* and allowed the distinguished morning *World* to die.

A number of other Jews became successful newspaper publishers. Among them was Pulitzer's younger brother Albert, who founded the *Morning Journal* in New York and turned it into a successful daily. An enigmatic personality, he was completely estranged from his brother—the two never even referred to each other's existence—and his life ended in suicide in 1909. In 1885, E. P. Adler, then a boy of thirteen, began to work on an Iowa newspaper, and he eventually rose to become the head of the Lee Syndicate, which published papers in Iowa, Nebraska, and Wisconsin. Liberal in outlook, Adler favored labor unions, and unlike the Pulitzers, he also took an active part in Jewish affairs. Another successful Jew was Lucius W. Nieman, who worked as a journalist in Wisconsin and later became editor and publisher of the Milwaukee *Journal*. He endowed the Nieman Fellowships at Harvard University for working journalists, thereby contributing toward achievement of higher standards in the profession.

Moses Annenberg, born in Germany in 1878, climbed from newsboy to multimillionaire newspaper owner. Among his holdings were the Philadelphia *Inquirer*, the Philadelphia *Daily News*, the New York *Morning Telegraph*, the Miami *Tribune*, the *Daily Racing Forum*, several popular magazines, plus some radio stations. In 1939 he was convicted of income-tax evasion, for which he served twenty-two months in prison. He died in 1942. Both he and his children were philanthropic, among their beneficiaries being the Annenberg School of Communication at the University of Pennsylvania and the Mount Sinai School of Medicine. His son Walter in 1969 was appointed ambassador to Great Britain.

Other Jews in the late nineteenth century and later who made their mark in the newspaper world were David Stern of Philadelphia, who published the *Record* and for a time controlled the New York *Evening Post*; Paul Block, who owned newspapers in Pennsylvania, New Jersey, and Ohio; Eugene Meyer, who published the influential Washington *Post*; and Samuel I. Newhouse, who began with the Newark *Public Ledger* and gradually extended his control over newspapers in Long Island, Syracuse, Harrisburg, Portland (Oregon), St. Louis, Birmingham, and New Orleans.

In addition to publishers, a considerable number of Jews gained prominence as reporters, columnists, editors, and executives on American newspapers during the first years of the twentieth century. One of the early columnists was Benjamin De Casseres. Henry Lowenthal served as city editor of the New York *Times*, and Louis Wiley distinguished himself as business manager of the same paper. Simeon Strunsky was an editor of the *Evening Post* before he conducted the "Topics of the *Times*" column. Fabian Franklin was a feature writer on the Baltimore *News* as well as a popular writer. Herbert Bayard Swope had charge of the *World*'s editorial page when it was at its literary best, and Franklin P. Adams (known as F.P.A.)

graced it with his column, "The Conning Tower." Walter Lippmann long made his column the sage's oracle. Charles Michelson, Frederick W. Wile, H. I. Phillips of the *Sun*, Arthur Krock, David Lawrence, and Lester Markell are others who have earned a prominent niche in American journalism.

8
Adolph
S.
Ochs

PUBLISHER
OF THE
NEW YORK *TIMES*

THE MOTIVATING forces in the life of Adolph S. Ochs are to be found in his parents and their influence. His father, Julius Ochs (1826–1888), was an idealistic youth of nineteen when he graduated from a Cologne gymnasium. Denied admission to a university because he was Jewish, he left Germany for the United States, where he became a teacher of French in a Kentucky school for girls. When the war with Mexico began, he enlisted, but saw little active service.

Religious and scholarly, Julius lacked the drive and aggressiveness necessary for success in business. In 1855 he married Bertha Levy, a refugee from the 1848 German revolutionary upheavals, a girl of strong conventional convictions. Although Julius favored the abolition of slavery, Bertha sympathized with the Southerners. At the outbreak of the Civil War, Julius enlisted in the Union army, rising in rank to Captain; Bertha, however, was once caught trying to smuggle quinine to Confederates across the river in Cincinnati.

At the end of the war Julius moved to Knoxville, where he earned a living with a draper's shop until the financial depression of 1867 left him penniless. Unable to re-establish himself, he and his family lived in poverty until they could be supported by their eldest son, Adolph.

Although Julius was a financial failure, he became a highly esteemed member of the community. In 1868 he was elected justice of the peace, and later served as tax assessor and as federal commissioner. Well versed in Judaic lore, he officiated for many years as a lay rabbi and head of the small Jewish congregation in Chattanooga.

Adolph Simon Ochs, the eldest of Julius's six children, was strongly influenced by his parents' outlook on life, but more by that of his mother than of his father. Born in Cincinnati in 1858, he was forced by family poverty to work, and he became a newsboy at the age of eleven.

> I had to appear at the office at five o'clock in the morning. The papers came from the press unfolded and the carrier boys had to fold the paper by hand. There were fifty papers to be delivered on my route, and I had to walk nearly four miles to deliver them—then home to breakfast and thence to school. For this task I received twenty-five cents a day ($1.50 per week).

His father often went along to help him. A kind neighbor noticed Adolph's threadbare pants and cut down a pair of her husband's trousers for him; years later, when the woman was widowed and in need, Ochs sent her monthly checks to the end of her life. Not long after, he was sent to Providence to work in an uncle's grocery store and remained there for a year, attending school in his free time.

At fourteen he became an office boy on the Knoxville *Chronicle*, was promoted to a full-fledged "printer's devil" two years later, and worked as a journeyman printer at seventeen. Restless and ambitious, young Adolph decided to make his way to California. Members of the *Chronicle* staff gave him as a parting gift a volume of poetry with the prophetic inscription: "We, the undersigned, your fellow workmen, appreciating your moral and practical worth, both as a friend and workman, present you with this our feeble tribute, with the hope that some day, soon or late, we shall be able to note you among the nation's honored sons." When his relatives in Louisville persuaded him to go no farther west, he worked for several months under Henry Watterson, the eminent editor, becoming assistant foreman. Learning that his family was in need, he sent his mother his entire savings—$56.00—and told her: "As for myself my prayer is that I may soon be able to make for you all a comfortable home where want is unknown and send my brothers and sisters on their different roads rejoicing."

Returning to Knoxville, he worked on the *Tribune* as a reporter and assistant business manager. In April 1877 he joined two of the *Tribune* executives to start the *Daily Dispatch* in Chattanooga, but like so many local periodicals it failed to establish itself. During its slow decline Ochs supplemented his income by compiling data for *Chattanooga City Directory and Business Gazetteer*, which made him known to many local businessmen. Though still a minor, he was so well regarded that he became the receiver for the bankrupt *Dispatch*. The rival *Times* was also in financial difficulties and it was offered to him for $800 plus a lien of $1500. He managed to borrow $300 and arranged to buy a half ownership for $250, with the right to purchase the other half within two years for an amount to be fixed by arbitration; when he was ready to exercise this right the arbitrator fixed the price at $5500! Since he was not yet twenty-one, Adolph needed to have his father sign the necessary documents. The first issue of the *Times* with "Adolph S. Ochs, Publisher" on the masthead appeared on July 2, 1878. After paying sundry expenses he had only $12.50 of capital left, so that for some time he had to borrow to pay wages and later supplied his employees with goods and services obtained from advertisers in lieu of cash.

When Ochs came into possession of the *Times* it was, according to G. E. Govan and J. W. Livengood, "utterly dilapidated, demoralized and publicly and privately anathematized," with a circulation under 250. He announced his policy in the first issue: "It will be the foremost purpose of its manager to make it the indispensable organ of the business, commercial and productive, of Chattanooga, and of the mineral and agricultural districts of Tennessee, North Georgia and Alabama." He promised the latest news, adherence to "the Conservative Democracy of the South," and affirmed the then novel principle of full independence in both news and advertising. To this policy he adhered throughout his career as a newspaper publisher.

From the outset, eager to establish his credit, he insisted on clearing bills promptly, for a time borrowing from banks to do so, but he also demanded punctual payment from advertisers. He was ready to accept goods and services instead of cash, knowing that he could dispose of them to his employees in the form of barter.

When a yellow fever epidemic broke out during his first summer as a publisher, leading to an exodus of readers putting him $600 in debt, he persisted in bringing out the paper, reducing it to a single sheet. The first frost brought the citizens back to town, and business confidence was restored. Toward the end of the year Ochs sent for his family, appointed his father treasurer, and put his younger brothers to work for him during their free time while financing their education through college. On March 12, 1879, he proudly announced that he had reached his twenty-first birthday and that the *Times* was prospering.

In the 1880s Ochs gained prominence as a civic leader, being active in all community affairs but always avoiding party politics. His large home had become a guest house for visiting journalists and persons of prominence from all over the country.

In 1883, on a visit to Cincinnati, he met a daughter of Rabbi Isaak M. Wise and married her soon after. The painful experience of two miscarried pregnancies before the birth of their only daughter seems to have strenthened their union and their dependence on each other.

The *Time*s had by then established itself as an alert, reliable, and attractive daily, superior to the others in the area, and it had become highly profitable as well. Ochs also published *The Tradesman* and *The Rural Record*, and he operated a sizable job-printing plant. He began to envision Chattanooga as a future industrial and commercial center. Materialistic in outlook, very much a man of his time, he was eager to take advantage of prospective gains and invested heavily in outlying realty and in business ventures. In 1892 he erected a sumptuous building to house the *Time*s, fitted it with the most modern printing plant in the South, and was honored by Chattanooga citizens on its completion. In response to praise, he declared: "If I have in any measure merited such an expression of good-will from the people of Chattanooga, I believe it is because I have always endeavored to do that which I thought best for the city of Chattanooga and in doing so have understood that my own interests were thereby being best promoted."

When the boom collapsed, Ochs was sued for debts on which he had co-signed and he had to remit in excess of one hundred thousand dollars. Financially embarrassed but refusing to take shelter in bankruptcy, he borrowed money from every possible source and arranged a bond issue on his assets in the prosperous *Times*. He determined thereafter to concentrate on his journalistic endeavors, subsequently refusing even to take investment opportunities offered by friends in Wall Street.

Again solely dependent on his newspaper, Ochs was interested in buying a poorly operated daily and making it profitable. A search in the South did not uncover one that met his requirements. In 1895 a friend advised him that the New York *Mercury* was for sale, but it was primarily a political sheet unlikely to become the kind of organ he envisioned. Intrigued, however, by New York possibilities, he wrote to a fellow journalist: "There is going to be a great change in the newspapers of New York in the next five years, for I believe in less than five years Mr. Dana will die of old age, Pulitzer of nervous prostration and Bennett of riotous living."

In the spring of 1896 Henry Alloway, a newspaperman, who had visited Ochs in 1890, telegraphed: "Would New York Times proposition be attractive now? Answer confidential." It was, and Ochs went to New York without delay, leaving the Chattanooga *Times* in the care of his brothers.

The New York *Times*, established in 1851 by Henry J. Raymond and George Jones, had fought Reconstruction extremism, Grant administration corruption, Tammany and the Tweed gang, and it had distinguished itself generally by its earnestness and polished intelligibility. With both founders dead by 1891, a decline set in and within five years its circulation had dropped to around 9000, so that it was losing nearly two thousand dollars daily. Its owners were anxious to sell it, but the amount they asked was beyond Ochs's means.

Eager to obtain control, certain that there was room in New York for a newspaper that presented the news fairly, accurately, and intelligibly, Ochs began to make complex financial proposals. A basic factor in these transactions was the confidence he generated in everyone concerned. He asked about fifty men of prominence, most of whom had been his guests in Chattanooga, at one time or another, to write letters of commendation to him. President Grover Cleveland responded handsomely:

In your management of the Chattanooga *Times* you have demonstrated such a faithful adherence to Democratic principles, and have so bravely supported the ideas and policies which tend to the safety of the country as well as of our party that I would be glad to see you in a larger sphere of usefulness.

The controlling stockholders were impressed, but since Ochs lacked the desired capital they offered to employ him as manager, intimating payment of up to $50,000 a year—an extremely high salary in 1896. He refused, adding: "Unless you offer me eventual control of the property—based, of course, on my making good—there is no sense in keeping on with these negotiations." He proposed to form the New York *Times* Company with 10,000 shares at $100 par and an issue of $500,000 in bonds paying 5 percent; to give a bonus of 15 shares with each $1000 bond; to buy 75 bonds himself and to receive 3876 shares after the *Times* had become profitable for three years—thus gaining 5001 shares and control.

> I hope to be able so to manage the property, while conducting it as a decent, dignified and independent newspaper, that this deficit will be extinguished, and that it will earn and pay 5% interest on $500,000, and create a sinking fund of $15,000 a year; thus turning an annual deficit of more than $100,000 into a surplus of $40,000, requiring more than $140,000 per annum increase in the receipts, as compared with the last two or three years.

Ochs wrote to his wife that this offer was "the supremacy of gall for a country newspaperman burdened with debts." Spencer Trask, the banker to whom he made the proposal, was at first shocked by the terms, but a month's reflection persuaded him of their feasibility. When some minor stockholders wanted to merge the *Times* with the *Recorder*, Charles R. Miller, editor and in nominal control (whom Ochs had won over previously), put the paper into receivership. In June the major stockholders accepted Ochs's proposal, and he trudged from office to office to persuade the owners of the old *Times* bonds to accept new bonds in exchange. When he came to Jacob Schiff, who had earlier bought 250 shares for $25,000, he was offered the stock as a gift, but Ochs insisted on the exchange—much to Schiff's subsequent profit.

On taking hold of the paper, Ochs did nothing radical or startling. He found the staff comparatively competent and kept it almost intact. He proceeded slowly to plug areas of inefficiency, reduce or eliminate wasteful expenditures like overprinting—nearly twice as many copies had been printed daily as were actually sold—and brought about changes in the business office to encourage greater proficiency. Familiar with every aspect of newspaper publishing, he was able to reduce daily losses by half.

Taking control on August 1, 1896, Ochs announced his policy in the first issue under his management—a policy very similar to the one he had proclaimed eighteen years earlier.

> It will be my earnest aim that *The New York Times* give the news, all the news, in concise and attractive form, in language that is permissible in good society, and give it as early, if not earlier, than it can be learned through any other reliable medium; to give the news impartially, without fear or favor, regardless of party, sect or interest involved.

It should be stressed that he carried out this program with scrupulous zeal.

Ochs offered a striking contrast to his chief rival, Joseph Pulitzer. Unlike the older man, who was primarily an intellectual and a crusader, Ochs was in the main a merchant of news, an upholder of his mother's notion of conventional respectability. Both Pulitzer and Ochs were exceptionally able and successful publishers, but one was a maverick liberal and the other prided himself on his conservatism and on his dignified presentation of news. Like his father, Ochs was a man of probity and good will; but more influenced by his mother, he practiced the "ordinary virtues" which she extolled. His policy was: hurt no one; do not stir up trouble; give the aura of authority to news.

Pulitzer, with some justice, charged that under Ochs's management the *Times* had become an "apologist and friend" of big business; that "it is muzzled and no longer represents honest conviction in the treatment of public questions." Yet Ochs was essentially correct when he later stated: "There was never a man or interest that could require me to do his or its bidding or consult his or its wishes, and I am proud to say that I am today, as is *The New York Times*, firmly entrenched in that independence. We are our own master, beholden to no one." His independence and his remarkable success ensued from his ability to reflect accurately and sensitively the attitudes of businessmen as well as the conventional decencies of most Americans. When he was later praised for his extraordinary success, he countered ingenuously: "I do not understand the tributes that come my way. I merely proved that, given the chance, the reading public would choose a newspaper that served up the news without coloring. I knew it would work out that way."

He was not long in eliminating the weekly deficit. He reduced the detailed reports of prices in commodity markets, which were dealt with in trade journals, and added the illustrated Sunday magazine and the Saturday review of books, both features of popular appeal. When the loose pages of book reviews were discarded by most readers who rode to work on Saturday morning, and a cartoon referred to the section as "The Littery Review," Ochs changed the date to Sunday and had the pages stapled. Additional features included were the weekly financial review and the section of letters from readers. Later features added were the Review of the Week and the drama section. Each of these innovations brought new readers, and Jason Rogers of the New York *Globe* stated: "If ever a newspaper was built brick upon brick, through the recommendation of one reader to a friend who was not yet reading it, *The New York Times* was so built." With the paper prospering, Ochs remarked: "There is no doubt that I have got the chance that comes only once in a century." Two months after he began publishing the *Times*, he put on its masthead his slogan, "All the News That's Fit to Print"; and although he later ran a contest for a new one and received thousands of suggestions, he and his staff thought none more apt.

Adhering to his established policy, he early rejected city advertising amounting to $33,000 a year on the ground that New York did not need that much publicity. Although Ochs did this at a time when he needed additional income, the act gained him more in prestige than he lost in money.

When the *World* and the *Journal* were spending thousands of dollars during the Spanish-American War to obtain news "beats" on the fighting, the *Times* began to suffer financially. Aware that he needed to act drastically to retain early gains, Ochs reduced the price of the paper from three cents to a penny. Such an act, in the face of strong opposition by his staff, was one of the boldest moves of his career. In less than a month, circulation jumped from 26,000 to 75,000—more than justifying the change, especially in view of the increased income from advertising. In essence, the reduction in price was based on Och's firm belief that a good many poor people appreciated solid, dignified news and preferred the *Times* to the "yellow" dailies sold at the same price. That he was right was evidenced by a profit of $52,252 for the year 1899.

By 1900 Ochs was in full control of the *Times*, having received the shares held in escrow when he fulfilled his obligation to show a profit during three successive years.

To make the *Times* better known in Europe, Ochs had his brother George arrange for an exhibit at the Paris Exposition, where the daily printing of the newspaper attracted wide and favorable attention. He considered this expenditure justifiable because he was planning to give the *Times* full international coverage and had begun to employ European correspondents to this end.

With circulation expanding and profits increasing at a

rapid rate, Ochs found himself in need of larger quarters. He looked for a site on which to erect a building that would symbolize the importance of the *Times* in New York in the same way that the *Times* building in Chattanooga symbolized its pre-eminence in the South. With the aid of his friend Henry Morgenthau, he bought the land that became Times Square. The cornerstone for the tall and dignified structure was laid in 1904, and the building was ready for occupancy by the end of the year. Yet so rapid was the growth of the newspaper that it soon needed additional space. An annex was completed in 1913, and even larger additions were made in 1923 and 1930. The skyscraper on Forty-third Street became the best equipped newspaper edifice in the world. A separate rotogravure building was erected in 1924, and a plant in Brooklyn was built in 1930.

Independence in advertising redounded to the paper's prestige. Regarding advertisements as a form of news, the publisher insisted that they be accurate and ethical. To a group of journalism students he once declared: "You can more readily judge the character of a newspaper by its advertising columns than by any other outward appearance." Again and again the *Times* refused advertising that it suspected as fraudulent or not in the public interest. Ochs made a point of omitting advertisements when space was needed for special news coverage. That he should take this attitude after he had fully established the leading position of the *Times* was understandable; to maintain it when he was still struggling for existence evidenced courage and foresight. Thus in 1901, replying to a complaining advertiser, he boldly asserted his policy:

> We consider it a privilege to any one to be permitted to make an announcement in the columns of *The Times* aside from the fact that our rates for advertising space are far from commensurate with the service rendered. . . . We are seeking to secure the good will and confidence of intelligent, discriminating newspaper readers. The advertiser is a secondary consideration.

In 1915 the management of the Schubert theaters objected to the adverse criticisms of its plays by Alexander Woollcott and stopped giving him the customary complimentary tickets to new plays. Ochs told him to buy tickets, but Woollcott was refused admission when he did so. Thereupon Ochs rejected Schubert advertising, and this contest of wills continued for nearly a year—until the Schuberts apologized and invited Woollcott back to their openings.

In 1901 Adolph Ochs bought the Philadelphia *Times* and a year later the *Public Ledger*, where he put his brother George in charge. Although these dailies were operated at a fair profit, Ochs found himself too involved in the operations of the New York *Times* to give them his full attention and sold them in 1913 to Cyrus H. K. Curtis. Yet in that same year he started *The Analyst*, a journal growing out of the weekly financial reviews, which became annually more important to businessmen. Concurrently, he began publishing *The New York Times Index*, which soon established itself as an indispensable guide to past events, one used by other newspapers as well as by scholars and students. In 1914, with interest in the European war becoming widespread, he began to issue *Current History Magazine*, a repository of current speeches, articles, and documents. In 1917 he originated a ragpaper edition of the *Times* for libraries. Earlier features that promoted the popularity of the paper were "The Hundred Neediest Cases," since 1911 appealing daily during the weeks before Christmas for gifts to the needy, and the rotogravure pictorial section added in 1914.

Early in the 1900s Ochs perceived the value of wireless telegraphy and aviation. He offered financial assistance to Marconi, and in April 1904 the *Times* received its first wireless report—the fall of Port Arthur—from its own ship. In 1907 it began getting wireless messages from Europe. The *Times* also gave featured space to the Wright brothers as well as to later aerial achievements. The paper took a leading role in the encouragement of polar exploration and subsidized Robert E. Peary in his successful effort to reach the North Pole; later it arranged for the exclusive reports of other explorers. Such features helped to increase circulation and profits. By 1910 the *Times'* daily sale averaged 260,000 and eleven years later Ochs reported that during the twenty-five years of his association with the paper, its income was a hundred million dollars, of which only 4 percent had been paid to stockholders.

Consistent with the policy of placing what he regarded as the public good above all other considerations, Ochs, while adhering to President Wilson's policy of neutrality, generally favored England over Germany in the war that began in 1914—although the *Times* printed the official documents of both sides. After the American entrance into the war, the *Times'* complete coverage of the fighting spurred circulation to 390,000 daily.

In September 1918, the *Times* suffered a severe temporary shock when Charles R. Miller stated in an editorial that the Allies might consider favorably Austria's proposal for a "preliminary and non-binding" discussion of peace terms. With "unconditional surrender" the prevailing attitude, the statement was widely condemned as near-treason. Ochs had not seen the editorial before it was printed, and the reaction literally stunned him. He accepted responsibility, and for months thereafter remained in a condition of melancholia. Not even the award of the first Pulitzer gold medal in journalism for meritorious public service, presented earlier in the year, offered him solace.

In 1921, the foregoing incident not quite forgotten in the celebration of his twenty-five years with the *Times*, Ochs declared: "We have little to regret for what has appeared therein, but in no issue was principle ever surrendered or subordinated to expediency." This was not, however, true of the newspaper's reporting of the Russian revolution during its first three years. Walter Lippmann and Charles Merz, in a supplement to the *New Republic* called "A Test of the News," demonstrated that in reporting

the news about Bolshevik Russia the *Times* was consistently biased, printing propaganda as accurate information.
Oswald Garrison Villard, a pacifist and caustic critic of
American journalism, also wrote harshly about the *Times*
in this connection:

> The *Times* is no more independent than it is swayed
> by a desire to be just. It is a class paper, pure and simple.
> . . . No journal has exceeded it in disseminating falsehoods,
> misrepresentations, and half truths during the unparalleled
> era of wholesale lying in which the whole world lived
> since 1914. . . . Petrograd has fallen six times, been on the
> verge of capture three times more, been burned to the
> ground twice, been in absolute panic twice and in revolt
> against the Bolsheviks on six different occasions—all with-
> out the slightest foundation in fact.

Although Ochs and his associates publicly ignored this
unanswerable criticism, they did cease to rely on the anti-
Bolshevik propagandists outside of the Soviet Union by
sending Walter Duranty to Russia to report the news as he
found it, which he did with distinction and fairness. In
1931, with the demise of the *World*, Charles Merz, its critic
a decade earlier, was engaged by the *Times*, becoming its
editor in 1938.

Throughout the 1920's the *Times* continued to improve
and extend its news coverage of the world. In 1927 Ochs
engaged Waldemar Kaempffert as science editor, and three
years later W. L. Lawrence became his assistant, thus giving the *Times* the best science news coverage in any daily
newspaper. The result of all this effort was augmented
income—$25 million in 1926—and an average circulation
in 1930 of 431,931 daily and 728,909 on Sundays. Since
most of Ochs's policies continued long after his death, it is
worth mentioning that these circulation figures soared by
1970 to well over a million.

Ochs's understanding of the public good was sometimes warped by his allegiance to the business community.

Never the social reformer, ever the defender of the status quo, he tended to ignore or minimize evidence that might reflect discredit on business. An example of this attitude was the *Times'* early treatment of the Teapot Dome scandal. At the outset it not only made little effort to investigate the rumors and allegations then current, it even sought to quash them. When the Senate investigators brought out the facts, the *Times* called them "scandalmongers and assassins of character . . . throwing the government into disorder and demoralizing those charged with the duty of conducting public business." Later, however, when the graft and corruption in connection with government concessions became a public scandal, Ochs blithely told a reporter:

> We had early information concerning the oil scandals, but we could not print one word about them until the reports were confirmed in Washington. I could mention numerous other instances to you. The point I am making is that a responsible newspaper is always very careful to see that the news it publishes is true.

If he was hypocritical on this occasion, especially in the light of the early Russian reporting, he behaved responsibly on others. A case in point is the *Times'* handling of the news concerning the tottering Bank of the United States in 1930. Arthur Hays Sulzberger, Ochs's son-in-law and successor, explained:

> We were up against a conflict of responsibilities that morning and had come to the conclusion that our duty lay in doing our utmost to prevent financial panic and in protecting the deposits of many thousands of people rather than in giving the news, which, if the worst happened—as it did—would be bound to reach the community in any case, and, consequently, was not being withheld from it improperly.

That year, in accepting the gold medal from the University of Missouri for the *Times'* excellence in journalism,

Sulzberger praised Ochs's extraordinary success as a publisher: "Mr. Ochs is the perfect newspaperman. He pos-
sesses evenness of spirit and a catholicity of interests. He
is simple and direct, able to strip the most difficult problem of its complexities and put his finger on underlying and
motivating facts."

Adolph S. Ochs grew up with a fierce and abiding loyalty to his family, with an intense belief in the "ordinary
virtues" held dear by his mother, with a fealty to "the God-
of-things-as-they-are."

Adolph S. Ochs was influenced early by his father's religious earnestness and ethical integrity, and he manifested an unquestioning acceptance of Reform Judaism—
a loyalty later strengthened by association with his rabbinical father-in-law:

> Judaism is a conception of religion that spells respon-
> sibility—responsibility to society, to neighbor, to family
> and to one's self. It distinguishes man from the brute,
> civilizes his life, makes him human and justifies his exis-
> tence. Everything that my religion teaches me, if adhered
> to and practiced, would make me a better man and a
> better citizen. . . . The Jew who stands up for his Judaism,
> of his faith, invariably has the respect and admiration of
> his fellow citizens of every creed.

He could say this in all sincerity because he grew up
in the state of Tennessee at a time when few Jews lived
there, and perhaps for this reason none of their neighbors
discriminated against the Ochs family because of their
religion. Years later, by then a leading citizen of Chattanooga, a man held in high esteem and experiencing none
of the slights to which Jews in other parts of the country
were then exposed, Ochs could never persuade himself
that Gentile exclusion of Jews forced them to develop a
distinctive ethnic culture, one that might be only tenuously
associated with the religion of Judaism. He commented

that to him Jews were "no different from other people," except that they practiced the Mosaic faith instead of one of the other religions.

In the 1920s, however, after a decade of persecution and pogroms in Eastern Europe, with anti-Semitism in Germany becoming virulent, and with anti-Jewish prejudice in the United States fomented by Henry Ford's *Dearborn Independent* and the screeds of the Ku Klux Klan, many Jews began to feel threatened, and many turned inward— some to Zionism and others to a greater cultural identity with their fellow Jews. Not so Ochs. In 1925 he said, "I have nothing of Judaism in me that does not spell religion. Religion is all that I stand for as a Jew." Zionism he considered a philosophy alien to his Jewishness, and he generally opposed it. When he was in Jerusalem in 1922 he admitted that the Zionists had accomplished a great deal— but thought that the direction in which they were going was wrong. When he gave $25,000 to relieve distressed Jews in Europe he protested against calling the organization to which he contributed a "Jewish" fund, since he felt the relief of the distressed should concern all human beings.

His rejection of Jewishness in other than its religious aspect may have been one reason that Ochs made great efforts to forestall any impression that the *Times* favored Jews in the slightest way. Consequently, he tended to minimize or suppress evidences of anti-Semitism. When a non-Jewish tenant in a Washington Square cooperative sued the other tenants to permit her to sublease her apartment to a Jewish lawyer, the *Times* was the only New York newspaper not to print the story. Even more reprehensible was its handling of the Sir Stuart Samuel report in 1920 on Polish pogroms. The *Times* first printed the inaccurate Associated Press statement that the treatment of Jews in Poland was being "gradually mitigated" and would "abate when peace has been restored." Later, when the corrected Associated Press condensation arrived (followed by the report itself), the *Times* refused to use it. The *Times* did

print the report finally—as a paid advertisement! Oswald
Garrison Villard rebuked Ochs:

> For not even the Jews, Mr. Ochs's own race, has it
> pleaded as ardently as have others, apparently for fear lest
> it be further decried and criticized as a Jew paper; how else
> can one explain its refusal to print the British report on
> the Polish pogroms save as paid advertising? Mr. Ochs
> cannot deny that his newspaper printed a false Associated
> Press summary of Sir Stuart Samuel's report, making it
> acquit the Polish Government when Sir Stuart actually
> held that Government guilty, or that his trustworthy and
> impartial journal refused to print either the Associated
> Press correction of its error or the full text of the report
> when it arrived—save as an advertisement paid for at the
> hands of some of his coreligionists.

If Ochs dissociated himself from the cultural and so
cial aspects of Judaism, he remained loyal to his religious
belief. He became an active member of Temple Emanu-El.
In 1924 he expressed his devotion to his deceased parents
as well as to his co-religionists in the South by presenting
the Julius and Bertha Ochs Memorial Temple and Community House to the Mizpah Congregation in Chattanooga.
A year later he undertook the chairmanship of a committee
to raise an endowment of five million dollars for the Hebrew
Union College, founded by his father-in-law, and he began
solicitations by announcing his own contribution of five
hundred thousand dollars. In the same year, as a demonstration of good will toward Christianity, he presented to
the Cathedral of St. John the Divine a pair of large,
menorah-shaped candelabra designed by the Cathedral's
architect, Ralph Adam Cram.

With his wealth increasing steadily, he enjoyed giving
to worthy causes. In addition, he provided pensions and
other benefits to *Times* employees. Among his notable contributions was $532,000 toward the publication of the
twenty volume *American Dictionary of Biography*, sponsored by American scholarly organizations. He also under-

took to publish the *American Year Book*, a valuable source history requiring a considerable subsidy. His generosity and his outstanding success as a publisher brought him a number of honorary degrees as well as the gold medal from the National Institute of the Social Sciences.

His devotion to his family was genuine and pervasive. He provided not only for its immediate members but for many more distant relatives. When he began to travel abroad, he took along with him as many of the family as were able to accompany him. In all matters of personal concern he sought his mother's advice, and later his wife's. He doted upon his only daughter and gave much time to her instruction. In 1917 she became attracted to Arthur Hays Sulzberger, whose father was a textile merchant. Ochs felt distressed until the young man agreed to join the *Times*, and he trained him as successor with parental diligence and devotion. He was equally helpful to his two younger brothers, Milton and George, whom he trained as newspapermen from early youth, and to his nephew Julius Ochs Adler, whom he made a leading executive of the *Times*.

In the 1920's Ochs began to take long vacations abroad. By that time he was everywhere respected as an influential publisher, and he was honored by leading men in each country he visited. In 1933 his heart began to weaken, and he had to curb some of his activities. When his long-time associate and close friend, Louis Wiley, died early in 1935, Ochs became very melancholy, but after a while he recovered sufficiently to visit old Chattanooga friends. At a luncheon with several of them, he suffered a cerebral hemorrhage and died where he sat. In Chattanooga, in New York, and in Washington he was mourned publicly as one of the nation's eminent citizens.

MAIL-ORDER
MERCHANDISING

The decades from 1865 to 1900 were a period of egregious *laissez-faire* in the American economy. While the nation as a whole was engrossed in the conquest of a continent, enterprising men were equally energetic in exploiting its seemingly inexhaustible natural resources for their own enrichment. In high places and low, the rule was *caveat emptor*. As late as 1914 Julius Rosenwald told the Committee on Business Ethics of the National Civic Federation, "Not long ago the general practice in business was to let the buyer look out for his own interest. The man who sold made little effort to protect the man who bought."

East of the Mississippi River, where distances between plantations and farms were not prohibitive, peddlers, many of them Jewish immigrants, brought their packs or wagon loads to kitchen doors. In addition, most farmers lived near enough to a village general store to obtain supplementary provisions. But in the vast stretches of the West, where hardy settlers were beginning to make their homes in relative isolation, a trip to the nearest store meant traveling for days on horseback or wagon. And then they might find only a part of the goods they needed.

To cater to these customers, some merchants began to promote the sale of goods by means of a catalogue. The farmer who received a mail-order catalogue was, in effect, getting the described contents of a large emporium for his leisurely inspection and selection. His order, sent on a penny postcard or in a two-cent letter, was promptly filled by mail, express, or freight. The establishment of rural free delivery in 1896 greatly furthered such purchases.

One of the first national mail-order houses was started shortly before the Civil War by E. C. Allen of Augusta, Maine. A much more important entrepreneur was Aaron

Montgomery Ward. Born in New Jersey in 1844, he went to Chicago in 1865 to work for Marshall Field. Later, as a traveling salesman, he came to know intimately the ways and needs of the rural and farm population. In 1872 he entered the mail-order business and advertised himself as "the cheapest cash house in the country." He began by promoting 50 items, all under a dollar. Shrewd enough to associate himself with the then popular National Grange, he got the approval of the organization's officials and called his firm "The Original Grange Supply House" in the catalogue he sent to its large membership. He stressed low overhead, cash practice, and the absence of middlemen, and offered goods at prices lower than those in local stores. By the middle 1880's his sales were large and profitable.

Not many Jewish merchants entered the mail-order business, seeming to prefer the surer, if not always so profitable, trade of the local store. May, Stern and Company was established in 1882 and sold goods by mail on the installment plan, but success was elusive until the firm was taken over by the Spiegel Company. The National Cloak and Suit Company began in 1888 to promote its wares by mail order. Some of the larger department stores, R. H. Macy and Company for one, added mail-order divisions to their activities, but none of these efforts made much headway. In the 1880's a number of jewelry firms started selling merchandise by mail, including a few unscrupulous ones who would send a fictitious order to a local dealer. When he refused the package, the firm offered to let the express agent keep it at half the "regular" price—which had previously been doubled—to sell to his local acquaintances. Fairly often the ruse worked, and the agent, seeing a chance to earn extra money, turned jewelry salesman. One of these agents was Richard W. Sears.

Born in 1863 in Minnesota, the son of a blacksmith, Sears got his first introduction to the mail-order business as a boy when he ordered merchandise from a Ward catalogue. He learned telegraphy in his teens and worked as an operator for a railroad. To add to his modest wages, he bought wood, coal, and other staples from the railroad and sold them at a profit to local merchants. When a rejected package of watches from a jewelry house was offered to him at a "bargain" price, he accepted it and sold the watches to other express agents at a profit of two dollars each. He ordered more watches, sold them, and within a relatively short time had earned several thousand dollars.

In 1886 he started a watch company of his own in Minneapolis. Having learned his lesson well, he, too, sent fictitious orders to local jewelers and then persuaded express agents and others to accept the merchandise. Through clever and venturesome promotion, he increased his business, and within a year moved to Chicago to widen his market. When customers began to ask for watch repairs, Sears hired A. C. Roebuck, a self-trained watch tinker from Indiana. This aspect of the business grew so rapidly that Sears soon had eight watchmakers working under Roebuck's supervision. Meantime he continued to advertise heavily in newspapers and by catalogues, with highly lurid copy, merchandise he had bought cheaply as discontinued styles or at bankruptcy sales. Like Ward, he stressed his low prices and the guarantee of his goods.

Restless and impetuous, Sears sold his firm in 1889, but he soon started another jewelry company in Minneapolis under a new name. Two years later he sold that company to Roebuck —only to rejoin it as a major partner shortly afterward. In 1893 the firm of Sears, Roebuck and Company began to sell various other items by mail, and later that year Sears moved to Chicago. But the depression had hit Chicago hard and the company's liabilities rose threateningly. Roebuck, in poor health, insisted on selling his minor equity to Sears, and the latter, to save himself from the danger of bankruptcy, decided to sell half of the firm's assets for $75,000.

Paradoxically the mail-order business, which had begun on a somewhat shady note, soon became a force to raise ethical standards in retail merchandising generally. Ward, and Sears after him, although no more scrupulous than other traders, learned that they could not get the farmer's orders without first gaining his confidence. Moreover, catalogue prices not only had to be attractive to the potential buyer but also had to remain fixed for the life of the catalogue, thus forcing a one-price system upon mail-order houses. In addition, to overcome customer resistance to unseen wares, mail-order houses had to guarantee that the merchandise advertised was exactly as described. This, in turn, led them to insist that their producers also conformed to contractual specifications. In time, despite the persistence of shoddy items at various prices, the one-price system and the qualitative assurance of merchandise was the general rule not only among mail-order houses but also among department and other retail stores.

9
Julius
Rosenwald

MERCHANT
AND
PHILANTHROPIST

WHEN SAMUEL ROSENWALD arrived in the United States from Germany in 1854 at the age of twenty-six, he followed a common pattern of Jewish immigrants and became a peddler. Not long afterwards, the Hammersloughs, his brothers-in-law, hired him to work in one of their clothing stores; in 1862 they sent him to Springfield, Illinois, to take charge of their sale of army uniforms. Six years later, in 1868, he opened his own store in Springfield and advertised himself as "The C. O. D. One-Price Clothier." His business prospered, and he became a charter member of the city's Board of Trade. In a few years he would be able to state that his assets were close to $33,000, and that it cost him $3,000 annually to provide for his family and $4,000 to operate his store. In time he became the father of four sons and two daughters. He took an active part in Jewish affairs, and in 1881 reported to relatives in Germany that Jews in the United States, while tolerated, were "not on the same level with Christians." His long-time friend Moses

Newborg called him "a typical, upright, principled, hard-working successful small merchant."

His son Julius was born on August 12, 1862. As a school boy he helped his father in the store, sold papers, and worked at odd jobs. On his thirteenth birthday he was confirmed at a Bar Mitzvah ceremony and began to work summers in the "Boston 99¢ Store" at $2.50 a week. After two years of high school he went to New York as an apprentice in one of the Hammerslough clothing stores, living with an uncle "in much finer surroundings than I had been accustomed to."

In 1884, when he was 22, Julius and his brother Morris opened a clothing store under the name of "J. Rosenwald and Bro." Business in New York was poor in 1885, and the brothers left for Chicago where, together with their cousin Julius E. Weil, an experienced clothing manufacturer, they opened a clothing factory. The elder Rosenwald, having helped them financially, joined the enterprise.

Julius was the most energetic member of the family business; he bought cloth in New York and sold the finished products in southern and western cities. Although he was doing fairly well financially, he seemed not to have great ambition to become rich. "The aim of my life," he stated at the time, "is to have an income of $15,000 a year—$5,000 to be used for my personal expenses, $5,000 to be laid aside, and $5,000 to be used to go to charity." This philanthropic generosity early manifested itself at a Jewish charity meeting when, emotionally aroused by the speaker, he impulsively announced his gift of $2,500—much more than he could then afford. When he confessed his rash act to his wife, the former Augusta Nusbaum, whom he had married in 1890, she assured him he had done the right thing and they would manage.

Rosenwald's brother-in-law Aaron Nusbaum in 1893 obtained the soda-water concession at the Chicago World's Fair-Columbia Exposition and by the time the Fair closed he had made a net profit of $150,000. He was shrewd and conservative, but also irascible and meticulous. Concerned about the best way to use the money, he learned that half of Sears-Roebuck Company could be acquired for $75,000. The opportunity tempted him but, loath to act alone, he interested Rosenwald in becoming his partner. Rosenwald, who had sold men's suits to Sears, and was impressed with his dynamism, borrowed money from the family to make up the $37,500 for his quarter share. Later he said, "An opportunity opened before me. . . . I did not create it. . . . I accepted the opportunity more in behalf of a relative than for myself." The firm was incorporated with a capitalization of $150,000, with Sears receiving 800 shares as president, Rosenwald 350 shares as vice-president, and Nusbaum 350 shares as treasurer.

At that time Sears was promoting the business as the "Cheapest Supply House on Earth! Our Trade Reaches Around the World." He was primarily an intuitive and exuberant advertising man, and wrote all the copy for the 527-page catalogue of 1895. One advertisement read: "Costs nothing—for $4.98 we will send you C.O.D. subject to examination etc. a fine black cheviot suit." When the catalogue was mailed he had not a suit in stock, but before the sale ended 25,000 suits had been manufactured and mailed. For all his successful advertising, he was a slovenly merchandiser and careless administrator, so that chaos always threatened the order and accounting departments.

Rosenwald severed his connection with the clothing factory, and assumed an active role in Sears-Roebuck in 1896. Economic conditions were improved, and sales that year rose to $1,273,000 and continued to increase at a rapid rate in the ensuing years. Quantity purchases made it possible for Sears and his associates to buy more economically and sell more cheaply than competing houses, and, with the rapid growth of population and the paucity of stores in western rural areas, the demand for goods seemed inexhaustible. In 1898 Sears catalogue extended to 1,206 pages, was called *Consumer's Guide* and was generally regarded as an important factor in the broadening of farm life. One of these catalogues was recently republished, and its nostalgic content made it a best-seller. With Rosenwald's introduction of prompt and efficient order handling and a tighter administrative routine, the firm continued to prosper.

An amiable, if somewhat aloof man, naturally sanguine, sincere, and ethical, Rosenwald concentrated on customer satisfaction, attending to complaints and seeking to minimize their recurrence. Sears's flamboyant advertising perturbed him, and he sought diplomatically to modify it, especially when inferior items did not match the glowing description in the catalogue. He stressed integrity as the firm's standard and urged the highest quality consistent with established prices. Since Sears prices were generally lower than others, both farmers and townspeople took advantage of them, to the detriment of local merchants. In 1897, for instance, the firm managed to obtain sewing machines at a greatly reduced price and promoted their sale so energetically that 19,000 orders arrived in a single month. This policy of lowering prices to increase volume was extended to many items. The result was reflected in the increase of sales from $3,020,557 in 1897 to $8,505,577 just two years later.

From the outset Sears and Nusbaum irritated each other. The impetuous and aggressive operations of the former annoyed the fussy and finical Nusbaum. By 1901 the relationship had become so strained that Sears told Rosenwald that either he and Nusbaum should buy him out or the two of them should buy out Nusbaum. Since neither wished to leave the business, they agreed to make Nusbaum an offer. After some haggling they paid him $1,250,000 for his quarter equity. Nusbaum joined Inland Steel Company and fared very well.

In the realignment of management, Rosenwald became treasurer as well as vice-president. Albert H. Loeb, Rosenwald's lawyer, who had become the firm's counsel in 1897, was appointed secretary. His sympathetic interest in the personnel and ability to keep harmony among his fellow executives enhanced his importance in the company.

In 1904 Sears-Roebuck had outgrown its quarters, and a new plant, sizable enough to accommodate it for the foreseeable future, was started the next year. In need of $5 million to pay for the building, Rosenwald went to New York to see his friend Henry Goldman, of Goldman, Sachs and Company, about a loan. He was advised to raise the money by an issue of stock, a decision which made Sears-Roebuck the first merchandising company to "go public." Preferred stock of $10 million and common stock of $30 million were sold without difficulty, and Sears and Rosenwald received $4,500,000 each for their divested holdings. Goldman and Philip Lehman became directors of the newly incorporated firm.

Sears persisted in advertising and promoting items which were cheap but of dubious quality. If his questionable ethics troubled the upright Rosenwald, his intuitive undertakings often proved highly successful. On a hunting trip he visited a farm and saw a cream separator that cost over a hundred dollars. He decided that an equally serviceable separator might be produced to sell for much less, and, on his return to Chicago, found a manufacturer who agreed. Once the separator was in production, Sears launched an advertising and promotion campaign that resulted in the sale of many thousands, to the firm's substantial profit. On the other hand, a 1904 experiment in opening retail grocery stores proved unprofitable and they were discontinued. On the whole, the house maintained its primacy in the mail-order field.

Never really seeing eye to eye, and with minor irritations cropping up between them from time to time, the rift between Sears and Rosenwald deepened in 1905. The agitation against unsanitary and contaminated food as well as against questionable patent medicines, which resulted in the 1906 Pure Food and Drug Act, greatly troubled Rosenwald who insisted that truth in the firm's advertising was essential to its good reputation. When he urged the discontinuance of items that were highly profitable but of inferior quality, Sears opposed him. Sears's plan to intensify advertising in 1908 in order to augment sales seemed to Rosenwald a waste of money and he objected strenuously. Nor was he in sympathy with Sears's decision to open a branch plant in Dallas, although he later admitted his overcaution.

In spite of his own success, Sears was never fully convinced of the permanence of the mail-order business. He went abroad in the hope that a change of climate would help his ailing wife, and for more than two years remained away from his office. Although he wrote regularly to give advice and directions, his interest in the firm gradually declined. When his health began to fail in 1908, he resigned from the presidency and sold his stock to Goldman, Sachs for $10 million. Rosenwald thereupon succeeded him as head of the firm. Now he could insist on making the catalogue copy clear and truthful and exact, and refused to sell questionable patent medicines. His policy raised the level of confidence in the company and resulted in greatly increased business. Loeb was made vice-president and treasurer. In 1911 Rosenwald's son Lessing was taken into the firm and ultimately became head of the gigantic concern.

The act of 1912 authorizing parcel post delivery, which lowered the cost of mailing, proved a boon to the mail-order business, and Sears-Roebuck became the chief beneficiary, sending out as many as 20,000 parcels daily at a cost of $6,000 in stamps. By 1914 its sales reached $101,121,000.

Although Rosenwald's income was reaching into millions of dollars annually, with much of it given to philanthropy, he acted on the principle of not paying employees more than the prevailing wage. In 1913 the 4,732 female workers at Sears-Roebuck averaged $9.12 in wages weekly, with a minimum wage of $5 to girls under 16, $6 to girls under 18, and $8 to $22 to those above 18. Men over 21 averaged $18.82 weekly. Employees with the firm longer than five years received annual bonuses of up to 10 percent of their earnings. Rosenwald maintained that these wages were normal for the industry. In 1916, however, he instituted a profit-sharing plan—the most comprehensive and generous than in existence—which within two years would cost the house up to $5,000 daily. In 1923 the firm began to put a minimum of 7 percent of its profits into a pension fund, and Rosenwald declared, "It is good business to treat people right."

In 1916, with the Wilson Administration preparing for the likelihood of war, Rosenwald was made a member of the Council of National Defense and head of the Committee on Supplies. He devoted himself zealously to the efficient procurement of supplies, refusing to let Sears-Roebuck participate in government business or make a profit in those few instances when the company was asked for goods unobtainable elsewhere. His work lessened only when purchasing was taken over by the War Industries Board. In 1918 he went to France to visit the armed forces. He took with him few personal belongings but four large wooden boxes of Sears-Roebuck catalogues, which he knew would interest farm boys recuperating from wounds.

During his three years' absence from the firm Rosenwald accepted no salary and Loeb acted as *de facto* president. Upon his return Rosenwald found considerable laxity in the management of the company. Sales in 1919, with the coming of peace, had spurted to $233,482,584, $52 million above the year before, when some goods were unavailable. Merchandise was being ordered on the basis of high current demand rather than on estimates of probable sales once acute shortages were over. When the depression of 1921 set in and a "buyers' strike" ensued, the firm was caught with a very large inventory as well as with commitments for goods it could not sell. That year Sears-Roebuck had a deficit of $16,435,468 and a critical shortage of working capital. To keep the company fluid, Rosenwald gave it $5 million outright and enough other financial assistance to see it through the crises.

By 1924, with operations again efficient and highly profitable, Rosenwald was ready to relax control. Loeb was ailing and eager to retire—he died soon after—and Rosenwald began a search for high-level replacements. He had great respect for the efficiency of railroad executives, and the man he finally engaged as president was C. M. Kittle, a brusque railroad expert; he himself becoming chairman of the board and chief executive officer. General Robert E. Wood, who had served in Panama under General Goethals and who had just resigned as vice-president of merchandising at Montgomery Ward, was named vice-president in charge of factories and retail stores. Kittle, whose bluntness had antagonized his fellow executives, died in 1928, and Rosenwald named Wood to succeed him as president. He did so on the theory that because Wood was young, and not yet rich, he would work harder than Otto Doering or Max Adler, who had been top administrators at Sears for many years. When the other two were passed over, they resigned.

The travel revolution brought about by the automobile, and the consequent trend toward urbanization, acted in two ways to reduce rural dependence on mail-order purchases. Not only were farmers able to drive to stores in town, the great chain stores expended outward from the cities to open branches in smaller communities. The chain store was a fairly early phenomenon in American life, with small local chains even predating the Atlantic and Pacific Tea Company which, in 1858, became the first of the nationwide chains. It was followed by F. W. Woolworth Company in 1879, United Cigar Stores Company in 1901, J. C. Penney Company in 1902, and W. T. Grant Company in 1906.

Wood perceived this trend and, on joining Sears, urged Rosenwald and Kittle to open stores in strategic areas. In 1925 he installed a retail outlet in Chicago; seven more stores were opened by the end of the year. During the next two years nineteen more stores were put in operation, all

"A" grade because they were located in large cities. With Rosenwald's full cooperation, Wood greatly increased the number of stores after he became president. By 1931 the company had 391, mostly "B" grade, located in smaller cities, with a few "C" grade in rural areas. Within a year, sales in these outlets made up 57.7 percent of the company's total income. Subsequently the number of Sears stores increased to over 600.

The economic depression that began in 1929 affected Sears-Roebuck as severely as it did most business firms. Sales declined drastically; some stores were closed, and Sears-Roebuck stock dropped sharply. On his own initiative Lessing Rosenwald announced that employee shareholders would be helped to keep their holdings. His father, pleased with his son's generous gesture, took upon himself the responsibility of guaranteeing about 300 stock-market accounts held by employees, although he had to borrow $7 million to do so. According to Edwin R. Embree, this ability to help others made him happy despite his own losses. "He saved hundreds of persons from immediate bankruptcy. He saw his own fortune in the collapse which culminated this day, reduced by a hundred million dollars. He saw his business and his personal affairs plunging irresistibly into the most troubled waters. It was one of the happiest days of his life."

Mrs. Rosenwald died in 1929. The following year Rosenwald married Adelaide R. Gutkind, but he himself was in poor health and continued to suffer from various ailments until his death on January 6, 1932. In his will he left $11 million to the Rosenwald Family Association, established some time previously.

Julius Rosenwald's munificent philanthropy was characteristic of traditional Jewish charity at its noblest—his ideal was one third of his income, as compared with Jacob Schiff's 10 percent minimum—enhanced by phenomenal wealth. Neither an extraordinarily aggressive manipulator like Rockefeller nor the inventor of a revolutionary product like Henry Ford, Rosenwald reaped his millions by associating himself with a timely merchandising enterprise.

> It was not till I reached my early forties, however, that fortune smiled upon me in a big way, and no one was more surprised at my sudden landing in the midst of America's multimillionaire class than I was myself. . . . Genius does not make men rich; very often luck does. By luck a man stumbles into an unusual opportunity and by more luck he holds on to it. This, in any business of great money-making possibilities, means becoming a millionaire.

He was modest enough to appreciate his good fortune and was often apologetic about it—"whatever it is, it's too much"—and sincerely sought to put the millions that came to him to the most effective use. Charles S. Johnson, president of Fisk University and an eminent sociologist, wrote, "That generosity by which he became so justly famed overshadowed the shrewd social intelligence and prophetic wisdom which gave it direction."

One of the early influences upon his charitable inclinations came from Rabbi Emil G. Hirsch's sermons, which advocated social and community service. Later Judge Julian W. Mack brought various benevolent causes to Rosenwald's attention. Jane Addams was another friend who inspired his sense of philanthropy, and he early began to contribute to Hull House, as well as to the Immigrant Protective League headed by Grace Abbott, and to various other Chicago organizations.

As a very young man, as we have seen, he would pledge more to a Jewish charity than he could afford. Once his income increased, he became the largest donor to the Associated Jewish Charities in Chicago, his gifts to it totaling nearly two million dollars during his lifetime. Elected president of the organization in 1902, he told its members how he felt about the pleasure of giving.

My friends, it is unselfish effort, helpfulness to others that ennobles life, not because of what it does for others but more what it does for ourselves. In this spirit we should give not grudgingly, not niggardly, but gladly, generously, eagerly, lovingly, joyfully, indeed with the supremest pleasure that life can furnish.

As president he established the policy that contributions should be made unconditionally to be used at the discretion of the directors.

Rosenwald was interested in conciliation between Reform and Orthodox Jewish factions in Chicago and donated to both while urging harmony between them. As a founding member of the American Jewish Committee and influenced by Rabbi Hirsch, he opposed the Zionist movement, yet contributed to Palestine institutions. In 1910 he became strongly interested in Aaron Aaronsohn's discovery of wild wheat in Palestine and served as president of the Jewish Agricultural Experimental Station which was established at the foot of Mt. Carmel. His visit to Palestine in February 1914 confirmed his belief that the country would never become self-sufficient and that Zionism would remain an unrealized dream. Some months later, when the outbreak of war caused great hardship among Jewish colonists, he agreed to contribute $1000 monthly for their relief. Jacob Schiff, who was also opposed to the idea of a Jewish state, told Rosenwald that "bitter experience tells me that we must make it possible for the unfortunate and unhappy Jew to go somewhere where he will be welcome, and where else can that be than Palestine in due time?" Rosenwald, however, maintained that Jews must seek to establish their rights in the lands of their birth. Yet in 1925 he gave $75,000 to help build the Hebrew Teachers College in Jerusalem.

At first rather lukewarm to the needs of Jewish war sufferers in Eastern Europe, he made an anonymous donation of $10,000 in 1914, and increased the amount to $15,-

ooo the following year. As conditions worsened in 1916, his attitude changed and he contributed $100,000. In 1917 he offered to give an additional 10 percent, up to a million dollars, of all money collected for relief, and actually donated $778,925.28. It was on this occasion that Jacob Schiff commented, "I believe there is no one who has done so much to make the name of Jew respected, to raise it, not only in the eyes of our countrymen, but everywhere, as Julius Rosenwald." In 1918 he offered to add 25 percent to the sum collected in Chicago, and his share came to $212,530.

Maintaining his belief that Jews must seek civic equality in their own countries, he lauded Dr. Joseph Rosen's efforts to settle Russian Jews in farming communities on land provided by the Communist government in its idealistic phase. "It is the duty of Jews in America," he asserted, "to look after the Jews in Russia. I am simply doing my duty." During the 1920's he contributed a total of $3,600,-000 to help settle a quarter million Jews on farms. It was largely as a result of this benevolence that he was awarded the Gottheil medal in 1929 in recognition of having done most for Jews during the previous year. At that time, stimulated by a letter to him whose death occurred that year, from Louis Marshall, he gave a half million dollars to the Jewish Theological Seminary as an endowment to be known as the Louis Marshall Memorial Fund.

Rosenwald was also a generous contributor to non-Jewish local and general projects. The University of Chicago received from him a total of four million dollars plus a half million specified for a medical center at the urging of Abraham Flexner. A noteworthy adjunct to his benevolence was his successful effort to persuade other wealthy men to follow his example. On his fiftieth birthday in 1912 his own public gifts came to $687,500. At the end of World War I he was ready to provide five million dollars to help restore devastated Europe, but the project remained unrealized. In 1923 he did give $100,000 for German relief. A year later, in honor of Charles W. Eliot's birthday, Rosenwald gave $100,000 to the Harvard Chemistry Department.

Julius Rosenwald's real fame as a philanthropist was established by his imaginative and magnificent grants to Negro education and culture. Americans had earlier made individual contributions to Negro education, but none before or since has approached Negro problems with, for his day, the intelligence, persistence, and generosity exercised by Rosenwald. Booker T. Washington's *Up From Slavery* and J. G. Brooks's *An American Citizen: The Life of William H. Baldwin, Jr.*, which dealt with Baldwin's endeavors in behalf of Negro education, sparked Rosenwald's interest and moved him to devote millions in money and years of effort to the post-slavery Negro generation.

On the principle that philanthropy is most useful when it stimulates both cooperation on the part of its beneficiaries and additional giving by men of means, in 1910 Rosenwald announced that he would give "$25,000 for a YMCA building for colored people in any city in the United States where an additional $75,000 is raised among white and colored people." He added, "I believe that the Young Men's Christian Association is the best medium I know for accomplishing what I would like to see done for colored men, and this does not mean that I am the less a Jew." This offer was so widely accepted that his share came to $637,000 for YMCA's and $75,000 for YWCA's. In 1911, at a luncheon in honor of Dr. Washington, he gave $50,000 toward a YMCA hotel in Chicago and persuaded nine other wealthy Chicagoans to do the same.

At the Hampton Institute he made a plea for racial tolerance. "As an American and a Jew, I appeal to all high-minded men and women to join in a relentless crusade against race prejudice, indulgence in which will result in the blotting out of the highest ideals of our proud nation." Later that year he visited Tuskegee Institute, became one of its trustees, and helped it financially. When Washington died in 1915, he gave the Institute $100,000 as a memorial.

It was from Washington that Rosenwald learned about the shocking neglect of Negro education. In 1912, when he became involved, only 20 percent of Negro children went to school, and even these went to schools that were open only four months of the year under teachers with little general knowledge and less pedagogical training. There was not one standard eighth-grade school for Negroes, and of course no high school. In 1913 Rosenwald offered to help build one-room schools for Negroes provided both whites and blacks in the area contributed toward their construction. At first the offer was greeted skeptically by Negroes and antagonistically by some whites; soon, however, attitudes altered, and Negroes turned to his offer with the enthusiasm of a religious revival, offering their pennies and dimes to the amount of $150 plus a similar sum in labor. Rosenwald's share was $300 and white residents gave $350.

Rosenwald had also stipulated that as soon as the school was ready it should be made a part of the local school system, with the school board guaranteeing five months of schooling plus equipment and maintenance. This was at first opposed by the white population because it entailed increased taxes and because the "Rosenwald" schools were often superior to existing schools for white children. It took considerable campaigning and persuasion to overcome this hostility. Once the precedent was established, however, Rosenwald's assistance was welcomed and he underwrote one third of the cost of over 300 schools. The state superintendent of Tennessee wrote to him, "No greater work than yours is now being undertaken in the South and the Tennessee authorities are delighted at any opportunity to cooperate with you."

In 1917 the Julius Rosenwald Fund was established as a clearing house for his philanthropy. It began with 20,000 shares of Sears-Roebuck shares and was added to from time to time, so that by 1928 it had received a total of 227,874 shares valued at more than $40 million. Its chartered purpose was to help "the well-being of mankind," and as a family-operated fund it spent $4,049,974 by 1928. Much of the money went to the building of Negro schools in town and villages where community cooperation was obtained from local officials and black and white residents. The Fund gave from $200 to a one-room school to $6,000 to a high school having 12 teachers. It also furthered the development of library services, teacher training, and higher education.

Rosenwald felt that it was unwise for contributors to perpetuate their gifts. In 1912, when he learned that Carnegie had given Tuskegee Institute an endowment of $750,-000 with the stipulation that only the income be spent, he persuaded Carnegie to remove this condition. Thirteen years later he affected a similar change in the Baron de Hirsch Fund. He applied this principle to his own Fund.

In 1925 Abraham Flexner encouraged him to further his efforts in behalf of the Negro.

> You have acquired a prestige in the field of Negro education, which ought not to be wasted and which perhaps no one else will ever again acquire. There is no more important single field, whether looked at from the standpoint of the Negro himself or from the standpoint of our international well-being. There exists no agency with funds or personnel capable of exercising the influence which the development of the Negro race and the evolution of public opinion have now rendered feasible.

Thus encouraged, Rosenwald decided to place the Fund under more objective and efficient management. He engaged Edwin Embree as its president, added to its assets, and stipulated that both the Fund's principal and its income must be spent within 25 years after his death. He gave Embree complete freedom to use the Fund's millions as he thought best. "I am not in sympathy," he declared, "with this policy of perpetuating endowments and believe that more good can be accomplished by expending funds as Trustees find opportunities for constructive work than by storing up large sums of money for long periods of time."

This philanthropic principle, which influenced other benefactors, among them Rockefeller and James Couzens of the Ford Motor Company, he expounded on various occasions. It was his view that accumulated fortunes should be spent soon after they were made "in support of such educational, benevolent or humanitarian enterprises as will benefit their contemporaries—them and their children; no more." He further asserted that while charity in itself was good, "perpetual charities tend to do evil, blessing neither him that gives nor him that takes," since they become subject to misuse, disuse, and abuse. As examples of such endowments he cited J. E. Thompson's $2 million fund for daughters of railroad workers killed while in service and B. Mullanphy's fund to assist travelers from St. Louis westward. In a talk before the American Academy of Political and Social Science he said, "Permanent endowment tends to lessen the amount available for immediate needs; and our immediate needs are too plain and too urgent to allow us to do the work of future generations."

Embree was in sympathy with Rosenwald's aims and made efficient use of the Fund toward their realization. He continued to stimulate the building of rural schools for Negroes, but gave less money as public funds for them increased. By 1932, when the program was virtually ended, 5,357 "Rosenwald" schools were in existence in 15 states and 883 counties. Their total cost was $28,408,520, of which 64 percent came from taxes; more was given by Negroes than by the Fund—Embree's aim being "to give as little as possible for as short a time as possible," and to interest local people and officials in building and maintaining the schools themselves. Thus the Fund served as a spur and not as a crutch. It contributed five industrial high schools for Negroes; where needed, it provided buses for schools. Gradually the Fund gave more attention to teacher training in Negro colleges, spending $1,646,181 for this purpose and influencing state officials to provide a considerably larger sum. By 1935 nearly 15,000 teachers were instructing 650,000 Negro children in "Rosenwald" schools.

The Fund stimulated library development in Negro schools by actually establishing a number of them and by urging county officials to maintain those which it had started. It also furthered the expansion of four major centers for higher education: Howard University in Washington, a federally supported institution; Fisk University in Nashville; Atlanta University, and Dillard University in New Orleans. In each of these it established or enlarged departments, at a cost of $2,739,312. Many other Negro colleges also received its aid.

Another of its benevolences consisted of fellowships to Negro college students and grants to Negro scholars and artists. Among the recipients were Ralph Bunche, Marian Anderson, Katherine Dunham, Charles S. Johnson, and the biologist E. E. Just. The latter subsequently wrote to Rosenwald, "You will never know how much you meant to me and what an abiding light you and your life have been to me." A total of over 1,500 of these recipients obtained grants totaling $1,659,911. Executives of the Fund also spent several million on agencies aiming to develop understanding and cooperation between whites and blacks.

Still another function of the Fund was the improvement of health facilities and personnel for Negroes. It offered medical services at a nominal cost for those suffering from syphilis and tuberculosis, and also provided maternal and child care. Yet although the Fund spent $1,701,928 on Negro health care, its primary aim was to act as a catalytic agent between private and public agencies. The Fund, Embree pointed out, "offered leadership and resources and helped to chart the direction and change along the boundaries of these new frontiers."

By 1932, the year Rosenwald died, Sears-Roebuck shares had shrunk greatly in value and the income from them had almost stopped. To carry out his several programs, Embree spent about a million dollars from the principal and also enlisted the help of the Rockefeller and Carnegie Foundations to enable him to make good on his pledges. Nor did he hesitate to spend the principal in the ensuing years. By this procedure he exhausted the Fund by 1948, nine years before the limit set by Rosenwald. Abraham Flexner summarized its accomplishments. "It had done important work, often in collaboration with the [Rockefeller] General Education Board and always under expert guidance, in improving elementary, secondary, and higher education for Negroes of the South."

What stands out in Julius Rosenwald's career are the ease with which great wealth came to him, once he had joined Sears-Roebuck, and the imaginative use to which he put it. He was quick to admit his lack of financial genius, his lack of education, his ordinary human traits and capabilities. A solid citizen, a normally devoted Jew, a sound and capable businessman, upright in his dealings and conservative in outlook, he considered himself an average American Jew. His political naiveté is revealed in his effort to serve democracy and good government by offering F. L. Smith of Illinois a large financial bonus to resign his notorious candidacy for the United States Senate. If his accidental association with Sears-Roebuck had not materialized, he might have remained a fairly successful clothing manufacturer, charitable according to his means, and as obscure as thousands like him.

Yet he must have been potentially exceptional, since his radically altered circumstances brought out in him the rare trait of genuine modesty combined with an altruistically sophisticated resolve to put his millions to the best possible use. For in addition to his normal generosity to Jewish and other general causes, he had the inspiration to dedicate his millions and his best thought to the education and uplift of a whole population fresh from slavery. As Charles S. Johnson stated, "The courage of Mr. Rosenwald was in the quiet fearlessness of his assumptions and in the daring to impute full humanity to a group that had not yet full stature. In venturing the mortality of his reputation he gained immortality for his name."

Fully aware that he could not by himself, for all his millions, lift the Negro populace to the educational level of white Americans, he used his money as a stimulus to both whites and blacks in the South, making them aware of the essential need of schooling and of the duty of the white majority to right a long-standing wrong. Thus, by providing only a relatively small percentage of the actual cost, he was instrumental in erecting over 5,000 schools for hundreds of thousands of Negro children who might not have any education otherwise. And he did much the same for Negro higher education and medical care.

In his opposition to perpetual endowment, he had the perspicacity to realize that the living generation cannot foresee the needs and conditions of future generations. He therefore maintained that benevolence must be a contemporary action, and any effort to perpetuate a charitable contribution is unfair to the living who have need of it and a hindrance to those yet unborn. By publicizing this principle he influenced the direction of American charity. Rockefeller, Henry Ford, and others may have given away more than the $63 million which Rosenwald donated during his lifetime, but none used his wealth more intelligently or more imaginatively.

AN ILLUSTRIOUS
JEWISH FAMILY

The Flexner brothers exemplify an illustrious Jewish family whose achievements were the result of sheer intellectual endowment and dedication to the common good. Early in the nineteenth century their grandfather Michael Flexner produced the first Hebrew-Latin lexicon in his native Bohemia. One of his sons became a rabbi, but another, Moritz, who was born in 1820, migrated to New Orleans in 1853 in search of greater freedom and economic betterment. Shortly after his arrival, he contracted yellow fever. On his recovery he left for Louisville, where a family he knew from Bohemia had settled. He earned his living as a peddler, first with a pack on his back and somewhat later with a horse and wagon, saving his money to bring over other members of his immediate family.

In 1856 he married Esther Abraham, and a year later they became the parents of Jacob, the first of seven sons and two daughters. Moritz had in the meantime gone into the wholesale hat business, selling his product in the cities and towns of the southern states. No intellectual himself, his chief interest was the education of his sons and, like so many Jewish fathers, to see his boys become professional men. Although he was practically ruined in the panic of 1873, he did his best to keep them in school and away from what he considered the coarsening influences of trade. Although his business never recovered, he hoped that "our children will justify us"; and before he died in 1882 he saw the early evidences of his faith in them. For by that time four of his sons gave promise of achieving scholarly distinction.

Jacob Flexner (1857–1934) studied pharmacy because it took less time and money than medicine. He opened a drug store, and his interest in medicine made his pharmacy a gathering center for the city's doctors. When his father died, he took over the burden of the education of his younger brothers—carrying out his father's unfinished task even though it necessitated the further postponement of his own ambitions. It was he who sent Abraham to Johns Hopkins University, which he had heard was one of the best American institutions of higher learning, supporting him for two years with his hard-saved $1,000. When his brothers were launched on their professional careers, he sold his drug store and studied medicine both at the University of Louisville School of Medicine and at Johns Hopkins University. In time he became a highly regarded physician, and took a keener interest in his patients than in furthering himself financially. After his death Abraham said,

> We can never be sufficiently grateful to the memory of our oldest brother for the sacrifice he made in behalf of an ideal at a time when his own needs were pressing, but he was throughout his life a person of quick and remarkable intelligence, and he must have realized that we were all destined to humble careers unless at the first opportunity a break was made. Always serious in youth, he had, at our father's death, in a very real sense taken his place as head of the family.

Simon Flexner (1863–1946) worked as a drug clerk and then studied at the University of Louisville School of Medicine, graduating in 1889. Although his medical preparation was pitiful, he went to Johns Hopkins University to study pathology with Dr. W. H. Welch, an outstanding medical scholar. Despite his weak background, his native ability soon won him Dr. Welch's confidence and friendship. At the end of the year he won a fellowship of $500, to study in Germany and France for another year. By now well versed in pathological anatomy, he was engaged by Johns Hopkins in 1891 as a co-teacher with Welch. He remained there until 1899, when he became a professor of pathology at the University of Pennsylvania.

In 1901 the Rockefeller Institute for Medical Research was established and Simon was offered a place in its laboratories. He concentrated on research into poisonous substances in the human body, especially snake venom, and in time discovered the bacillus, now bearing his name, that causes dysentery. Another of his discoveries was the virus that causes poliomyelitis, and he devised a treatment which lowered mortality. As director of the Institute and an outstanding medical scientist, he had a worldwide reputation and was active in various medical organizations and on government commissions. He wrote extensively on his laboratory findings, and upon his retirement in 1935 he prepared, with the help of his son James, a distinguished biography of his mentor and friend Dr. Welch.

A third brother, Bernard Flexner (1865–1945), became an eminent liberal lawyer in Louisville and published books on the juvenile court and on probation. In 1928 he was the prime mover of a group of distinguished lawyers and philanthropists who published and distributed to law libraries the multivolume record of the Sacco-Vanzetti trial. More than his brothers he took an active interest in Jewish affairs. In 1919 he went to Versailles as a delegate in behalf of Jewish minority rights. He also worked with the American Jewish Joint Distribution Committee as an authority on economics, as a member of its executive committee, and as chairman of its committee on medical affairs. Interested in Zionism, he served as a non-Zionist member of the Council of the Jewish Agency in Palestine.

Other members of the Flexner family have had distinguished careers in the arts and letters, notably Simon's wife, Helen Thomas Flexner, the author of A Quaker Childhood (1940) and other writings, and his son, James Thomas Flexner, who has written biographies and books of art criticism. Jacob's two daughters, Jennie M. and Hortense, have both had notable careers, the first in library administration and the second as a poet and playwright. Eleanor Flexner wrote on American playwrights as well as A Century of Struggle (1959). Marion K. Flexner is the author of cookbooks. Kenneth Flexner Fearing (1902–1961) was a poet and novelist of solid merit.

10
Abraham
Flexner

ABRAHAM FLEXNER'S career illustrates a remarkably fertile mind functioning boldly and imaginatively for the general good. Born in 1866, he graduated from Louisville high school in 1884. Although he was poorly prepared for college by eastern standards, being deficient in both Greek and Latin, Abraham quickly overcame his initial difficulty in keeping up with his Johns Hopkins classmates. In addition, since he knew his brother Jacob could not support him in college for more than two years, he carried twice the usual number of courses and managed to graduate within that time. He even found the leisure to attend public lectures and to write home daily.

Returning to Louisville in 1886, not quite twenty years old, he began to teach in a local high school, where he became a conspicuously effective teacher. He lived at home in the intimacy of his family and gave his entire salary to his mother, taking from her only what he needed for his few personal expenses.

In 1890 a wealthy lawyer, eager to have his unruly son prepared for college, arranged with four friends who had sons of a similar age to engage Flexner as tutor, paying him $500 tuition for each boy. This was the beginning of "Mr. Flexner's School." Flexner's approach was novel. He let boys have complete freedom, set no rules, and gave neither tests nor marks, meanwhile assuring them that he would prepare them for college. He encouraged them to pursue whatever subject interested them and gradually transferred this interest to other subjects. When the boys realized that they were not being forced to study but that they could not enter college until they learned the required subjects, they began to apply themselves to their studies and had no difficulty in being accepted by a college. Flexner had made clear to them the value of knowledge for its own sake as well as its value as a means to an end.

In the fifteen years of its existence Flexner's School was operated by Abraham with the aid of his two sisters. Although small, it had an exceptionally high reputation. President Eliot of Harvard wrote to Flexner inquiring how he managed to send him boys who were both younger and more capable than students from other preparatory schools. In reply Flexner wrote, "I treated these boys as individuals, and I let each go at his own pace. I took hold of pupils where they were strong, not where they were weak, and having whetted their appetites by success in one field, usually succeeded in arousing their interest in another." Eliot urged him to describe this method in a paper, and he complied in an article published in *The Educational Review* in 1891.

In 1890 he agreed to teach a girl, Anne L. Crawford, and tutored her for a year. Later, after waiting two years to help the younger members of his family, he married her. Since neither of them was religious, their differences of faith had no effect on their long and harmonious life or on the upbringing of their two daughters. Mrs. Flexner became a successful playwright in her own name, and among her comedies *Mrs. Wiggs of the Cabbage Patch* achieved notable popularity.

In 1905, after nineteen years of teaching, Flexner decided to close his school and take graduate work at Harvard "to make a career in education." On obtaining his M. A. degree, he went with his family to Europe for further study. After sojourning in England to observe its leading universities, he resumed his advanced study at the University of Berlin. While there he wrote *The American College: A Criticism*, a severe indictment of the elective system, lecture courses, and assistantships as he had observed them during his year at Harvard, making the point that the students whom he had sent to eastern colleges lost rather than gained in enthusiasm for scholarship.

The book appeared in 1908 and was generally ignored. A copy, however, was read by Dr. H. S. Pritchett, director of the Carnegie Foundation for the Advancement of Teaching, and so favorable was his reaction that he invited Flexner to make a study of American medical schools. At first Abraham thought he was being confused with his brother Simon, but was disabused of this assumption by Pritchett, who said the "professional schools should be studied not from the point of view of the practitioner but from the standpoint of the educator." These institutions, Pritchett added, must be examined to see if they are equipped and conducted in a manner "to train students to be efficient physicians, surgeons, and so on."

Flexner began his research in December, 1908, reading everything he could find on medical education in the United States and Europe. He also talked at length with Dr. Welch and others at Johns Hopkins before visiting the 155 medical schools then in existence. "Flexner," wrote John W. Gardner, "was entirely without the obvious qualifications of a medical background. All that he had was a razor-edged mind, fierce integrity, limitless courage, and the capacity to express himself clearly and vividly." He investigated entrance requirements and how they were enforced, the size and medical training of faculties, the endowments and tuition fees of the colleges, the quality of the laboratories, and the relation between laboratories and hospitals. What he found was a generally disgraceful situation: entrance requirements were low and usually unenforced, laboratory facilities were ridiculously inadequate, faculties were mediocre and too small, 140 of the colleges had no library or a very poor one, and the relations between medical schools and hospitals were simply "awful." He considered these conditions "sordid, hideous, unintelligent even where honest—and so little that is even honest." His detailed report, *Bulletin Number Four: Medical Education in the United States and Canada* (1910), shocked the medical profession and its sponsors. "Throughout," Flexner declared long after, "I struck from the shoulder, naming names and places. Pritchett stood behind me like a stone wall."

Robert S. Brookings, who had been giving $80,000 a year to the medical school at Washington University at St. Louis, read the criticism of the school with deep chagrin and complained to Pritchett that the indictment must be exaggerated and false. Pritchett arranged for Flexner to review his findings with Brookings. Persuaded of the accuracy of the criticisms, the philanthropist accepted Flexner's suggestion that the school be completely reorganized in line with President Gilman's procedure at Johns Hopkins, the one medical school which Flexner had found entirely satisfactory.

Elsewhere in the United States the *Bulletin* caused much consternation and a re-evaluation of conditions in medical schools. "Such a rattling of dead bones," Flexner later commented, "has never been heard in this country before or since. Schools collapsed to the right and left, usually without a murmur. A number of them pooled their resources." Of the 155 schools only 35 were left. Louisville, for instance, combined its seven medical schools into one, and in Chicago 15 were reduced to three. When the shouting and breast-beating subsided, American medical education was radically modified, although it continued to limp for lack of funds and trained faculty. Flexner asserted at the time that to place medical education on a solid scientific foundation required hundreds of millions of dollars.

In 1910 Pritchett sent Flexner to Europe to investigate medical teaching abroad. The fame of his brother Simon helped him obtain the cooperation of leading doctors in England, Scotland, France, Germany, and Austria. He sought no statistics, used no questionnaires, but met many people, sat in at lectures, observed students at work and talked to them. German medical schools impressed him favorably. "There were adequate entrance requirements and they were enforced; relation between laboratories and clinics were close; teachers were professors, not practicing physicians, though there were, to be sure, places in which consultations and fees were leading to abuses; research was held in high and proper esteem." He considered French teaching superior to German in its clinical emphasis, while in England stress was laid on practice rather than research. In Germany he received an honorary M.D. degree from the University of Berlin. His detailed report, published in 1912 as *Bulletin Number Six: Medical Education in Europe*, was impressive and well received.

Shortly after his return to the United States in 1911 Flexner was invited to lunch by F. T. Gates, philanthropic adviser to John D. Rockefeller, and told that *Bulletin Number Four* "is not only a criticism; it is also a program." In the course of conversation Gates asked him what he would do with a million dollars. Flexner replied that he would give it to Dr. Welch, who had accelerated sound medical teaching in this country. Gates thereupon asked him to go to Baltimore and study conditions at Johns Hopkins more specifically. Three weeks later Flexner reported that the most obvious need was the payment of adequate salaries to teachers in clinics so that they would not have to depend on their practice, and that to do this satisfactorily required an endowment of $1.5 million. Gates and his fellow members of the Rockefeller Institute for Medical Research appropriated the money and thereby introduced the idea of subsidizing clinical teaching to other medical schools.

The Bureau of Social Hygiene was established by John D. Rockefeller, Jr., to study prostitution and seek remedies for its elimination. In 1912 he persuaded Flexner to study the situation in Europe. For the next two years Flexner made a thorough investigation in several countries, interviewing police officials, women in and out of brothels, and social workers as well as social scientists. To a friend he wrote of his work as "the sordid and painful topic which now absorbs all my thoughts and time." His conclusions appeared in *Prostitution in Europe* (1914):

> By European thought and policy, prostitution has hitherto been treated in a lump and most illogically—partly as harmful, partly connived at as inevitable, partly punished as criminal, and partly ignored as human—and in contemporary practice all these various attitudes are simultaneously in evidence.

His three studies had made Flexner a leading educational investigator both in Europe and in the United States and in 1913 he was invited to join the General Education Board, which had been established by Rockefeller a decade earlier. He became secretary in 1917 and director in 1925. One of his first undertakings was a field trip to the South, where he inspected schools for both white and black children and found them equally poorly equipped and staffed. His published report and his talks with state and local officials helped to stimulate increased taxation for the improvement of educational standards and cooperation with the Rosenwald school program. Subsequently he made similar trips to other parts of the country as well as return visits to the South.

One result of these trips was the idea of a general modern school to serve as a model for the entire country in the same way as the medical school at Johns Hopkins was furthering improved teaching of medicine. In 1915 he presented the project to the General Education Board and was asked to describe it in a detailed report, which he did in *A Modern School* (1916). The Board received it favorably

and voted to establish the endowed Lincoln School in association with Columbia University's Teachers College. Subsequently he admitted his error: Johns Hopkins Medical
School could serve as a model for other medical schools
because their number was relatively small and their specialized nature made them amenable to stimulus and improvement; Lincoln School failed of its purpose because
elementary schools numbered in the thousands, were mostly
public, within established school systems, subject to political pressures and pedagogical inertia, required more tax
money than parents and officials were willing to give, and
drew a less selective group for students.

After 1918 Flexner concentrated on the improvement
of American medical education. In Chicago his plan to improve Rush Medical School miscarried owing to a change
of personnel. He thereupon persuaded Julius Rosenwald,
John D. Rockefeller, and President Judson of the University
of Chicago to help establish a university medical school,
obtaining $3 million for the purpose. Somewhat later when
Albert D. Lasker offered the school a million dollars for
cancer research, Flexner urged him to attach no strings to
his gift and let the faculty decide on the best use of the
money.

Aware that it would take hundreds of millions of dollars to raise medical education standards to a level of excellence, he conceived the idea of obtaining $50 million as
seed money from Rockefeller and using it to attract contributions to local schools from other wealthy men. At Gates's
suggestion he prepared a four-page memorandum for
Rockefeller's study. Several months later Rockefeller informed Flexner that he was ready to give him $20 million.
Flexner's response was that it was not enough if the improvement of medical education was to be carried out properly. He received the additional $30 million.

Flexner now devoted his energies and ingenuity to encouraging large gifts from wealthy men in different sections of the country. His first proving ground was Rochester,

where he believed a medical school should be added to the local university. Since George Eastman was the city's richest and most prominent citizen, Flexner arranged to see him and explained that he had the opportunity to perform a magnificent service to his fellow citizens by helping to finance a medical school for the University of Rochester. The project appealed to Eastman and he offered what he considered a very generous sum—$2.5 million. Flexner blandly countered that it was not enough, that the amount must be doubled if the school was to serve the community with the distinction Eastman would expect. Eastman added another million, but Flexner still insisted on the full amount and Eastman capitulated with the remark, "You are the best salesman I have ever seen." The General Education Board contributed the same amount, and the medical school established with these resources became one of the better institutions in the East.

Flexner next chose the state of Iowa in which to develop a good medical school. He believed that this action would spur neighboring states to emulate Iowa, since they "cannot afford to have it said in the Middle West that Iowa has something that [their] university lacks." When news of this venture became public, university officials in other states urged him to do the same for them. His reply was that the Board had not the means to help every state, but there was no reason why each state could not develop a medical school as good as the one in Iowa.

In New York City Flexner exerted his best diplomatic efforts over several years to persuade the heads of New York Hospital and Cornell University to join their resources in creating an improved medical school, and success finally came in 1926. His conversation with Payne Whitney about the Cornell Medical School's need of a high-level neurological division at a cost of $8 million persuaded Whitney to add a codicil to his will providing that sum for a neurological institute. In a chat with J. P. Morgan, Flexner explained that an institution suffering from annual deficits cannot function effectively and that if he wished to see the Lying-In Hospital, an institution which he supported, operating properly he should add $2 million to its endowment. Morgan made the gift and thanked Flexner for the advice.

Always interested in the South, Flexner next selected Vanderbilt University as the school most worthy of assistance in the medical field. With $4 million provided by the Board he helped reorganize its medical school, making it a model for others in the South. So pleased was he with its successful operation that when his brother Bernard wanted to endow a lectureship in his name, he suggested that the gift be made to Vanderbilt University.

For ten years, from 1918 to 1928, Flexner concentrated on the improvement of American medical teaching. In addition to establishing or reorganizing medical schools in pivotal sections of the country, he promoted good teaching by seeking out promising undergraduates and financing their advanced study abroad. A number of these men returned to the United States equipped to establish first-rate laboratories and clinics.

By the time he retired from the General Education Board in 1928, he had been instrumental in adding to the original Rockefeller gift more than a half-billion dollars, donated by individuals and states, to the resources and endowments of American medical Schools—largely by stimulating matching grants and by the use of key schools to encourage the development and improvement of schools in neighboring universities. Warmly appreciative of his successful efforts, John D. Rockefeller, Jr., wrote to him:

> I think it would be hard to overestimate the contribution which you have made to the development of education generally in the United States and especially to the establishment of a high, strong foundation of medical education. In the fifteen years of your relationship to the General Education Board, because of the splendid background of knowledge which you have brought with you

and your highly trained mind, you have been able to accomplish what another could not have done in twice the time, if at all.

Flexner's emphasis on medical education did not lessen his strong interest in general education. In 1923 he published his views in *A Modern College and a Modern School*. At that time Lincoln School was still in the process of hopeful realization, and in describing the liberal type of training it was developing, he wrote,

> I am one of those who believe that the current activities, opinions, and ideals of life—and "current" does not by any means exclude the past—contain the physical, intellectual, and spiritual elements, out of which an educational scheme, at once liberal and appealing, can be constructed. Hence, literature, music, and art were conceived as playing important parts in the curriculum, not less than science, industry, and modern languages.

All these elements, he pointed out, serve to "put the child into effective relation with the world in which he lives." The objective is to teach him the knowledge he needs to handle himself effectively in the world about him. "The modern school," he asserted, "would prove a disappointment unless greater intellectual power is procurable for its pupils on the basis of a realistic training than could have been procured from an education of any other type." He urged that in addition to the traditional subjects the child should be taught science, industry, aesthetics, and civics, courses to illuminate his daily life. He also encouraged the teaching of literature as a means of developing taste, interest, and appreciation in poetry, as well as "the surest way of liberating creative talent." He rejected the teaching of useless facts or obsolete writings simply because they had been taught in the past.

In 1928 he was invited to deliver the Rhodes Trust memorial lectures at Oxford University. His talks generated wide interest, and each one attracted a larger audience.

These lectures as well as the one entitled "Do Americans Really Value Education?" he incorporated in his book *Universities—American, English, German,* published in 1931. Highly critical of "applied" trends in American higher education, he deplored the fact that the American student "spends two years or more on work that should be included in a good high school." He referred caustically to the many high school and college courses with no intellectual contents, such as bookkeeping, typing, business letter writing, and marketing methods, on which students spend "a large part of their precious and unretrievable years. . . . None of them deserves recognition by a college and least of all does any of them deserve a place in an institution of learning." He did not believe that a trained intelligence can "learn the 'principles' of salesmanship from a Ph.D. who has never sold anything, or the 'principles' of marketing from a Ph.D. who has never marketed anything."

As in his earlier reports, he named names and specified courses taught. He referred astringently to the University of Wisconsin's five series of courses in journalism: the daily newspaper, the community newspaper, advertising, magazines, and teachers of journalism. "The net result is the further dilution of an already diluted education by the effort to teach under the guise of a profession a few practical tricks and adjustments that an educated or clever youth could rapidly pick up 'on the job.' " Consequently he held business schools in little esteem, and maintained that most college students are prematurely trained in various "practical" subjects. He also asserted that, in general, the graduate school "suffers from the curious cultural meagerness of American life . . . there is something lacking, something subtle and elusive, but vitally real and substantial." Particularly critical of Columbia University's Teachers College, he pointed out that its 200-page catalogue was "devoted to trivial, obvious, and inconsequential subjects, which could safely be left to the common sense or intelligence of any fairly well-educated person."

Despite the existence of "a saving remnant" of students

who manage to get a real education, he insisted that "universities must depend on ideas, on great men. . . . But great men are individualists; and individualists and organizations are in everlasting conflict." In American universities, however, the president is ranked above the teacher. "The executive is valued because the American loves administration and organization and esteems highly those charged with responsibility for it, whereas he gives less recognition to superior intellectual achievement." He regretted that Americans seemed to be unable and unwilling "to distinguish between genuine culture and superficial veneer," tending to lower "institutions which should exemplify intellectual distinctions to the level of venders of patent medicines." In sum, his criticism of American education rested on the premise that we have "jumbled together in secondary schools, colleges, or universities all sorts of persons, all sorts of subjects. Exceptions, brilliant and solid, may be noted, but they can also be counted."

He was more favorable in his evaluation of English and German universities. Although he criticized the University of London for faults similar to those he deprecated in American institutions, he found the English public schools articulating well with the universities, especially with Oxford and Cambridge. What perturbed him in the late 1920's was the general trend among nations toward spending for armaments rather than for education. "Nations have recently been led to borrow billions for war, no nation has ever borrowed largely for education. . . . Probably no nation is rich enough to pay for both war and civilization. We must make our choice; we cannot have both."

He tended to admire German universities. In that country, he explained, schools were "varied to *meet the cultural possibilities of the pupil—not the needs of the vocation* which he might subsequently enter." Yet the German university graduate, because he "tasted little freedom," was sometimes less successful as an adult than the American graduate despite his superior education. He pointed out, however, that in German universities teaching and research had long been stressed, and that their great investigators were often inspired teachers; that even German pedantry rested on solid scholarship.

In his lectures on higher learning Flexner outlined his ideal university, an institution where scholars could further their studies and research unhampered by rules and regulations. He was convinced "that if outstanding men are brought together and left free to pursue their research under favorable circumstances and without the necessity of producing practical results, great and practical results may be realized."

When Louis Bamberger sold his Newark department store in 1929 and he and his sister Mrs. Felix Fuld wanted to donate part of their wealth to a worthy cause, they approached Flexner for advice. His exposition of a research institute which would do for scholarship what the Rockefeller Institute was doing for medicine appealed to them, and they insisted that he become its organizer and director. He was given $5 million and complete freedom to establish the Institute for Advanced Study in Princeton.

Chartered in 1930, the Institute was opened some time later with a department of mathematics—because Flexner considered it fundamental to all research, because it required least "plant," and because he believed he could attract the highest caliber of scholars in that discipline. It was his idea that members of the department should pursue their high-level studies and also do a little teaching in an atmosphere of complete academic freedom. With this in view, he limited the functions of the trustees to business matters. He was fortunate to attract such eminent mathematicians as Albert Einstein, Hermann Weyl, John von Neumann, and Oswald Veblen. "Each was practically autonomous," he was pleased to point out. There was no routine, no formality, no opening or closing exercises, only the simplest records, and no committee meetings. There was in fact only one faculty gathering in the seven years of Flexner's directorship. When one of the newscomers asked what his duties were, he was told: "You have no duties—only opportunities." Subsequently, as he found the right men, Flexner established departments in economics, politics, and the humanities. By the time he retired in 1939 the faculty he had collected was indeed a galaxy of world-renowned scholars and scientists.

Even before he left the Institute he began to write his autobiography, which he published in 1940, entitled *I Remember*; shortly before his death in 1959 he completed an updated edition. Written with his wonted frankness, it recapitulated in some detail his efforts and achievements. He emerges as the concerned humanitarian and shrewd optimist despite his scathing criticism of American education. "Education was my strongest continuing interest," he wrote. "I have cared—cared profoundly—about education, ever since at nineteen years of age I began to teach. My interest has always had a pragmatic cast; I wished to see, hard, practical work done to improve the range and attitude of teaching in America."

His pioneering criticism had a salubrious effect, and he lived long enough to witness the higher standards which he had helped to establish in colleges and particularly in medical schools. Allan Nevins, in an introduction to the 1960 edition of the autobiography, indicated the rare combination of Flexner's qualities: "What gave his service its greatest impact in American life was, first, his imagination in seeing the possibilities of change and reform in society—particularly in education; second, his boldness in insisting on goals of the largest magnitude, not just limited achievements; and third, his grasp of organization."

Although he was over 70, his energy remained unabated. His next task was to pay public tribute to the man who had brought him into educational research and whom he greatly admired. In *Henry S. Pritchett* (1943) he discussed the development of astronomy in the late nineteenth century and Pritchett's part in it; his presidency of Massachusetts Institute of Technology; his leadership in the Carnegie Foundation for the Advancement of Teaching; his efforts to provide college teachers with adequate pensions; and his close relation to Flexner and his work to the end of his life in 1939. In this warmly appreciative estimate, Pritchett emerges as "a veritable statesman of education," and one of the most able utilizers of the wealth of others for the benefit of men of worth.

Three years later Flexner brought out a biography of another man whom he deeply esteemed and to whom he owed much—Daniel C. Gilman, first president of Johns Hopkins University. He depicted him as a highly endowed educator, with the vision and persistence to build Johns Hopkins on the basis of the soundest scholarship and to strive not for more buildings and a larger student body but for a faculty of "high intellectual quality."

In 1952 Flexner collaborated on a monograph entitled *Funds and Foundations.* In general he indicated that foundations must follow four basic principles if they are to achieve their humanitarian aims: Operate on a large plan; give money to a qualified man or institution, not to projects or problems; stimulate gifts from others by matching donations; choose gifted leaders to carry out plans. He intimated that these principles are frequently violated to the detriment of the intended benevolence.

In 1956 Flexner reached his ninetieth year. His wife had died the year before, and he lived alone, busy at work on matters which interested him. He was pleased that year to receive the Frank H. Lahey Memorial Award "for outstanding leadership in medical education." A year later the Association of American Medical Colleges established an annual Abraham Flexner Award "for distinguished service to medical education." At his publisher's urging, he brought his autobiography up to date. At his death in 1959 the New York *Times* commented that no other American of his time had contributed more to the "welfare of his country and of humanity in general." And John W. Gardner stated in an appreciation in *Science*,

In matters of intellect he was forceful, astringent, scornful of compromise, a warrior in behalf of wisdom and virtue as he conceived them. He had a sparkling wit which was equally effective in mischievous teasing of his friends, the needling of those he wished to stir to action, and the harpooning of those who won his scorn. . . . He fought a holy war against slackness, triviality, and educational quackery.

THE AMERICANIZATION OF JUDAISM

The mass migration of East-European Jews to the United States after 1905 subtly but surely affected the character of Judaism in America. The German Jews, who were by then fully Americanized and generally affluent, became a minority which retained its dominance for only another decade through the American Jewish Committee. They regarded the newcomers as their social inferiors and an ethnic responsibility. Some of the more tolerant and philanthropic German Jews did what they could to quicken the acculturation of the immigrants to the American way of life. Thus Jacob Schiff, Louis Marshall, and others supported the Jewish Theological Seminary, the seat of Conservative Judaism, in an effort to facilitate the religious enlightenment of the newcomers.

Many East-European Jews, and especially their children, were only too eager to establish themselves in the economy and culture of their new environment. They learned English, they worked hard to improve themselves materially, and not a few longed to attain the social status of their wealthy Germanic brethren. Arthur Hertzberg wrote in *The American Hebrew,*

> The great current represented by the children of the new immigrants can be characterized by three desires: the wish to upgrade themselves socially, either by joining congregations created by older waves of immigration or by establishing their own in an American image; the need to affirm an unideological, often not even overtly religious commitment to the Jewish way; and the desire to continue strong emotions which bound them to the Jewish communities overseas, from which their parents had sprung.

Among the earlier Jewish immigrants secularization had been fairly rapid, the process for a good many being helped along through adherence to a Reform temple, to membership in Ethical Culture or no religious association, to intermarriage, to a passive or complete loosening of Jewish ties. The immigrants after 1880 tended to follow a similar pattern, although circumstances kept most of them from its extremes. The American-born generation subsequently turned the Orthodox synagogues of their parents into Conservative or Reform temples. They began to develop Jewish Community Centers and to incorporate the existing YMHA branches into these social and educational institutions.

Time and the Americanization process served to merge the various Jewish groupings. Thus prosperous Jews of East-European parentage began to be accepted as members of Reform temples. Simultaneously anti-Jewish attacks in the 1920's strengthened the Jewish consciousness of many who were drifting away from Judaism. As explained by Rabbi Abba Hillel Silver, "When men are prosperous they find it easy to dispense with God—especially with a Jewish God"; but when anti-Semitism flared openly, many Jews "returned to their faith and their people as if to a shelter from a gathering storm." And the establishment of Israel in 1948 gave many a pride in their Jewishness which they had lacked before.

Religion currently has no stronger hold on Jews than it has on others. Although nearly sixty percent of American Jews are nominal members of a synagogue or temple, a much smaller percentage is either religious or interested in their Jewish heritage. And although more than half of Jewish youth of college age attend institutions of higher learning, few of them respect scholarship with the awe of their forefathers, and many are illiterate on Jewish culture and history. It was only recently that a number of them, stimulated by the establishment of Israel, have come to feel the need of rootage and identification.

Over the centuries two types of Jews dedicated themselves to the welfare of their people: "court" Jews, wealthy and influential, who endeavored to mitigate repressions and restrictions against the Jewish community, and rabbis within the ghettos, learned and esteemed leaders, who ruled the community in religious and civic matters. In the United States the role of the defender and apologist, assumed by the wealthy civic leaders, remained prestigious; that of the rabbi declined in importance. The lay board of a temple or synagogue is in full control, with the rabbi restricted to his duties as preacher and teacher. Only the exceptionally gifted rabbi succeeds in breaking through this restriction and lives up to his historic role as scholar and religious leader.

Emil G. Hirsch (1851–1923) was the son of the chief rabbi of Luxembourg. Brought to this country at the age of fifteen, he graduated from the University of Pennsylvania in 1872 and then studied in Germany. Influenced by his father and by his Jewish teachers in Germany, he assumed his role as rabbi with a strong consciousness of his mission. In 1880 he married the daughter of Rabbi David Einhorn and became rabbi of the Sinai Congregation in Chicago, succeeding his brother-in-law Kaufmann Kohler. In time he established himself as a scholar, civic leader, and orator. He gave a social emphasis to Judaism, helped found the Home Finding Society, and led the movement to federate Jewish charities. As a forthright liberal he opposed religious ceremonies which he considered obsolete and was the first Reform rabbi to limit the temple service to Sunday. Although a strong opponent of political Zionism, he favored its cultural program. Over the years he sought to bring sympathetic understanding between Jews and Christians, and became known as the "Jewish ambassador to the Gentile world." He was active in Chicago civic affairs and often asked to arbitrate labor disputes. In 1892 he helped found the University of Chicago and held a chair in rabbinic literature and philosophy there.

Samuel Schulman (1864–1955) was one of the first Russian-born rabbis to become prominent in Reform Judaism. Brought to this country in 1868, he studied at the College of the City of New York and did graduate work abroad. On his return to the United States he held several pulpits. In 1899 he became co-rabbi with Kaufmann Kohler at Temple Beth-El in

New York. When Kohler left to become president of Hebrew Union College in 1903, Schulman succeeded him as senior rabbi and distinguished himself as a preacher and in rabbinical activities, serving as president of the Central Conference of American Rabbis in 1911–1913. When Beth-El was merged with Temple Emanu-El in 1927, he became rabbi of the combined prestigious congregation until his retirement in 1934.

A strong exponent of Reform Judaism, he maintained that the Jews were solely a religious community. He strongly objected to the acceptance of Jesus as a Jewish prophet, maintaining that praise of Jesus was "the first step in the conversion to Christianity." Although vigorously critical of Jewish nationalism and the Zionist movement, he was greatly attracted to Palestine as the land of Judaism and visited it twice. In 1929 he became a non-Zionist member of the Jewish Agency.

Rabbi Judah L. Magnes (1887–1948) was born in San Francisco, the son of a rabbi. He graduated from the University of Cincinnati in 1898, from Hebrew Union College in 1900, and obtained his doctorate from Heidelberg University in 1902. As a rabbi in Brooklyn and New York he took an active part in Jewish and civic affairs, in 1903 leading a parade in protest against the Kishinev pogrom. An early adherent to Zionism, he was honorary secretary of the Federation of American Zionists from 1905 to 1908. He was also a founder of the American Jewish Committee and a leader of the Jewish Kehillah, (community) from 1909 to 1922. From 1906 to 1910 he officiated as rabbi of Temple Emanu-El, and from 1912 to 1920 he led the Society for the Advancement of Judaism. He also helped to establish the Hadassah in Israel and the American Jewish Congress. In 1922 he migrated to Palestine where he became chancellor and, after 1935, president of Hebrew University.

A pacifist and social reformer, Dr. Magnes derived his views from the Hebrew prophets. He maintained that "the conservation of Jewish piety and a thoroughgoing social radicalism are not antagonistic but complementary, and are both the outcome of the tradition of the prophetic morality." He differed from his fellow Zionist leaders in favoring a binational state for Arabs and Jews along Swiss lines because he believed that a Jewish state could only be founded on force. He opposed the violent acts of the underground in Palestine prior to 1948, and after Israel was established he pleaded for cooperation with the Arabs. Upon his death Sholem Asch said, "I consider Dr. Magnes the most characteristic example of Jewish idealism which America has yet produced."

Mordecai M. Kaplan, born in 1881 in Lithuania, reached this country when he was eight. He studied at the College of the City of New York, Columbia University, and the Jewish Theological Seminary. After a rabbinical career from 1903 to 1909, he became principal and later dean of the Seminary's teacher institute and taught homiletics at the Seminary. In 1916 he organized the first Jewish Center in New York, and from 1922 to 1944 he headed the Society for the Advancement of Judaism. A religious leader of the newer generation of immigrants, he wrote much on the philosophy of Judaism in an effort to reinterpret Jewish religious views. He called his philosophy Reconstructionism, and he founded *The Reconstructionist* in 1934 as a biweekly in which he expounded the concept of making Judaism compatible with our secular age. From 1932 to 1934 he was president of the Rabbinical Assembly of America.

One of the most illustrious of the rabbinical leaders, Abba Hillel Silver (1893–1963), was also born in Lithuania and brought to the United States as a boy of nine. His father, Rabbi Moses Silver, a scholar and Zionist, imbued his children with a love of Judaism and dedication to Zionism. He taught them Hebrew at an early age, and Abba and his older brother formed the Dr. Herzl Zion Club in 1904. After graduating simultaneously from the University of Cincinnati and Hebrew Union College in 1915, he served as rabbi in Wheeling for two years, then was called to The Temple in Cleveland. Although the leading members frowned upon his Zionism and his ideas of social reform, they tolerated him because of his superiority as a preacher and educator. Such was his popularity, indeed, that The Temple in time became one of the largest Jewish congregations. In 1925 he obtained his doctorate from Hebrew

Union College with a thesis entitled *Messianic Speculations in Israel.* Later he published several other volumes on Judaism.

Active in Zionist affairs, Silver sided with Brandeis and Mack in 1921 in the procedural dispute with Weizmann. He was one of the first, however, to rejoin the Zionist majority, and favored the extended Jewish Agency proposed by Weizmann and Marshall and ratified in 1929. In the 1930s he helped to organize the boycott against Nazi Germany and to raise funds for the Jewish refugees, as chairman of the United Jewish Appeal. During World War II he ardently advocated making Palestine a Jewish state. "When all the doors of the world will be closed to our people, then the hand of destiny will force open the door of Palestine." In 1943, as co-chairman of the American Zionist Emergency Council, he acted aggressively to reorganize American Zionists and to establish a bureau in Washington to keep closer contact with the American government. At this time he clashed with Dr. Wise on matters of policy—"Silver activists" opposing "Wise moderates"—but after 1945 both factions opposed British efforts to close Palestine to Jewish migration. When Weizmann, at the Congress of World Zionists in 1946, acquiesced in the partition of Palestine, Silver opposed the motion and won. The following year, he argued the case for the establishment of the Jewish state at the United Nations. To the end of his life he continued his dedicated service to Zionism and the Jewish people.

11
Stephen S. Wise

RABBI

AND

REFORMER

STEPHEN SAMUEL WISE, scion of several generations of rabbis, was born in Hungary in 1874 and brought to this country as a baby when his father accepted a rabbinical post in New York. With his grandfather Joseph Hirsch Weisz, the Orthodox chief rabbi of Erlau, Hungary, and with his father, the mildly Reform rabbi of Rodeph Sholem synagogue in New York, young Stephen grew up in an atmosphere of Jewish learning and traditional dedication, guided and encouraged by his father, with whom he remained intimate to the end. He attended the College of the City of New York and was graduated from Columbia University in 1892. Ordained as rabbi in Vienna, he completed his liturgical studies at Oxford University before returning to New York, where he soon became rabbi of Temple B'nai Jeshurun. He was a highly attractive young man, with remarkably strong facial features and a leonine head. His baritone voice, powerful and resonant, which he used dramatically to emphasize his natural eloquence, added a quality of sensuousness to his sermons. In later years his "flawless oratorical manner" made him one of the outstanding speakers in America.

In 1899, while on a visit to Alaska, he was invited to preach at Temple Beth Israel in Portland, Oregon. He made a favorable impression and was offered the rabbinate with a salary of $5,000, a high figure at that time. A strong motive for acceptance was his wish for a greater understanding of America as well as his feeling that he had not "touched and kindled the hearts of people" in New York. He hoped to be more successful in the Northwest. For, like Felix Adler, he wanted to be "the ethical leader of a church," though unlike Adler, he would not be "faithless to Israel."

To his fiancée, Louise Waterman, then a follower of Felix Adler, he wrote, "A great field of labor and opportunity awaits me in the North West. A number of cities within 500 miles of Portland have their Jewish communities, but no minister and nothing of religious teaching and striving. These I shall try to build up. It will be hard work, but I welcome it." At about that time he had completed his thesis, an edited translation from the Arabic of Solomon ibn Gabirol's *The Improvement of the Moral Qualities*, and he received his doctorate from Columbia in 1901.

Dr. Wise was a man of contradictory characteristics. Shortly before his marriage he described himself with exaggerated frankness to his intended bride as a "man of temperament . . . nervous, cross, petulant, irritable, selfish, vain, and even envious, with one miserable, unpardonable, besetting weakness, an unrighteous ambition which deadens the best within men in public life—love of fame, applause, popularity." This ambition notwithstanding, he remained all his adult life a dedicated and basically modest man.

In his inaugural sermon, which he called a "declaration of independence," he stated that "this pulpit must be free." Influenced by the writings of Theodore Parker, by the teaching of Thomas Davidson, and most of all by the social ethics of the Hebrew prophets, he soon broadened his activities into the spheres of civic affairs and the Christian community, his aim being "to promote a spirit of amity between Jews and Christians." He preached in Christian churches, addressed public meetings throughout the Northwest area, and took a liberal position on the current aspects of social reform stating, "I'll be damned sooner than be silent." In 1903 he was made a member of the state commission on child labor. He attracted not only Portland Jews to Beth Israel but also numerous Christians who came to hear him preach. He visited Jewish communities in adjacent states and encouraged the establishment of religious services where none existed. His growing prominence in the Northwest did not go unnoticed in the East.

Temple Emanu-El of New York, "the Cathedral of Reform Judaism," had become the most esteemed post in the American rabbinate. Dr. Wise was of course aware of it, but the hope of attaining it was tempered by qualms of doubt. As early as 1900 he had written to his fiancée,

> Emanu-El will never get a *man* in its pulpit until the snobs forget the millionairedom long enough to acquire some respect for a man who is not rich, but is some other things. They must learn that a "call" to Emanu-El is not an "honor" but a burden and a responsibility, and that if "honor" there be, it belongs to the God whom congregation and the minister should serve.

In 1902 he expected to be asked to preach in Emanu-El during a visit to New York, but he was not invited. He confided to his wife that it would be a "responsibility appalling in magnitude"; that to be invited to "preach a trial sermon" was "an abomination"; that he would never "preach in Temple Emanu-El save as its minister." An invitation did come in 1903, but illness prevented acceptance. To his wife he wrote, "I may conceive it my duty to read Emanu-El administrators an installment of a much-needed lesson."

The invitation was repeated in 1905, and he accepted it despite his strong reservations and his maturing plans for a new venture.

When his sermon was received favorably and he was offered the post, he made certain conditions, chief among them being that he must have an "absolutely independent pulpit." Asked to explain, he stated, "This is what I mean. In Oregon I have been among the leaders of a civic reform movement in my community. I would want to do the same in New York no matter whom it affected"; moreover, he added, he might oppose the trustees politically and economically. When Louis Marshall explained to him that the rabbi of Temple Emanu-El was responsible to the board of trustees, Dr. Wise declined the post. On December 1 Marshall wrote him formally, "In view of the traditions of the Congregation and out of consideration of the church policy which has always prevailed therein, it was considered as a necessary condition, applicable to any incumbent of the office of rabbi in the Congregation, that the pulpit should be subject to and under the control of the Board of Trustees."

In reply Dr. Wise declared, "I beg to say that no self-respecting minister of religion, in my opinion, could consider a call to a pulpit which, in the language of the communication, shall always be subject to, and under the control of, the board of trustees." James Seligman and Daniel Guggenheim, prominent members, assured him that he would have no difficulty speaking his mind; Jacob Schiff informed him he would back him if any dispute arose. But Rabbi Wise remained adamant. On January 5, 1906, with pleas and rumors continuing to reach him, he made public "An Open Letter" which he had mailed to the trustees, and which declared in part,

> The chief office of a minister, I take it, is not to represent the views of the congregation, but to proclaim the truth as he sees it. How can he serve a congregation as a teacher save as he quickens the minds of his hearers by the vitality and independence of his utterances? But can a

man be vital and independent and helpful, if he be teth-
ered and muzzled? . . . A free pulpit will sometimes
stumble into error; a pulpit that is not free can never
powerfully plead for truth and righteousness.

By this time his mind was made up. Months earlier he
had written to his wife that he planned "to found a new
and free and living synagogue movement in New York in
the event of not being called to Emanu-El, or of my probable decision not to become assistant-keeper of the morgue
even if called." Certain that liberal Judaism tended to become "an unvital sect of the Jewish faith, at the periphery
of Jewish life rather than at its inmost core," he determined
to revitalize it by battling "for freedom of the pulpit, for the
freedom and the moral supremacy of the Synagogue." If
such a victory could be won in New York, he hoped it would
"influence for good the destinies of American Israel." Rejecting the pleas of both Jews and Gentiles to remain in
Portland, he left for New York to establish his Free Synagogue.

By now a well-known figure in the American Jewish
community, Dr. Wise publicized his plan to sympathetic
audiences. At an early meeting he asserted that the Free
Synagogue would remain "loyally, unswervingly, uncom-
promisingly Jewish in its ideals, in its free and democratic
organization"; that it would "reassert the democratic ideals
of Israel, and present the teaching of Judaism in the light
of today to the light of yesterday"; that its aim was "not to
innovate but to renovate, not to destroy but to reconstruct."
His principles for the Free Synagogue were these:

Absolute freedom of the pulpit.
Abolition of distinction between rich and poor as to membership privileges.
Direct and full participation of the synagogue in all social
services required by the community.
Complete identification not only with the Jewish faith, but
with Israel's faith and future.

To his wife he wrote, "The hardest year of my life is before me—and I hope the best. I have set out to do a great work. If only I have the strength to do it worthily." The Free Synagogue was formally organized in April, 1907, and among its initial 192 members were Henry Morgenthau, Oscar Straus, Adolph Lewisohn, Charles Bloch, Max Steuer, and representatives of other leading families. This number increased to 400 in 1908 and the membership continued to grow until the Free Synagogue became one of the largest congregations in New York. Its early meetings were held at the Hudson Theater, but when Felix Adler vacated Carnegie Hall to move to the newly constructed Ethical Culture building, the Free Synagogue occupied it Sunday mornings for many years thereafter. It also opened a branch on the East Side in Clinton Hall and soon started a social service department. That the undertaking was highly successful was evidenced by a 1908 editorial comment in *Harper's Weekly*:

> The Free Synagogue has made a beginning so notable, so effective, that the merest sketch of it challenges the interest of all who would benefit their fellow men. . . . The people of the Free Synagogue do charity, but they do not talk charity. With them every means by which man can be helped is known as Social Services. Their work is constructive, re-creative.

Letters from and interviews with potential rabbinical students who wanted to study under Dr. Wise suggested the idea of a seminary based on Free Synagogue principles. For years, however, the idea remained unfulfilled, deferred by other interests, the war in 1914, and, primarily, lack of funds. In this connection Wise knew he was not helping his cause when he condemned the rich for exploiting their workers. As he wrote to his wife, "It will be serious, even fatal, to synagogue building and above all to the Institute if I speak. It will be a mournful decision but an inevitable one. The rich and powerful are such 'rotten sports,' taking it out of the workers because of their losses for a time.

A dozen years after he first initiated the project he finally received enough financial support to establish the Jewish Institute of Religion and went to Europe to enlist part of the faculty. He gave a great deal of his energy to the affairs of the Institute in addition to teaching classes. His concern for its progress and scholarship continued over the years, and shortly before he died he arranged a merger of the Institute with the Hebrew Union College. By that time, as he pointed out, "Liberalism as a mood had come to take the place of Reform as an end. The plans of union are such as to satisfy the friends of both institutions. The union means the creation of a great teaching institution of liberal and progressive Judaism, minimizing the things that seemed to divide, magnifying the things that unite."

Dr. Wise sought to help the poor, defend the workers, and advocate political and social reform. At the start of his rabbinate in 1895, when a street-car strike resulted in the death of several pickets, he condemned the killing in a forthright sermon. Subsequently he explained,

> Convinced that the ideals of religion, separated from their day-to-day application, were meaningless, I early entered into one area of controversy after another that many might call political, and which I recognize as part of the socio-political life of America. There were many state, national, and international issues in which I felt as a minister of religion I had a place.

In New York, Wise found frequent occasions to criticize the activities of Tammany politicians. When Richard Crocker was given a dinner on his return from Irish exile in 1907, Wise condemned it publicly as "New York's night of shame." He castigated office holders who thrived on civic corruption and social injustice. In this he was soon joined by John Haynes Holmes, the Unitarian minister who later founded the Community Church and who was an equally ardent reformer. The two men, indeed, formed a lifelong intimate friendship. Wise also participated in the establishment of the National Association for the Advancement of Colored People and remained in close sympathy with its activities. In advocating the acceptance of Negroes in labor unions, he called discrimination of any kind "doubly damning—it damns the man who discriminates, and it damns the man discriminated against. No man can proclaim himself superior and set out to prove his superiority by degrading the so-called inferior, without making himself a victim of the very degradation that he seeks to impose upon another."

In 1911 he lectured on the McNamara dynamite case in Los Angeles and indicated that as long as labor was refused the opportunity to organize it would resort to violence and illegal activities. Despite severe criticism from industrialists, he joined other prominent liberal citizens in urging President Taft to appoint a Commission on Industrial Relations. When the President complied but named mediocre men to it, Wise and other liberals were openly disappointed.

The fire in the Triangle Shirtwaist Company, in which 147 lives were lost, deeply shocked Dr. Wise. At a protest meeting he declared, "If this thing is avoidable, I want to see those responsible punished. If it was due to some corrupt failure to enforce the law, I want to see that determined. And I do not trust public officials to determine it for us; it is our own task to do for ourselves." He asserted that the fire was "not the action of God, but the inaction of men," and urged fire protection supervised by a permanent citizens committee. He also called for such a committee to investigate the police department in connection with the murder of Herman Rosenthal, a notorious underworld figure. He offered to mediate between textile mill owners and their striking employees, and stated later, "Throughout this experience, I was struck by the degrading conditions of the workers, including small children, their inability to win even the most modest wages, which were not sufficient to buy the merest necessities of life."

As a prominent civic reformer, he was reproachfully

described by the New York *World* as the "professional de-
nouncer of the times." A contrary opinion was expressed
by Charles S. Whitman, the energetic New York prosecuting
attorney. In thanking him for his help, he wrote, "The knowledge that men like you have understood—have supported
me during the most trying experience I have ever known,
has been of itself a real inspiration—and I shall never for-
get it."

Rabbi Wise invited New Jersey Governor Woodrow
Wilson to address his congregation at its fourth annual
meeting in 1911. Impressed with his liberal views, Wise
later was active in his behalf during the presidential campaign. After the war broke out in 1914, he and Holmes,
both pacifists, praised Wilson for his advocacy of complete
neutrality. In the year of 1917, however, when America
entered the war, Wise went to work as a common laborer
in a shipyard as his contribution to the war effort, differing
in this respect from Holmes's persistent pacifism. At that
time and later he was vigorously opposed to Bolshevism and
pacifist socialism and campaigned against Morris Hillquit's
candidacy for mayor and Meyer London's candidacy for
Congress because they were socialists and opposed to the
war.

In 1919 Rabbi Wise toured the country to arouse support for the League of Nations. When the steel workers
struck that year, he preached against the ruthless steel
companies, consciously hazarding the loss of contributions
toward his planned synagogue buildings. A number of
wealthy members did leave, and enough contributions were
withdrawn to postpone the building for many years, but
his offer to resign was rejected by the executive committee
headed by Oscar Straus. Replying to the accusation of sensationalism, Wise maintained that

> I for my part have found that the term sensationalist or
> sensation monger is oftenest applied to the men in the
> pulpit by those of their colleagues who have a peculiar
> genius for leaving their congregation undisturbed in their

weekly church or synagogue slumber. . . . In a world of shame, the truth bravely uttered is bound to sound sensational.

He persevered in his advocacy of improved labor conditions, in the defense of Tom Mooney and other worker prisoners, in the support of strikes where he could offer help and sympathy, often in collaboration with Sidney Hillman.

Always on the alert to civic corruption, Wise and Holmes in 1931 preferred charges against Mayor James Walker to Governor Roosevelt, accusing Walker of neglecting his duties and of spending too much time on pleasure trips. Roosevelt, with an eye on the Presidency, was unwilling to antagonize Tammany politicians; he admonished them curtly that they would do better to pay more attention to religion than to politics. Chagrined, they joined Norman Thomas, John Dewey, and others to organize the City Affairs Committee, and were instrumental in forming the Hofstadter Committee to investigate the charges against Walker. With Samuel Seabury as counsel, the Committee found damaging evidence of graft and made charges which Roosevelt could not ignore. Walker resigned and went to Europe rather than face examination.

In 1932 Wise voted for Norman Thomas, but four years later he and Roosevelt became reconciled. To Holmes, Wise explained his change of heart on the basis of Roosevelt's reactionary enemies and because of "my feeling that I might help him see the light and the right about the Nazi situation." Two years later, on news of the Munich pact, he described it to Holmes as "one of those tragic days of all human history. I feel as my forefathers must have felt on that day in the year 70 which witnessed the destruction of the Temple. Human liberties are fled, democracy is a sham, standards have gone, the moral realm of mankind is laid waste. God help us!" That Sunday his sermon was "Dishonor Without Peace." When Holmes, an ardent pacifist, stated that the pact avoided war, Rabbi Wise asserted that "the evil day has only been put off."

When the war in Europe was going full blast in 1941 and Holmes continued to preach nonresistance, Wise informed him that he expected too much in urging Jews "to set the example to the world of being what Christians profess to be in the matter of nonresistance to force." The following year, with news of Nazi atrocities reaching him from Europe, he confided to his pacifist friends, "I have had the unhappiest day of my life. . . . Jews, unarmed and defenseless, have been unable to do anything for themselves; and the world has done little, if anything, for them. I don't want to preach to you. I don't want to turn my heart inside out, but I am almost demented over my people's grief."

From early youth Wise was imbued with a love of Zion, stimulated by his father's devotion and his own absorption in Jewish history. When Theodor Herzl convoked a congress of Zionists in 1897, young Wise urged the founding of the American Zionist Federation. The following year he attended the second Zionist congress as a delegate and met Herzl, who impressed him as a prophet.

Appointed English-speaking secretary of the World Zionist Organization, Wise returned to New York aglow with the fervor of his Zionistic faith. As Dr. Richard Gottheil stated subsequently, "Friend of Herzl in a peculiar sense, comrade of Nordau, helper of Wolfsohn, he gained and held a place of honor in Zionist leadership throughout the difficult and formative years of the movement." This difficulty was aggravated by the antagonism of wealthy and influential Jews to whom Judaism was only a religion and who dismissed the ethnic and historical factors which kept Jews a distinct entity mindful of their separateness and hoping for "the next year in Jerusalem." Even so warm a Jew as Jacob Schiff belonged to this group. When he and Wise were in Europe early in 1904 and the latter urged him to meet with Herzl, Schiff's response was, "If he wishes to discuss Zionism am unwilling to do so, as with deepest attachment to my breathren in faith and race I am an American pure and simple and cannot possibly belong to two nations." Over the years Wise advocated the ideal and the logic of Zionism among his fellow Reform rabbis, most of whom were opposed to it, and among Christians as well, speaking on the subject in many cities and strengthening the small Zionist organization in every way he could.

The outbreak of World War I disrupted the center of world Zionism in Germany and caused great hardship to Jews on the Russian front. American Zionists joined with other Jewish organizations to succor the refugees in Poland and Russia. Louis D. Brandeis headed the effort, and Wise and other Zionists cooperated in the urgent appeals for money.

It soon became evident that American Jews, the largest and most influential Jewish community in the world, must no longer depend for their spokesmen on the self-appointed American Jewish Committee, but must elect its representatives democratically and have them responsible to the entire community. The affluent Germanic Jews strongly opposed the idea of a congress, but yielded reluctantly to maintain temporary unity during the critical war period. A preliminary meeting of the congress proponents was held in Philadelphia in March 1916, and Dr. Wise gave the keynote address. He maintained that the Jewish people must create their own organs through which to express their needs and demands—"a democratic organization of all the forces of American Israel save for such as may will to exclude themselves." Having the American Jewish Committee in mind, he declared,

> A people is not worthy of respect which does not insist on the right to be heard touching its own affairs, but surrenders the right of judgment and decision to a company of men, however wise and benevolent, who substitute their own opinions and wishes for the convictions and determination of the whole people.

The following year 335,000 Jews, paying the traditional shekel dues, voted for representatives to the first American Jewish Congress. The entrance of the United

States into the war postponed its first session to December, 1918. By that time the Balfour Declaration was already a fact and the Peace Conference a few weeks off. The delegates voted to seek equal rights for Jews the world over and for recognition of Jewish historic rights to Palestine, and sent its representatives, headed by Judge Mack, to Versailles. The following May, after hearing the report of the Conference, the leaders of the Congress agreed to establish it on a permanent basis—upon which the American Jewish Committee withdrew.

The now permanently established Congress held its first meeting in 1922, and Dr. Wise addressed it, insisting that the function of the Congress was "to speak and to act on behalf of Jews in all matters affecting the Jews as Jews." He asserted that "the enemy, unscrupulous and destructive," might disregard the representations of the "well-to-do and powerful, but he can hardly bring himself to question the purpose of an assembly such as this, made up largely of the lowly and ill-circumstanced of our people, whose sole power lies in their resolution unitedly to demand justice for themselves and for all peoples." This the Congress did during the ensuing years of woe in Europe, intensifying its efforts on behalf of Jews and other minorities as the Nazis increased their activities.

When the proposal for a Jewish national homeland in Palestine began to be seriously considered by the British government, Dr. Wise, then president of the Zionist Organization of America, solicited President Wilson's influence in its favor. Before 1917 Zionists did not want to antagonize Turkey for fear of the consequences to Palestinian Jews. As Wise pointed out, "We do not want Palestine to come to us from the blood-stained hands of the Turkish assassinocracy." Once the land was liberated, Zionists in England and the United States intensified their efforts to obtain a favorable decision. Lord Rothschild submitted a text draft of the Balfour Declaration, which was amended by American Zionist leaders and submitted to President Wilson for approval before it was issued by Balfour on November 2, 1917, stating:

> His Majesty's Government view with favour the establishment in Palestine of a national home for the Jewish people, and will use their best endeavours to facilitate the achievement of this object, it being clearly understood that nothing shall be done which may prejudice the civil and religious rights of existing non-Jewish communities in Palestine or the rights and political status enjoyed by Jews in any other country.

In August, 1918, when the Palestine situation required further clarification, President Wilson, urged by Wise and Brandeis, agreed to send Wise a letter supporting the Balfour Declaration and welcoming "the progress made by the Zionist movement in the United States and in the Allied countries since the Declaration by Mr. Balfour in behalf of the British Government." Upon this, Felix Frankfurter wrote to Wise, "And the nations of the world, no less than the people of Israel, will arise and call you blessed."

In December, 1918 Dr. Wise went to England to champion the Zionist cause. In an interview with Balfour he asked that England act as trustee for the Jewish Commonwealth in Palestine, to which Balfour replied, "American Jews have honored my country and its Government by this request." When Balfour was asked for an interpretation of the phrase "a national home for the Jewish people," he explained, "This means that Jews who either wish or require, now or in the future, to go to Palestine shall have the right to do so."

Wise went from England to the Peace Conference and joined other Jewish leaders in an interview with President Wilson concerning minority rights, and Wilson approved the statement: "The delegation of the American Jewish Congress found the President, as always, sympathetic with the incontestable principle of the right of the Jewish people everywhere to equality of status." At the Conference Wise also pleaded the cause of the Armenians. Back in the United States, Wise sided with Brandeis, whom he greatly admired, against Chaim Weitzmann, whom he considered too political and lacking in an appreciation of Palestinian economic needs.

All through the 1920s and later, Wise and other Zionist leaders watched with increasing concern as the politics of oil plus Arab intransigence combined to veer the British administration in Palestine from the pledge of the Declaration. At first, shortly after the end of the war, British diplomats continued to favor the Jewish cause. Lord Robert Cecil said, "Our wish is that Arabian countries shall be for Arabs, Armenia for the Armenians, and Judea for the Jews." Ramsay MacDonald, after a visit to Palestine in 1922, said,

> The Arab population do not and cannot use or develop the resources of Palestine. . . . To the older Jewish settlements and agricultural schools are owing, to a great extent, both the Jaffa orange trade and the cultivation of vines; to the newer, agricultural machinery, afforestation, the beginnings of scientific manuring, the development of schemes of irrigation and of agricultural cooperation. Palestine not only offers room for hundreds of thousands of Jews, it loudly cries out for more labour and more skills.

In the same year, however, the Winston Churchill White Paper was a stepdown from British promises. The government in London, while insisting that the Balfour Declaration must be affirmed and implemented, began setting restrictions which handicapped its realization, chief among them the limitation of immigrants. Lord Balfour was aware of this reversal and defended the aims of the Mandate, "If ever there was a Declaration which had behind it a general consensus of opinion, I believe it was the Declaration of November, 1917." But in 1922, his voice had lost its political potency.

Every year saw a deterioration of Zionist hopes in Palestine. Wise and Jacob De Haas stated in *The Great Betrayal*, "Every day of those eight years [1922–1930] officialdom has found means of retardation, procrastination, of turning the Jewish dream into a Penelope robe. What was woven in the day was unraveled at night." British officials in Palestine acted as if it were one of their possessive crown colonies and not mandated territory under certain specific conditions. Older British leaders, aware of the nature and purpose of the Declaration, spoke out critically in 1929. Lloyd George, Balfour, Smuts found the current Palestinian administration faulty and urged a commission that "would be an advertisement to the world that Britain has not weakened in a task to which her honour is pledged and at the same time an assurance to Jews and Arabs alike that any proven defects in the present system of government will be made good." Contrary to their expression of good will, the commission headed by Colonial Secretary Lord Passfield, the professed socialist Sidney Webb, made public its findings in a White Paper, issued in October 1930, which in effect abrogated the Balfour Declaration. Jewish leaders felt tricked and troubled. Felix Warburg resigned in protest from the Administrative Committee of the Jewish Agency and stated that "Lord Passfield's representations to me made me the innocent vehicle of misstatements to my colleagues of the Jewish Agency." Lord Melchet, a leading Zionist in England, said, "This grotesque travesty is an insult to the intelligence of Jewry and an affront to the Mandate Commission." Wise was very active in this protest against British duplicity and in *The Great Betrayal* he and De Haas presented the case against England in historic detail.

Meantime the Nazi menace worsened. Dr. Wise condemned it publicly, consulted frequently with Washington officials, and mobilized the American Jewish Congress against it. He urged the admission of refugees to the United States and campaigned for a boycott of German goods. After one of his visits to Washington he wrote to his wife, "We have friends—thank God that I have helped to win them for the cause of my people." He saw Justice Brandeis on his trips to the capital, and wrote to his wife that "every visit to him is a spiritual experience," adding that Brandeis had told him: "You are the foremost Jew in the country." The two leaders agreed, as late as 1932, that most German Jews were shortsighted and that, with Hitler in power, they should leave Germany without delay. After a trip to Europe in 1933 Wise told a group of ministers. "The racial fanaticism of the Hitler Reich may be a most immediate and deadly peril to us Jews, but it is no less truly a threat and a danger to all races and to all nations. . . . Only one thing is certain, namely, that the most vulnerable of the neighbors of the Reich will be singled out for doom."

After Hitler's election Wise planned a protest meeting in Madison Square Garden. Various persons urged cancellation, and the day before it was to be held the German Embassy telephoned Wise to tell him that persecution of the Jews would be lessened if the meeting were stopped. Wise consulted with Brandeis and was told: "Go ahead and make the protest as good as you can." In 1934, angered by persistent suggestions that he placate Nazidom in the hope of moderating its fury, Dr. Wise addressed the World Jewish Congress against "the unexpiable sin of bartering or trafficking with it in order to save some Jewish victims." He declared that "Hitlerism means war" and deeply regretted that no country was doing anything to stop it. To provide himself with a forum, he began to edit *Opinion*, a periodical devoted to Jewish interests.

In 1935, on a visit to Palestine, he was greatly impressed by the steady development of the land. "I have looked upon the results of that effort and I have never been prouder of my fellow Jews than I am at this hour, having seen what all of us together, Zionists, have done." Yet he was very troubled by the British "sharpness and ruthlessness" in their administration of the mandate.

The following year he made arrangements for a meeting in Geneva of the World Jewish Congress and was elected its first president in concurrence with his presidency of the Zionist Organization of America. While in Europe he visited Poland and was appalled by the poverty of the Jewish slums. "What I beheld of Jewish misery and learned of Jewish nobility touched my heart with sorrow not unmingled with pride."

In the late 1930s Wise intensified his efforts in behalf of Jewish refugees. As a member of the Jewish Agency he condemned British hostility, to Jewish immigration to Palestine, stating, "Nothing could be clearer than that the 1939 White Paper was just as truly an item of appeasement as the Munich agreement between Chamberlain and Hitler." During World War II, with Jewish genocide under way, he was met by stony indifference from bureaucrats in the State Department. Documents from Europe, addressed to Dr. Wise in care of the American ambassador in Switzerland and testifying to the murder of Jews in German concentration camps, were withheld from him until Under-Secretary Sumner Welles gave them to him privately to be made public. Somewhat later the Geneva director of the World Jewish Congress transmitted information to the American ambassador that some 70,000 Jews from Poland and Hungary might be ransomed. When this document reached Washington, both President Roosevelt and Secretary of the Treasury Henry Morgenthau, Jr., approved the required funds, but State Department officials held up the money for five months, when it was too late.

Dr. Wise had taken a leave of absence for the war's duration in order to devote himself to Zionism and Jewish interests. When the American Zionist Emergency Council was formed, he and Rabbi Silver served as co-chairmen. With the war over, Wise wrote to Holmes that with six million Jews dead and over a million "homeless on the European continent [and] with only one place to go—Palestine," it behooved him to speak up: "Lift your voice in their behalf and let your trumpet tones demand justice for the Jew and the restoration of the Jewish National Home, which represents exactly one-hundredth of the Arab territory." In 1946 he spoke before the Anglo-American Commission of Inquiry into Palestine with all the passion and pathos at his command, describing Zionism as an historical continuum, to use that awkward Latin term which has come to us through German metaphysics: there has never been a time in the nineteen and more Christian centuries during which there has been an abandonment or a waiver of relation to Zionism on the part of Jews. . . . We have blessed the Christian world; we have given the Christian world its noblest treasure. The Christian world, if Christian it be, cannot do less than say to the Jewish people, 'You have labored, you have grieved, you have suffered, you have long been injured. Palestine shall be yours."

Denied entrance to Palestine in 1947, Wise nevertheless favored an American loan to Britain and later remarked to Ernest Bevin that he had "acted with true Christian charity the day after I was denied a visa to Palestine by your Government."

Ill for some time, Dr. Wise felt physically exhausted by 1947. Regretfully he withdrew from Zionist leadership. When his wife died about that time, part of his own life died with her. But when a meeting was held in May, 1948 in Madison Square Garden to celebrate the establishment of Israel, he addressed the large gathering with his former vigor and the joy of a great hope realized. Meantime he was devoting himself to the writing of *The Challenging Years*, his personal memoirs. He also attended the World Jewish Congress in Geneva, bidding the assembly a wistful farewell at the end of his address.

On March 17, 1949, 1,200 guests in New York celebrated his seventy-fifth birthday. A month later he spoke at the Ford Forum, where he had long been a frequent speaker: "I have lived to see the Jewish state. I am too small for the greatness of the mercy which God has shown us." And for the first time in his many visits to this non-Jewish hall he gave the benediction in Hebrew.

Shortly thereafter he underwent surgery and failed to recover. In a letter to his son and daughter found in his wallet he had written: "I most deeply care for: The State of Israel and freedom and justice for the Jews everywhere." And he ended, "Into the Hand of God I commend my spirit. May He continue to vouchsafe me His grace and mercy."

The Jews of New York, and elsewhere, mourned him as one of their great men: a dedicated rabbi, a superb orator, a lover of justice, a fighter for right.

JEWS
IN
GOVERNMENT

The patriotic and political activities of Jews in the early decades of the American republic were described in previous chapters. As their number increased during the past century, their participation in government accelerated considerably in every section of the country. They were among the western pioneers in almost every state and territory; in California particularly, but also in less populated western areas. Still later, as Jews from Eastern Europe became Americanized, and began taking an interest in government affairs, a number of them made their mark in state legislatures and in various federal agencies. The following are brief sketches of some Jews who have served the government in one or another capacity.

Otto Mears (1840–1931), one of Colorado's leading citizens, was born in Kurland and emigrated to the United States in time to enlist in the Civil War. Settling in Colorado years before it became a state, he set up a sawmill and a gristmill. Later he built roads—300 of them over hills and across plains —and the Rio Grande Southern Railroad over the mountains. Mears Peak and Mears Highway were so named in recognition of his contribution to the state's development. He was elected to the state legislature and successfully negotiated with the Ute Indians for cession of their lands to the territory of Colorado.

Isidor Reyner (1850–1912) was graduated from the University of Virginia and practiced law. In 1878 he entered the Maryland state assembly and became chairman of the judiciary committee. Subsequently he was elected to the state senate, to the House of Representatives for three terms, and to the United States Senate for two terms. In 1901 he distinguished himself as defense counsel for Rear-Admiral W. S. Schley, in command of the battle of Santiago, over the controversy with Admiral W. T. Sampson as to who deserved most credit for the victory. Reyner's appeal for justice, according to one historian, "thrilled the country as have few orations in all our history."

Moses Alexander (1853–1932) was brought to this country from Germany in 1868. In Missouri, where the family first settled, he operated a clothing store. During his lifetime he was councilman and mayor of Chillicothe, Ohio, as well as mayor of Boise, Idaho, and governor of that state. He was considered a liberal and effective administrator. A participant in Jewish activities, he contributed generously to charitable institutions, and was for a time president of Beth Israel Synagogue in Boise.

H. M. Goldfogle (1856–1929) was an active Tammany politician and the first Jewish Congressman from New York. He began practicing law in 1877 and served as judge of the municipal court from 1886 to 1900 when he was elected that year to the House, where he retained his seat for eight terms. While in Congress he led the attack on Russia for refusing to admit American citizens of Jewish origin.

The Henry Morgenthaus, father and son and grandson, though not elected to office, were influential in Jewish and governmental affairs. Henry Morgenthau, Sr. (1856–1946), was brought from Germany in 1865. He was a graduate of Columbia Law School, but earned a considerable fortune in real estate.

In 1912 he was active in Woodrow Wilson's campaign for President and treasurer of the Democratic National Committee. Rewarded with the ambassadorship to Turkey, he followed Oscar Straus's example in aiding Christian missionaries. When World War I caused great hardship to Jews within the Turkish empire, he came to their support and cabled to New York Jews for help, having been assured by President Wilson that "anything you can do to improve the lot of your co-religionists is an act that will reflect credit upon America." During this period, as the representative of a neutral country, he took charge of the affairs of nine embassies. In 1916 he returned to the United States to campaign for Wilson's re-election. At the end of the war he was appointed head of a commission to investigate the treatment of Jews in Poland. Four years later he presided over the Refugee Settlement Commission sponsored by the League of Nations. He also helped to arrange the interchange of populations between Turkey and Greece. For many years he was prominent in Jewish affairs. His diplomatic activities are discussed in four books he published during his lifetime.

Henry Morgenthau, Jr. (1891–1967), was trained as an agriculturist and operated a 1,500-acre farm for many years. In 1928, appointed chairman of the New York agricultural advisory commission by Governor Roosevelt, he helped in the enactment of highly constructive legislation. Three years later he served on the conservation commission; he put unemployed workers on a reforestation and soil conservation program which later became a model for the federal CCC and WPA agencies. In 1933, as chairman of the Federal Farm Board, he saved many farmers from bankruptcy. The following year he was appointed Secretary of the Treasury, an office he held for the next eleven years. He led the campaign to strengthen confidence in the nation's fiscal policy and banking system. He also obtained permission from Congress to sell savings bonds directly to the public and thus facilitated the financing of the oncoming war. During the 1930s he was greatly concerned with the relief of the unemployed. In the late 1960s his son, Robert M. Morgethau, led in the combat against organized crime in his capacity as United States Attorney for the southern district of New York.

Julius Kahn (1861–1924) was born in Germany and brought to San Francisco in 1865. Until he was twenty-nine, he made his living as an actor; subsequently he practiced law and was elected to the California state legislature in 1892. Active in Republican politics, he entered the House of Representatives in 1898 and served, with the exception of one term, until his death in 1924. He supported President Wilson's foreign policy as an influential member of the House Committee on Military Affairs, of which he was chairman after 1920. He was a founder of the Jewish Educational Society of California.

At the turn of the century graft and corruption were rife

on the Pacific Coast. Abe Ruef, another San Francisco Jewish politician, yielded to temptation and was duly punished. A writer in *Overland Monthly* described Ruef as

> an unscrupulous lawyer who had wormed his way into the labor party and manipulated the "leaders" like puppets. Ruef's game was elementary. He sold his omnipotence for cash, either under the respectable cloak of "retainer" or under the more common device of commissions and dividends, so that thugs retained him for their freedom, contractors for the favors they expected, and the public service corporations for their franchises.

Lincoln Steffens, however, found Ruef an intelligent young man who lacked the strength of character to withstand temptation on the part of leading businessmen. His downfall came in 1905 when a citizens committee succeeded in sending him to jail.

Solomon Guggenheim (1867–1941), the sixth of the family of well-known brothers, was president of the Philadelphia Smelting and Refining Company of Pueblo, Colorado. His election to the Senate in 1907 was rumored to have been obtained more by financial favors than by popular choice—a not uncommon arrangement when elections were held in state legislatures. As a Senator he supported the establishment of the Children's Bureau and the direct election of Senators. In 1912 he refused to run for re-election. His strong interest in higher education stimulated him to finance the construction of buildings in several Colorado institutions. When his son died in the 1920's he and his wife gave $3 million to establish the John Simon Guggenheim Memorial Foundation, which has aided scholars and artists ever since, through Guggenheim Fellowships. He also founded the Guggenheim Museum. Like his brothers he was a generous contributor to various philanthropic enterprises.

Abram I. Elkus (1867–1947), a lawyer, acted as special federal prosecuting attorney in bankruptcy frauds in 1908; three years later he was counsel for the New York state factory investigation commission. Elkus succeeded Morgenthau as ambassador to Turkey in 1916. On his return to the United States he was made chairman of the New York state reconstruction committee for the reorganization of the executive branch of the state government. In 1919 he was appointed associate justice of the New York State Court of Appeals. The following year he served as the League of Nations commissioner to settle the dispute between Finland and Sweden over the control of the Aland Islands. Prominent in Jewish affairs, he was president of the Free Synagogue from 1919 to 1927.

Sol Bloom (1870–1949) was a builder and then a music publisher in his native Illinois. Moving to New York in 1903, he became a real estate broker and builder of theaters. In 1922 he was elected to Congress, where he remained to the end of his life. As chairman of the influential House Foreign Affairs Committee after 1939, he was instrumental in getting an additional 30,000 Jewish refugees admitted to Palestine. In 1945 he was a member of the American delegation to the San Francisco conference which established the United Nations. With little formal schooling, he gradually made himself an authority in American history and in 1932 was appointed director of the George Washington Bicentennial Celebration and, in 1939, of the Constitution Sesquicentennial Commission.

Meyer London (1871–1926) came from Russia in 1891, worked his way through law school and practiced law on New York's Lower East Side. Very closely associated with needle trade workers, he helped shape their union efforts and policies. He ran for various political offices from 1896 on, and in 1914 he became the first Socialist elected to Congress. He was re-elected in 1916, was defeated two years later during the war hysteria, and regained his seat in 1920—only to have his district gerrymandered to assure his defeat thereafter. In Congress he opposed anti-immigration bills and the tariff, and at the end of the war he urged amnesty for political prisoners. Idealistic and humanitarian, he dedicated himself to the welfare of the poor. In 1926 his career was cut short by death in an automobile accident.

Julius L. Meier (1874–1937) was the son of a Bavarian immigrant who established himself in the hamlet which became Portland, Oregon. Julius, trained as a lawyer, became a junior partner of Senator G. W. Joseph. In 1899, however, he joined his father's store, expanded it into the Meier and Frank department store, one of the largest on the Pacific Coast, and became its president. Active in civic affairs, he was a member of the chamber of commerce and a promoter of aviation, highways, and agriculture. During World War I he was regional director of the Council on National Defense and chairman of the Liberty Loan drives in Portland. He was also active in Jewish affairs and president of several organizations. When Joseph died suddenly in 1930, Meier replaced him as the liberal candidate for governor and won against conservative opponents of both major parties. He injected sound business practices into state government and cleaned house in every department, saving $6 million in his first year. An advocate of relief for the unemployed and the conservation and public ownership of water power, he was called a dangerous radical by his opponents, but most Oregonians regarded him as the best governor in the state's history.

William I. Sirovitch (1882–1939), son of a well-known Orthodox rabbi, was raised in quiet poverty. He worked his way through college and was graduated from the medical school of Columbia University in 1906. After practicing privately for five years he became superintendent of People's Hospital, a position he held for eighteen years. Living on New York's Lower East Side, he was devoted to the welfare of the underprivileged, especially the children. In 1919 he was made commissioner of child welfare, and in 1926 he was elected to Congress as a Democrat in a normally Republican district; he retained his seat to the end of his life. In Congress he advocated social-welfare legislation and supported New Deal measures. He also led the campaign to reform the federal courts in New York. In the 1930s he sponsored the Federal Theater Project.

Samuel Dickstein (1885–1954) was brought from Russia at the age of two. Admitted to the bar in 1908, he soon developed a thriving practice. He was elected to the New York board of aldermen, to the state assembly, and, in 1922, to the House of Representatives, where he held his seat for twenty-four years.

In 1931 he became chairman of the House Committee on Immigration and Naturalization. Early in the 1930s, perturbed by the activities of the German-American Bund, he urged the establishment of a committee to investigate its un-American behavior. After five years of effort the House, in a reactionary mood, created the Committee on Un-American Activities but refused to make Dickstein its chairman, as would normally have been the case, or even a member, presumably because of his foreign birth. In 1946 Dickstein resigned his seat to become a judge on the state supreme court.

Emanuel Celler, born in 1888, practiced law until elected to Congress in 1924. Retaining his seat to the present, he has been a conscientious worker in the fields of foreign trade, civil rights, and immigration. He has long been chairman of the House Judiciary Committee. An active participant in Jewish affairs, he has been an officer in several organizations.

Laurence A. Steinhardt (1892–1950) entered the foreign diplomatic service in 1933 and was sent to Sweden. In 1937 he became ambassador to Peru. Afterwards he served as ambassador to the Soviet Union, Turkey, Czechoslovakia, and Canada. During this period he not only represented the United States with distinction, as evidenced by the award of the Medal of Merit, but displayed humanitarian effort that gained the respect of men everywhere. He was the author of books and articles on medical jurisprudence, trade unions, economics, and finance.

Jacob Javits was born in 1904. An active trial lawyer, he became special assistant to the chief of Chemical Warfare Service in 1941 and served until the end of World War II, attaining the rank of colonel. After three terms in the House and a term as attorney general in New York, he was elected to the Senate in 1956 and twice re-elected by large pluralities. He has distinguished himself as a liberal Republican and favored various measures concerned with civil rights and social welfare.

Abraham H. Ribicoff, born in 1910, has held political office since 1938, when he was first elected to the state legislature. Since then he has served as judge in the Hartford police court, as a member of Congress for two terms, as governor for two terms, as Secretary of Health, Education, and Welfare, and as senator since 1963.

The foregoing list, while incomplete, indicates the varied political activity of Jews in American government. Among them Herbert H. Lehman achieved singular distinction.

12
Herbert H. Lehman

BANKER, POLITICIAN, HUMANITARIAN

I suppose my whole life has been in one way or another a seeking to advance the cause of liberalism and human welfare. Social responsibility has been a key concept in my thinking—the obligation upon each of us to fight against discrimination and for the rights of all men. My entire public career has been based on my firm belief that there is a responsibility on the part of society to protect the individual when he cannot protect himself and to provide a government with a heart.

THIS INSISTENCE on "a government with a heart" was the motivating force of Herbert H. Lehman's public career. Born in 1878, the youngest of eight children, he was reared in a home governed by Victorian decorum and Jewish benevolence. His parents early indoctrinated him with a sense of social responsibility. As a boy, he was taken by his father to Mt. Sinai Hospital, one of the elder Lehman's charitable interests, and to the poor neighborhoods on the East Side. Lehman recalled, "I saw the squalor, the con-

259

gestion, the disease, the misery of people forced to live under conditions which seemed to me at the time subhuman, in quarters that seemed utterly uninthinkable." While he continued to enjoy the amenities of his wealthy boyhood— summers in the Adirondacks, trips with his parents to Europe in 1884 and 1887—what he had seen on the East Side never quite left his consciousness. He recalled, "I'm sure I couldn't have described my feelings to anybody. How much direct effect it had on my later thinking I don't know, but probably a good deal."

Neither so serious nor so intellectual as his immediately older brother Irving, to whom he was very close, he had to study hard to do well at school. His father thought Herbert might become an engineer and considered sending him to a technical college, disregarding the fact that he was poor in mathematics and had no interest in science. Fortunately, one of his teachers, aware of his predilections and limitations, persuaded Mr. Lehman to send Herbert to a liberal arts college and recommended Williams College, his own alma mater. There Herbert went in 1895.

Lonely and homesick at the outset, ill at ease in the Yankee atmosphere, he tried hard to adapt himself to it. No scholar, he sought activity in extracurricular interests; although he was not naturally athletic, in time he became manager of the track team and acting manager of the football team. He also took part in debating and worked on the literary monthly. Good-natured, conscientious, and affable, he was the first Jew to be invited into the exclusive Gargoyle Society. Years later, as a loyal alumnus, he donated Lehman Hall and an endowed professorship to Williams and was elected an alumni trustee by acclamation.

Back in New York in 1899, he lived with his widowed mother—his father had died in 1897, leaving an estate of $5 million, of which Herbert inherited $400,000. His first job was with the textile firm of J. Spencer Turner at $5.00 a week, but he was not long in becoming a successful salesman of duck cloth. His pleasant personality and conscientiousness attracted numerous customers and his energetic sales efforts were duly rewarded. Over the next years he gained familiarity with the general conduct of commerce and rose to be the firm's treasurer and vice-president. "Whatever knowledge I have had of business came much more from my ten years' experience in a merchandising house than from the investment banking business."

When his oldest brother Sigmund died in 1908, his partnership in Lehman Brothers went to Herbert, partnerships in the firm being then restricted to the males in the immediate family. In the twenty years he was with Lehman Brothers, its activities greatly expanded, mainly in financing mass production and large merchandising corporations such as Sears Roebuck, Studebaker, Woolworth, Continental Can, and Underwood. By helping to float their securities amounting to billions of dollars, the firm earned commissions amounting to millions. Herbert was an active partner, hard-working and conscientious rather than enterprising. As one partner pointed out, "He liked the excitement of putting through a big deal. He liked the process of negotiating a complicated arrangement. But he was not heart and soul a businessman."

Lehman's preoccupation over the years with schooling, business, and banking did not obviate help to those less fortunate than he. Upon graduating from college he joined the Henry Street Settlement, in which his family had long been interested. There he came under Lillian Wald's "immediate and powerful influence." Inspired by her and other social workers, he "developed an understanding of positive and constructive humanitarianism." At Miss Wald's suggestion he organized a teen-age boys club. His interest in the settlement and his intimate friendship with Miss Wald continued through the years. In 1910 he worked with her on legislation for a child-labor bureau, and in 1917, he became a member of the board and remained on it to the end of his life.

In 1910 Lehman married Edith Altschul, an attractive and intelligent daughter of a San Francisco banker.

For more than a half century she was his constant adviser and associate. They adopted three infants and raised them with solicitude and affection. The gift of a boxer dog led to their breeding boxers, and in time they became leading American specialists in this breed. They gave up their kennel only when Lehman became governor and they moved to Albany.

The forced evacuation and brutal persecution of Jews in Eastern Europe during World War I brought into being the Jewish Joint Distribution Committee. Lehman was an active participant and served as treasurer until 1917.

When the United States entered the war, Lehman enlisted in the Navy and was assigned to textile procurement. In this capacity he had frequent dealings with Assistant-Secretary Franklin D. Roosevelt. Some months later he was transferred to the Army and was eventually put in charge of textile procurement in the War Department Ordnance Bureau. His work gained him advancement to colonel and a Distinguished Service Medal.

When he returned to civilian life in 1919 and resumed his place in Lehman Brothers, he was made chairman of the sub-committee on economic rehabilitation or the Joint Distribution Committee. The war had left hundreds of thousands of Jews in Poland, the Ukraine, and adjacent countries practically homeless and completely impoverished. It was Lehman's task to provide them with housing and re-establish them in business by means of credit cooperatives and loan societies. In 1923 he reported, "During the last eighteen months 353 individual loan associations have been set up and these have a membership of 144,896, all heads of families. This means that we reach more than 650,000 persons, all sufferers from the war."

For several years he and his associates strove to rehabilitate the economy of these Jewish communities. In the process he met people who were similarly engaged in behalf of non-Jewish groups and learned the most effective ways of fund-raising. He deeply appreciated the eagerness with which the sufferers were ready to revive their religious and cultural institutions, even in preference to their economic restoration. His decade of devotion to this relief work served to deepen his interest in both public welfare and world affairs, preparing him for later and much broader efforts to alleviate distress on a worldwide scale.

Lehman's father had been a loyal Southerner. Living in Montgomery during the Civil War, he did what he could to help the Confederacy. Governor I. H. Watts of Alabama in a letter to Jefferson Davis, referred to Lehman as "one of the best Southern patriots." After moving to New York he joined the Democratic party, and his youngest son also identified himself with it. He and his brother Irving, however, were the only members of the Lehman family to remain Democrats; the older brothers and cousins became Republicans, like most affluent Americans.

Up to 1912 Herbert Lehman had only a passive interest in politics. In that year he favored Woodrow Wilson's candidacy and argued heatedly for his preference. Four years later he campaigned in Wilson's behalf. When the election depended on the outcome in California and there was apprehension that the ballot boxes might be tampered with by Republican officials, Lehman wired his uncle, the banker I. W. Hellman in San Francisco, to give the California Democrats, who were without funds, $5,000 to hire guards for the ballot boxes and assure an honest count.

For the next decade he was preoccupied with war work and the Joint Distribution Committee. In 1924, having become friendly with Governor Alfred E. Smith, he was strongly perturbed by the evidence of Ku Klux Klan influence at the Democratic Convention. Chagrined by the deadlock which resulted in a compromise candidate, he took no part in the national campaign. He did, however, become treasurer of the Citizens Committee for Governor Smith and devoted himself to his election for a third term. What pleased him most about Smith was that "he has never shown either favoritism or prejudice because of race, religion, or social condition." He accepted Smith's appointment to a commission to settle the garment strike and dealt conscientiously with both workers and manufacturers, gaining insight into the complexity of labor problems. When the strike was settled, he lent the union $50,000 to rehabilitate itself. Two years later he again worked for Smith's nomination and election as President. When Smith's liberal legislation was called "socialistic," Lehman countered: "If this is Socialism, I thank God for it and am proud to be arrayed under its banner."

During this period he readily accepted Mayor James Walker's appointment as chairman of a committee to investigate New York's financial condition. He paid researchers from his own pocket to bring out the facts, and some of the reforms proposed by the committee were later adopted.

In the 1928 presidential campaign Lehman was chairman of the Democratic finance committee. By September, Smith's chances of election seemed to hinge on victory in New York. All leaders agreed that Franklin D. Roosevelt would make the likeliest winner and help carry the state for Smith. Roosevelt, however, was in Warm Springs, Georgia, working anxiously to strengthen his crippled legs, and he refused to interrupt the treatment. Smith and his associates desperately pleaded with him to accept, and he was finally persuaded by the assurance that Lehman would take the nomination as lieutenant-governor and would relieve him of the routine duties as governor. Lehman had not expected to give up banking for political office, but yielded to Smith's urging on the assumption that he would resume his partnership after two years. Smith lost the Presidency but Roosevelt and Lehman were elected by narrow margins. The Democratic deficit amounted to $1.4 million, and Lehman vainly urged wealthy Democrats to make it up—he himself contributed $150,000.

The lieutenant-governor in New York had been largely a figurehead, but Roosevelt made Lehman an important adjunct of the state executive. He delegated numerous functions and duties to Lehman and had him serve as acting governor during his frequent absences from Albany. Always scrupulously conscientious, Lehman attended to his various assignments with the utmost care. In October, 1929, apologizing for not being able to accept speaking invitations, he wrote, "I am devoting all my time to my present job and my mind is so full of the budget, state hospitals, prisons, etc., that I could not leave Albany." He was especially helpful to Roosevelt in financial matters, in the improvement of various state agencies, and in the settlement of emergency situations such as recurrent garment strikes and severe prison riots. In one of the latter events Lehman, as acting governor, refused to make any concession to embattled rioters and insisted on full submission. "As long as I am here," he declared, "there will be no compromise, no matter what circumstances or what the result may be." Instead he ordered the state police and the militia to enter Auburn prison and release the kidnapped warden and guards, which they did without loss of life. On subsequent investigation, however, he was appalled by the dreadful conditions in the state prisons and effected improvements and reforms. At the end of his term the New York *World* hailed him as one who had "lifted a routine job out of routine mediocrity and made it a vital and helpful agency of the state." There was now no question of returning to banking, and in the 1930 election he polled a plurality of nearly 800,000 votes, even larger than Roosevelt's.

The two men began their second terms in the midst of economic crisis and human misery. Businesses were going bankrupt, banks were on the verge of failure, unemployment was rising precipitously, and relief became urgent. Because of his banking experience, Lehman endeavored to save distressed banks from having to close their doors and ruin their depositors. When the City Trust Company, catering largely to Italians, was about to collapse, Lehman pleaded with leaders of the banking community to save it by necessary loans, and he himself invested a million dollars to that end. When the larger Bank of the United States, which was controlled by Jewish officers and served 450,000 depositors, most of them Jewish, was in the same plight, he again called leading bankers into consultation. This time, however, they did not cooperate. Although the bank failed, causing temporary distress to its depositors, its assets proved adequate to repay most deposits. The behavior of the bankers greatly disturbed Lehman, and he later stated, "I made the strongest possible plea not to let the bank fail. . . . I was unsuccessful, but never in all my life have I fought harder to save others."

In 1932 Roosevelt, nominated for the Presidency, wanted Lehman to succeed him as governor. Tammany leaders, however, feared that he would be even stricter than Roosevelt on political largess. Unable to sidetrack him altogether, they planned to nominate him for the Senate and to name Robert F. Wagner as governor. Informed of this, Lehman at Roosevelt's suggestion told them he would refuse the nomination to the Senate and that he would be the candidate for governor. At the convention both Smith and Roosevelt named him—the only thing on which they then agreed—and in the ensuing election Lehman won handsomely, 2,659,519 to 1,812,080 for "Wild Bill" Donovan.

Lehman assumed office in the nadir of the depression. Millions of unemployed were in dire want, and the state, already greatly in debt, could not cope with the tremendous demands upon it. Lehman sought assistance from the federal government and increased taxes in the effort to feed the hungry. Day after day and often long in the night he struggled with crisis after crisis, among them the liquor situation (Prohibition was still in effect), city finances, and banking difficulties. After a special session of the legislature, during which he had to combat stubborn Republican opposition, he underwent an appendectomy and developed a pulmonary embolism, which fortunately soon dissolved. On his recovery his brother Arthur reprimanded him for risking his health. "You cannot possibly—if you are to continue in public life—continue under the same strain as you have been under during the last year."

For Lehman this was much more easily said than done. Along with his scrupulous conscientiousness was the awareness that he followed two of the best governors of his time and that he had to deal with an economically paralyzed state and millions of people in want. Worried about the poor, he exerted himself to the utmost to find ways for their relief. Simultaneously, he faced dozens of other pressing problems, including a legislature that stubbornly resisted his proposed bills to protect the rights of workers, provide for the needy, curb the demands of big business, and further social reform.

An instance of his persistent eagerness for even-handed justice was his veto of a bill giving a judge's widow a pension which was not wholly earned. Frequently confronted with similar bills—legislators acted generously in such cases —he could not in conscience favor a few over the many, and explained to the widow, "It isn't quite fair to do this in the case of men who earn $20,000 a year, and not do it in the case of a fellow who earns $1,800." His conscience nevertheless troubled him and he wrote to Irving, "I never felt worse about vetoing any bill, but I do not see how I could have done anything else."

In running for re-election in 1934 against Robert Moses, a popular and highly picturesque public figure, Lehman achieved another unprecedented victory. In the 1935 legislative session he struggled for each bill, but the laws finally enacted were a remarkable achievement in social legislation. Concurrently he had to deal with organized crime in New York City. Disturbed by the inefficiency of the city prosecutor, he arranged to engage young Thomas E. Dewey as special prosecutor. Dewey's energetic aggressiveness pleased him, but when Dewey wanted to lessen the prison terms of convicts in order to have them inform on others, Lehman refused, declaring that it would be unfair to the accused to tempt prisoners to testify under such an inducement. In 1936 he supported legislation against organized crime based on a study by penologists, police chiefs, and social workers. He accused opposing legislators of being men who "took almost a delight in killing bills instead of in bills to prevent killing."

Eager to return to private life, Lehman was reluctant to run for re-election, but Roosevelt and others urged him to do so. The President, mindful of his own candidacy, wrote him, "The more I look at it from every angle the more I'm convinced of the very great importance of your running —important to the social security of the whole nation in all that implies." Lehman accepted the nomination, won by a sizable majority, and continued to broaden and deepen social reforms against the persistent opposition of the legislature.

No doubt influenced by his brother Irving, then a judge, and from the first his close adviser, as well as by his own deep respect for law, Lehman was strongly perturbed by Roosevelt's effort to "pack" the Supreme Court. In a letter he assured him of his own disappointment at the conservatism of the Court, but indicated that the proposed plan was no solution. Roosevelt did not appreciate this advice, and was even more irritated to learn that Lehman had written Senator Wagner to urge him to vote against the bill. The relationship between them was further strained when Lehman objected to Roosevelt's attempt to "purge" some of the conservative senators, on the ground that a government executive had no right to punish legislators for opposing him.

In 1938, Lehman was again reluctant to continue as governor, wishing "relief from the tremendous strain and responsibility under which I have been working for the past many years." When an opening in the Senate occurred, he thought that would be more to his liking and announced his candidacy without consulting Roosevelt or the leading state politicians. When Dewey declared his candidacy for governor on the Republican ticket, it was obvious that Lehman was the only Democrat who could defeat him, and Roosevelt joined other Democrats in pleading that a Dewey victory would endanger the social legislation Lehman had fought so hard to enact. Moved by what the *Christian Science Monitor* called his "prodigious sense of public stewardship," he yielded, winning by a small plurality.

For the next four years, Lehman, with less opposition from the legislature than previously, proceeded to strengthen the social-welfare laws to which he was dedicated. In 1940 the *Nation* stated editorially, "In his quiet and methodical way this ex-banker has achieved far more than was accomplished by either Smith or Roosevelt in liberal legislation."

All through his years as governor Lehman felt keenly the evil of Hitlerism. Son of a German Jew and devoted to Judaism, he followed with horror and heartache the Nazi persecution of Jews. The Lehman family established a trust fund to help relations abroad, and anyone remotely connected with it was assisted with money and guidance. Lehman, however, received so many appeals from other European Jews that he had to refer them to the Jewish relief agency. He was opposed to Zionism—"While I am deeply sympathetic with the idea of building up Palestine economically, socially, and spiritually, I did not want to align myself with any political group doing it"—yet the suffering of Jews in Europe gnawed at him.

In 1940, as the war in Europe was worsening for the Allies, Lehman felt that Roosevelt was needed in the Presidency and campaigned for his election to a third term. When Roosevelt won, Lehman urged him to mollify his business and isolationist opponents by stating "that you are the chief protector of our capitalist system, that you have not wanted and do not want autocratic power, and that you are determined to bring all classes together in harmony."

In 1942 Lehman was determined not to seek re-election. He had held the governorship for ten years and had achieved a liberal record of which he was justly proud, and now he wished to broaden his activities in the international field. Distressed by news of wholesale murder of Jews and liberals in Nazi-controlled Europe, he longed to do something to assuage their suffering. Roosevelt sensed this wish and called Lehman to Washington in November to head the projected Office of Foreign Relief and Rehabilitation Operations. It was as if he considered it poetic justice— apart from the fact that he had great confidence in Lehman's administrative ability—for a Jew to head the relief of Nazi victims. Lehman eagerly accepted this assignment, resigning at once to give his friend Lieutenant-Governor Charles Poletti the opportunity to act as governor for a month.

With the need of relief urgent in the liberated North African areas, Lehman lost no time in providing it as best he could. He was disappointed when both Roosevelt and Churchill vetoed the shipment of food to Nazi-held countries. Lehman felt, as Herbert Hoover had in World War I, that hungry people should be fed regardless of who controls them politically. Churchill, as early as 1940, was emphatically opposed to this view,

> Let Hitler bear his responsibilities to the full, and let the people of Europe who groan beneath his yoke aid in every way the coming of the day when the yoke will be broken. Meanwhile we can and will arrange in advance for the speedy entry of food into any part of the enslaved area when this part has been wholly cleared of the German forces.

Despite this and other frustrations—since winning the war was of first priority, the armed forces commandeered everything in sight—Lehman strove to bring relief to people as soon as they were liberated. He had difficulty finding able associates; he lacked adequate authority and was opposed by men in other departments who considered their priority superior to his. When he complained to Roosevelt and others in command, he got sympathy but not much else. Moreover, what relief he managed to provide was strongly criticized by isolationists in Congress.

Meantime the idea of the United Nations Relief and Rehabilitation Administration was assuming concrete form, and in April, 1943 Lehman went to London to formulate its basic principles and to prepare for joint military and civilian control of liberated areas. It was soon agreed that some countries would get supplies free and others would be charged in proportion to their ability to pay. When this information reached Congress, certain members denounced the entire idea of UNRRA, but consent was obtained by making fund allotments subject to Congressional approval.

In November, 1943 delegates from 44 nations signed a compact creating UNRRA. To finance the obvious tremendous needs of the millions to be liberated from Nazi domination, it was agreed that the uninvaded countries should contribute 1 percent of their national annual income. The United States was thus to give the lion's share—$1.35 billion; Great Britain, $330 million; and Canada, $90 million. Lehman was appointed director-general.

In December, 1943 he set up his headquarters in Washington. As his biographer Allan Nevins stated, "His strong belief in justice, his conviction that the rich should share with the poor and the strong help the weak, were satisfied by the whole basis of UNRRA." Lehman made strenuous efforts to attract persons of ability and altruism as his associates; he began to collect supplies, and worked indefatigably to overcome opposition from the armed forces when he saw no interference with their legitimate needs; he also went personally to the liberated lands to arrange for the speedy and efficient distribution of immediate relief.

While in Algiers in March, 1944 to arrange for the UNRRA relief work in liberated areas, he slipped on a rug in the British Embassy and broke a leg at the knee. His other engagements being urgent, he flew to Cairo as soon as the leg was put into a cast. There, from his bed, he carried on conferences with local officials, army leaders, and representatives from the Middle East and the Balkans. Informed of the critical condition in that part of the world, he strove resolutely to supply food and medicines to each country as soon as it could be reached. His task was made more difficult by intrigues and quarrels between rival factions as well as by the natural reluctance of army leaders to supply UNRRA with provisions which they might need for their own forces. When he returned to the United States a month later, exhausted and in pain, he learned that his oldest son Peter, who had flown fifty-eight missions over Germany and earned the Distinguished Flying Cross, had been killed in an airplane accident.

Through all of 1944 Lehman had to practice patience while waiting for the armed forces to let UNRRA officials enter areas gradually being liberated. In the interim he built up UNRRA personnel and accumulated what supplies and transportation facilities he could obtain—both being scarce and in control of war officials. In his trips to Europe that year he was shocked at the misery of civilians in the various countries and sick at heart because of his inability to help them adequately. He felt that it should be possible to feed the hungry without handicapping the war effort. To the various criticisms of presumed UNRRA inefficiency, he could only reply, "We want desperately to get to work. But even if we had supplies, we would have no means of getting them into the needy areas of Western Europe unless the military ordered them forward. And the military declines."

When conditions became desperate, Lehman cabled President Roosevelt to urge that additional shipping tonnage be given to UNRRA to move supplies to Europe. Roosevelt granted the necessary facilities, and food and goods began to be supplied to millions in desperate need. At the end of the fighting in May, 1945 UNRRA's problems of relief and rehabilitation became complicated by the flight of Germans from the Russian-held zones and by the liberation of survivors from concentration camps. Both groups were in charge of the army but in need of help from UNRRA. In addition there were in Germany millions of forced laborers from other countries, and some of them, like the Poles, refused repatriation and had to be fed and clothed by UNRRA. All these pressing and perplexing problems were dealt with heroically—though not always effectively. By the end of

June, 1.25 million tons of supplies were shipped to Europe and distributed, but that was not nearly enough.

At an UNRRA council meeting Lehman elicited the support of various governments by a factual and passionately worded presentation of the needs and facilities of UNRRA. Thereupon the council recommended that each uninvaded country repeat its grant of 1 percent of its national annual income. It also decided to cease shipments of supplies at the end of 1946 and to terminate the work of UNRRA in March, 1947.

The need to mitigate suffering and to revive the economy of the ravaged countries the world over, once the fighting in the Pacific stopped in August, was far greater than UNRRA could fill. Its total income of $3,872,749,021 was simply inadequate to meet obvious requirements, and they were scaled down accordingly. It cared as well as it could for the camps of displaced persons and helped to repatriate or rehabilitate them—approximately 725,000 refugees were returned to their native countries under very difficult conditions. It did much to revive economically devastated communities in the face of self-interest and prejudice on the part of local functionaries. In 1946 the greatest needs were for raw materials with which Europeans could make their own clothing and shoes, build homes and factories, and thus start their industries anew, and UNRRA supplied these materials from every obtainable source. It also provided quantities of locomotives and rolling stock, trucks and petroleum products, with which to maintain essential transportation. In addition it rendered many services in the fields of health and welfare and agriculture; farmers, for instance, were supplied with fertilizers, tractors, seeds, livestock, and implements.

Lehman worried about every problem confronting UNRRA, and the criticism directed at it caused him deep distress. In March, 1946, exhausted and depressed, and offended by President Truman's arrangement with Herbert Hoover to survey food needs in Europe and Asia without prior consultation with him or any reference to the work of UNRRA, he resigned his post with the statement, "I have carried a very heavy responsibility without interruption for many years—in particular during the last three years when I have had both the horror and the task of creating the first international organization with great executive responsibilities." In retrospect, however, he was proud of his achievement. "Perhaps the work that has given me the deepest satisfaction and which I consider the highlight of my career was my service in the United Nations Relief and Rehabilitation Administration."

At the next meeting of the UNRRA council, members vied with one another in praising him, and elected him honorary chairman. The French representative called him "one of the greatest world citizens, one who put all his energy in aiding destitute humanity and to rehabilitating the countries which suffered most from war." The Greek member said, "One of the outstanding achievements has been to have kept this first practical experiment in international economic collaboration above political rivalries and national jealousies and to have shown that the things that unite men are more important than the things that divide them."

Opposed to political Zionism and recoiling from the terrorism of the Irgun and Stern rebels, Lehman was nevertheless in sympathy with the Jewish refugees who sought to enter Palestine despite British opposition, which he considered "not only indefensible but unwise." At a meeting of the United Jewish Appeal in 1947 he said,

> I have visited many countries, and I have seen with my own eyes the indescribably pathetic plight of the pitiful remnant of Jews which survives in Europe—a million and a half out of six million. The physical handicaps they have endured cannot be fully pictured. And yet they stand before us not as beggars, pleading for crumbs of charity. They stand before us with a stirring faith and will . . . as

have men and women who are anxious to take their right-
ful place in the world.

Nominated to the Senate in 1946, he failed of election for the first time in his political career because he refused to acquiesce in the "cold war" psychology, which was
gaining prevalence. He would not reject the nomination of
the American Labor party, led by Sidney Hillman but stigmatized for its communist associations, nor would he express himself critically of Henry A. Wallace, who was advocating co-existence with the Soviet Union. Again a free agent
politically, he devoted himself to his charities, to the Jewish
Theological Seminary, to the campaign for President Truman's election in 1948.

Deeply perturbed by the talk of a "preventive war"
when the communists gained control of China in 1949, he
expressed his concern to Secretary of State Dean Acheson.

> The first principle of the American people in foreign policy
> today is a search for peace, justice, and the well-being of
> all peoples. It is not to maintain a particular battleline
> along the Asia coast or to resist by force those ideologies
> which are not reconcilable with ours. . . . We must not
> practice evil to halt it. There is a slower and harder but
> surer way.

Thus he later approved Truman's dismissal of General Mac-
Arthur for threatening to extend the Korean War.

When Cardinal Spellman publicly castigated Mrs. Eleanor Roosevelt for favoring the Barden bill to aid public but
not private schools, Lehman was shocked. Having always
believed that one had a right to express one's views, he
came to her defense in a letter to the *Times*. "Her whole life
has been dedicated to a constant fight for tolerance and
brotherhood of men as children of one God." He did this
after he had been asked to oppose John Foster Dulles for a
temporary term in the Senate, aware that his criticism of
the Cardinal might hurt his chances at the polls. To his sur-
prise the letter was generally well received, and although

such agents of public opinion as the *Times* and Walter Lippmann opposed his election, he won by a majority of nearly 200,000 votes.

Lehman had long wanted to serve in the Senate, expecting his duties to be relatively light and life in Washington attractive. As a freshman Senator he knew he had to listen and learn, but he also had a "simple and clear" understanding of his duties as a member of the federal government. In a speech the previous fall he had declared,

> I believe with all my heart that government is *for* the people. It must be clean and honest and efficient. But it must be more than a mere administrative machine. It must ever concern itself with the solution of human as well as material problems. It must satisfy the needs and aspirations of its people, and in order to satisfy these needs and aspirations it must be flexible enough to meet the changing conditions of the world today.

His disappointment with the antiliberal trend of many Senators was immediate, and his annoyance with the Republican-Dixiecrats coalition forced him to oppose them with the fervor of his solid liberalism.

Conscientious and hard-working as always, he assembled the largest and most efficient research staff of all the Senators, paying the salaries of more than half of it himself. He followed the debates and compromises with increasing anxiety, aware of the mediocrity and perversity of some of the Senators and angered by the machinations of the inner clique. He particularly detested Patrick McCarran's behavior, and after 1950 he fought Joseph McCarthy without let. He was disappointed in the liberal Senators who seemed to him afflicted with a "failure of nerve," too confused and frightened by the bogey of communism to oppose the reactionary bills under consideration. What grieved him was their readiness to settle for a slice—and seldom getting it—rather than fight for the whole loaf. "I felt that not to make the case for the whole loaf was to lose sight of the whole, and thus to compromise the case for liberalism itself." When his liberal colleagues advised him not to oppose the Internal Security Act of 1950 if he wanted to win the oncoming election, he nevertheless condemned it, and won re-election by a sizable majority.

Lehman found himself working more strenuously as a septuagenerian Senator than he had as governor. On the subject of taxation he declared, "While the reactionary elements in Congress slash away at funds for public health, public power, and public housing—under the guise of economy—they move very slowly, indeed, to tax the unprecedented profits of big business." Incensed by the Immigration and Naturalization Act of 1952, sponsored by McCarran, he asserted, "This indefensible and evil act reflects a racist philosophy of fear, suspicion, and distrust of foreigners, and must be repealed or drastically revised in conformity with bills I introduced for four successive years."

He was equally outraged by McCarthy's behavior, and the timidity of liberal Senators in their reaction to it. From the first he challenged McCarthy's reckless and irresponsible assertions, insisting on proof which was never given and denouncing his misrepresentations and accusations.

> I have been shocked, as have many other members of this body and of the public, by attacks on individuals constituting character assasination, by charges unfounded, ungrounded, unproved. In the past two years a policy of indicting by smear has been indulged in, and the victim has no opportunity whatever to defend himself. There has been a policy of trying to prove guilt by association, not only of persons, but of ideas.

He courageously defended the men and women attacked by McCarthy and spoke up against him at every opportunity. In a speech in Milwaukee in 1953 he said, "As for me, I shall continue to fight, as long as I have breath and energy, against all the evils of McCarthyism, and against the spirit of fear which he and his associates use and invoke. I will not be intimidated. I will not be swayed from my course." When J. Robert Oppenheimer was judged a security risk by the Atomic Energy Commission in 1954, Lehman, as a member of the board of the Institute for Advanced Study, insisted that the victimized scientist remain as director. Similarly, when the Fund for the Republic, headed by Robert Hutchins, came under attack from reactionary groups, he joined its board in the belief that it "must not be allowed to perish for lack of support."

In opposing the 1954 Communist Control Act he called it "loaded with truly dangerous and self-contradictory provisions"; later he regretted his failure to vote against it. He had learned by then that "a fight is worth while, even if you know you're going to lose it. . . . And in the end I've seen many hopeless cases win out."

Lehman's liberalism and refusal to compromise alienated many Senators and made him a lonely and embattled figure among them. William S. White stated that he was "confined by niggling and almost brutal Senate action to the most literal inhibition of the least important of all rules." He was hurt by this ostracism but made no effort to modify his liberal ardor. He was primarily concerned with "how to make democracy and representative government work in a complex and interdependent world, in which the hydrogen bomb is the symbol of the final destruction threatening us all if our understanding does not measure up to our responsibilities."

In 1956, in his seventy-ninth year, he decided to retire. Colleagues and friends praised his long and devoted service to the public good. Senator Paul H. Douglas called him "the best man I have ever known in political life and the noblest Senator of my generation." Mrs. Roosevelt wrote him, "You were not only the conscience of the Senate, but I think you have been the conscience of a great many people in the inspiration which your life has given them to be of service to their country." Organized labor, in appreciation of his long support, honored him with the first annual William Green-Philip Murray Award.

Too public-spirited to relax in privacy, he resumed his work for Israel and was critical of the State Department for not protecting the rights of Jewish-American citizens in Arab countries. Pointing out that as far back as 1868 a statute required the Department to act in such cases, he referred to the American action when Austria-Hungary would not accept A. M. Keiley as our minister because his wife was Jewish, and to our abrogation of the treaty with Russia for the same reason. "I believe," he declared, "that the government of Saudi-Arabia will respect us more if we stand up for our principles and refuse to accommodate ourselves to the intolerable prejudices of the Saudi-Arabian Government in the name of either oil or base rights." He also continued his active participation in philanthropic and civic organizations. One of his and Mrs. Lehman's last gifts was the children's zoo in New York's Central Park, a unique and charming collection of animals and structures.

On his return to New York Lehman resumed his active interest in Democratic reform politics and joined the fight against Tammany control. Although an octogenerian, he did not hesitate to walk for miles on a hot summer day to demonstrate his adherence to the reform opposition candidates. In 1961, when Mayor R. F. Wagner, Jr., broke with Carmine De Sapio, the grand sachem of Tammany Hall, Lehman campaigned for his election. The year before, loyal to Adlai Stevenson, he had sought his nomination at the Democratic National Convention; when John F. Kennedy was chosen, Lehman worked for his election. To the very last day of his life—on December 2, 1963, when his heart gave way as he was preparing to leave for Washington to receive the Presidential Medal of Freedom—he took seriously his role as citizen and statesman.

A fitting memorial to him was The Herbert Lehman Education Fund, established in 1964 to assist poor Negro students in the South to complete their professional education.

Herbert H. Lehman lacked the popular flair of "Al" Smith or the political sophistication of Roosevelt. He was essentially a simple and modest man, born to wealth, bred in an atmosphere of conventional conservatism, long a businessman and banker, who was driven by a demanding conscience to devote himself to the welfare of the mass of mankind. A beneficiary of capitalism, he was critical of its tendency to exploitation. His aim was to imbue business leaders with the spirit of democracy, with a sense of responsibility to the people as a whole. Late in life, aware of his ineffectiveness in this respect and worried like Brandeis, about the gigantic growth of corporations, he wrote,

> One of my chief worries so far as big business is concerned is the lack of democratic controls, or of any controls. The huge corporations, with their tremendous power over so many phases of our national and individual lives, are responsible only to the balance sheet and to the profit-and-loss statement. This is the only responsibility which management has even to the stockholders, the theoretical owners.

His philosophy of government was similar. When he came to Albany in 1928 he was distressed by the insincerity, stupidity, and venality of men in public office. By nature more the mild reformer than the determined crusader, but increasingly aware of human frailty and the ease with which men tend to become corrupt, he made himself the conscience of state government—as later he did of the United States Senate.

This zeal in behalf of political democracy and human welfare, which distinguished the conduct of his adult years, he ascribed to his Jewish upbringing.

> My Jewish heritage has unquestionably affected my political and social thinking. All through my years of public life I have felt strongly the importance of keeping faith with the ethics of Judaism and its basic concept that "creed without deed" is meaningless. As a Jew and as a human being, I have accepted no boundaries except those of justice, righteousness, humility, and charity.

LAW SERVING
THE
PUBLIC GOOD

Many of the thousands of American Jews who are lawyers or judges tend to emulate the social ethicism that characterized the careers of Justices Brandeis and Cardozo. Not unlike men of law in general, Jews individually vary greatly on the scale of public service. Among them have been grasping and egregious lawyers, but a much larger number have devoted their talents to public advantage. Of the latter group the following few are representative and noteworthy.

Simon E. Sobeloff was born in Baltimore in 1893 and was graduated from the law school of the University of Maryland in 1914. Between alternating periods of private practice, he was assistant city solicitor, deputy city solicitor, United States Attorney for the District of Maryland, city solicitor, and, in 1952, chief judge of the Maryland court of appeals. Two years later he was appointed United States Solicitor General and argued numerous government cases before the Supreme Court. In 1954 he was made judge of the United States Court of Appeals for the Fourth District, and elevated to chief judge four years later. He was throughout his adult years actively interested in Jewish affairs.

Samuel I. Rosenman, born in San Antonio in 1896 and educated at Columbia University, was for four years a member of the New York state legislature. When Franklin D. Roosevelt was elected governor of New York in 1928, Rosenman became his counsel and speech coordinator. He was a state supreme court justice from 1932 until 1943 when he resigned to become special counsel to President Roosevelt, whose speeches he had continued to help write during their many years of intimate association. When Roosevelt died, Rosenman remained special counsel to President Truman for a year before returning to private practice in New York. In 1949 he was a member of the steel industry fact-finding board, and in 1963 he served as chairman of the railway labor emergency board. He wrote *Working with Roosevelt* and edited the multi-volume *Public Papers and Addresses of Franklin Delano Roosevelt, 1928–1945.*

Born in New York in 1900, Bernard Botein studied at City College and received his law degree from Brooklyn Law School in 1924. In 1929 he became an assistant district attorney, leaving in 1936 to serve as head of an accident-fraud investigation. In 1941 he became a justice of the appellate division of the state supreme court, of which he was presiding justice for a decade after 1957. Among his published writings are books on crime and the judiciary. A member of various Jewish and general organizations, in 1968 he headed the special committee on racial and religious prejudice in New York City.

Another New Yorker, born in 1903, Stanley Fuld was graduated from City College and from Columbia Law School. In private practice until 1935, he served as assistant district attorney until 1944, when he returned to private practice. Appointed to the court of appeals in 1946, he was elected to a full term the following year and re-elected in 1961. In 1967 he became chief judge. He was awarded the Joseph M. Proskauer Medal for his participation in Jewish activities. His eminence in law gained him the Cardozo Medal and the Harlan Fiske Stone Award given by the Association of Trial Lawyers.

Born in Boston in 1906, Charles E. Wyzanski was educated at Harvard University. He served as law secretary to Judges Augustus N. Hand and Learned Hand, was solicitor in the Department of Labor, and American delegate to the International Labor Conference in Geneva. Late in 1935 he was appointed special assistant to the Attorney General and argued the constitutionality of the Social Security and National Labor Relations Acts before the Supreme Court. In 1938 he joined a Boston law firm, but left in December 1941 to become a United States District Judge for Massachusetts. He lectured on government at Harvard and Massachusetts Institute of Technology, and served as president of the Harvard overseers from 1953 to 1956. In 1970 he made headlines for his landmark decision on war resisters.

Arthur J. Goldberg, born in Chicago in 1908, received his law degree from Northwestern University in 1930. Highly successful in private practice for many years, in 1948 he became general counsel to the CIO and the United Steel Workers Union and achieved notable successes as a labor negotiator until 1961, when he was appointed Secretary of Labor. Nominated to the Supreme Court in 1962, he served until 1965, when President Johnson prevailed upon him to succeed the late Adlai Stevenson as American Representative to the United Nations. His attempts to move the Viet Nam war into the Security Council were overruled by the advisers to President Johnson, and early in 1968 he submitted his resignation. President Johnson's curt acceptance was both ungracious and ungrateful. Long active in Jewish organizations, he received the Stephen S. Wise Award in 1965, and in 1968 he was elected president of the American Jewish Committee. In 1970 he became Democratic candidate for governor of New York.

David L. Bazelon was born in Superior, Wisconsin, in 1909, studied at the University of Illinois, and received his law degree from Northwestern University in 1931. He served as assistant United States Attorney from 1935 until 1940. In 1946 he accepted the office of Assistant Attorney General of the Lands Division, and two years later transferred to the Office of Alien Property. Appointed Judge of the United States Court of Appeals in 1949, he has been its Chief Judge since 1962. He has lectured widely on the legal aspects of psychiatry, and in 1960 was the recipient of the Isaak Ray Award of the American Psychiatric Association; the following year he chaired the task force on law in the President's Panel on Mental Retardation.

Born in Memphis in 1910, Abe Fortas was graduated from Southwestern University in 1930 and from Yale Law School in 1933, where he was befriended by Dean William O. Douglas. For the next five years he taught law at Yale and served in the legal divisions of New Deal agencies, ending as Under-Secretary of the Interior. In 1946 he resigned along with Secretary Ickes and turned down a professorship at Yale to became a founding partner of the law firm of Arnold, Fortas, and Porter, of which he was, according to Professor Fred Rodell, "the acknowledged biggest brain in that spectacularly successful firm." The firm had some large corporations among its clients; it also accepted the defended victims of McCarthyism, among them Professor Owen Lattimore and Dorothy Bailey. When the latter was deprived of her government job, the firm found a place for her in its own office. Probably Fortas's most conspicuous victory was in the *Gideon* case; his argument, according to Professor Rodell, "persuaded a unanimous Supreme Court to overturn an old Frankfurter-written ruling and required the state to provide, as does the Federal Government under the Constitution, free legal counsel for every poor defendant charged with an untrivial crime."

Fortas and Lyndon B. Johnson had a close client-lawyer relationship, and when Justice Goldberg resigned from the Supreme Court in 1965, Johnson appointed Fortas as his successor. In the summer of 1968, after Chief Justice Earl Warren expressed a desire to retire, at the pleasure of the President, Johnson named Fortas to his office. When hostile conservative Senators persisted in opposing confirmation, Justice Fortas requested the President to withdraw the nomination. The New York *Times* commented, "Associate Justice Fortas is the victim of a political dispute in a Presidential election."

Soon after, however, it became known that Fortas had accepted a lifetime retainer of $20,000 from the family foundation established by Louis Wolfson, a client of the firm with which Fortas was associated before joining the Supreme Court. Wolfson was then serving a prison sentence as a convicted stock manipulator. Fortas's apparent insensitivity to judicial ethics alienated even many of his erstwhile supporters, and he resigned from the Supreme Court in 1969.

13
Felix
Frankfurter

OUTSTANDING FIRST as a lawyer and civil libertarian and later as an exponent of judicial self-restraint,
Felix Frankfurter (1882–1965) was a man of complex character and exceptional achievement. He was born in Vienna
of a family rich in rabbinical and lay scholars. In 1893 his
father traveled to the United States to see the Chicago
World's Fair and was so impressed with the political freedom
and physical grandeur of America that he remained, and
some months later brought over his wife and six children.
He became a fur merchant on New York's Lower East Side,
earning a modest living.

Felix was twelve years old and knew no English when
he reached New York. Short, alert, bookishly inclined, he
made rapid progress at school. Living near Cooper Union
Institute, he used its library almost daily and attended its
lectures on current issues, from which, he later stated, "I
got most of my education." In 1896 he took an interested
part in Bryan's Presidential campaign—Bryan being to him

the golden voice protesting the exploitation of the poor by rapacious capitalists. In 1897 he went to City College, which then combined a high school and college course in five years. He was especially interested in Greek and history, and made a conspicuous scholastic record, graduating third in his class. Determined on a career in law, he worked for a year as a clerk in the Tenement House Department and saved his salary of $1,200 for law school expenses.

At Harvard Law School, in addition to his courses, he "satisfied a gluttonous appetite for lectures, exhibitions, concerts." He was "a social creature," and soon made friends with many students and teachers. Then and later he was eager to know everybody of importance and status. He was first in his class for three years, nearly equaling the still unbeatable record made by Brandeis. Long thereafter one of his papers was cited in class as a work of masterly legal analysis. On graduation he was asked by Professor John C. Gray to work with him for a month on his book *Property*, an honor which the youthful Frankfurter appreciated so much that he refused a check for $100 until Gray told him brusquely but amiably not to be "a damned fool."

In the spring of 1906 Frankfurter went to New York, armed with enthusiastic letters of recommendation. He made a special effort to find acceptance at Hornblower, Byrne, Miller and Potter—succeeding in spite of his Jewishness only because a junior partner, also of Harvard, was so strongly impressed by his record. By ironic chance Frankfurter later was the first to hold the Harvard Law School chair endowed by James Byrne, one of the senior partners.

After two months with the firm, he received a call from Henry L. Stimson, the new United States Attorney appointed by President Theodore Roosevelt to prosecute antitrust suits. With a free hand but little money, Stimson decided to attract the best recent graduates of leading law schools and wrote to the deans for suggestions. Frankfurter was first on the Harvard list, and Stimson asked him to serve as an assistant. Loath to leave a firm in which he was practically assured a successful legal career, Frankfurter was nevertheless strongly attracted to public service in a field of his preference, and agreed, satisfying his conscience with the thought that he was taking a reduction in salary from $1,000 to $750.

The decision had a crucial effect upon his future career: it not only oriented him to a life of public service, to which he had long been passively predisposed, but also brought him into intimate association with the first of the powerful public personalities who continued to influence his thinking and action. Like Brandeis, he was not interested in working for clients to whom he would have to be amenable; moreover, the prosecution of Roosevelt's "malefactors of great wealth" satisfied his yearning for social justice. The more he came to know Stimson, the more he admired him as "an incredibly effective and wholly scrupulous man."

For the next three years Frankfurter associated with a group of young men who were highly gifted and devoted to public service. Put in charge of the case against the American Sugar Refining Company, he found evidence that the firm was defrauding the Treasury Department through the use of false scales operated by corrupt custom-house officials. The company's president, Charles W. Morse was convicted and sentenced to prison. So impressive was Frankfurter as a "trust-buster" that Stimson took him to the White House to introduce him to President Roosevelt as a legal prodigy. He was similarly successful in cases against New York Central and E. H. Harriman. Following the leads of Roosevelt and Brandeis, he held ruthless enterprise inimical to the public good and insisted on fairness and honesty in business. It was, indeed, his work on the American Sugar case that brought him to Brandeis's attention and started their lifelong friendship. Later he stated, "Brandeis had a very important influence on me, particularly in his austere moral views, in matters where moral issues do not lie on the surface." In 1929 Brandeis returned the compliment when he told Harold Laski, "He seems to me clearly the most useful lawyer in the United States."

In 1909, with the coming of the Taft Administration,

Stimson returned to private practice and took Frankfurter with him; a year later Frankfurter helped him in his campaign for the governorship. When the defeated Stimson was appointed Secretary of War, he engaged Frankfurter as his legal adviser and personal assistant, with the official title of law officer of the Bureau of Insular Affairs. In this capacity Frankfurter served until 1913, making his personality felt powerfully among his increasing circle of friends. During the 1912 campaign, though Stimson felt honor-bound to favor Taft, Frankfurter worked for Roosevelt's election.

When Wilson became President, Frankfurter was ready to leave the War Department with Stimson, but the latter urged him to remain in office under Secretary of War L. M. Garrison in order to complete his work on the regulation of water power. During the years in Washington Frankfurter had been shifted from one administrative position to another, so that, to quote Professor Fred Rodell, he was "a sort of one-man brain-trust for his superiors."

Frankfurter found Garrison and Wilson dogmatic and without the human warmth radiated by Stimson, and in 1914 gratefully accepted an offer to join the faculty of the Harvard Law School. Claiming to be surprised at this stroke of good fortune, he later reminisced, "I no more thought of myself as a member of the Harvard Law School faculty than I would have felt myself as a member of the House of Lords—in fact, more easily, probably, considering the people who are in the House of Lords. . . . My first concern was that I wasn't qualified." Of that Brandeis told him it was for others to say.

For by 1914 this disclaimer was almost mock-modest. Frankfurter had already made an enviable record as a prosecutor and legal adviser. He was equally successful as a cultivator of influential friendships, with Justices Holmes and Brandeis heading the list. In fact, he always acted on the advice he gave Ella Winter in 1919, "Use every chance to make personal contacts. They are what count in life. You never know when one may become important."

Harold Laski in his letters to Holmes confirmed this talent for friendship. "I am amazed at the barriers he has over-leaped. People meet him, and the adjective 'dangerous' melts as the snow before the sun. . . . Felix, in his whirl-wind ways, sees everyone and everything. . . . No person I have ever met had the same genius for ultimate friend-ship." He further stated that Frankfurter "collects people" instead of books or pictures. And Holmes replied that Frank-furter truly enjoyed people—"with an unimaginable gift of wiggling in where he wants to." His investment in friend-ships was repaid when Brandeis recommended him for the Harvard position.

Both Holmes and Stimson advised Frankfurter against accepting the Harvard post, the latter pointing out that he was best fitted for public life. Frankfurter put on paper the likely advantages and disadvantages of teaching at the Har-vard Law School and concluded that he would both teach and engage in public service.

> I would keep my independence, or rather spread it, and say what thinking will lead me to say, and that, too, with-out any danger of having my thinking unconsciously softened or my underlying ardor impaired. It is a great big job that has to be done—to evolve a constructive juris-prudence going hand in hand with the pretty thorough-going overturning that we are in for. . . . The big thing, one of big things, is that I would go in for about five years of thinking, not cloistered, but in the very current of the problems that are *the* national problems of greatest appeal to me.

He envisaged five years of teaching, and assumed he would then "take new stock." As it turned out, he remained five times five years. As a teacher he wanted to be "a kind of loosener of other people's tongues."

It took time for Frankfurter to attain his stride, and he never managed to impress certain students, but those whose intellects and wits synchronized with his found him not only stimulating but also highly helpful in launching their legal careers. Paul A. Freund stated that he showed students "the illumination created by an incandescent mind." Perhaps his chief interest was in making students see law "as a vital agency for human betterment," and he sought to instill in them a desire for experience in public service before entering private practice. In a speech on students in 1915 before the American Bar Association he declared, "We fail in our important office if they do not feel that society has breathed into the law the breath of life and made it a living, serving soul. We must show them that law is an instrument and not an end of organized humanity." And he exerted himself to this accomplishment, placing hundreds of students with judges and the government as well as with private law firms.

True to his interest in public affairs, he helped Herbert Croly, whose *The Promise of American Life* had earlier profoundly affected his political thinking, start the *New Republic*, resisting the offer of an editorship but becoming a concerned godfather to the liberal weekly and writing frequently for it, many of his contributions were unsigned editorials. He also volunteered his legal services to the National Consumers' League and to the National Association for the Advancement of Colored People.

In 1916, when Brandeis was named to the Supreme Court, Frankfurter took over the legal appeal on the minimum-hour work law before the Court. Employing Josephine Goldmark, Brandeis's sister-in-law and a very able researcher, to supply him with the pertinent social and economic information, he prepared "a Brandeis brief," modeled after *Muller* v. *Oregon*, and won his case by a vote of 5 to 3, Brandeis not voting. In the O'Hara cases on the minimum wage law, which he took up next, the Oregon attorney general had submitted a "flimsy" brief. Upset by this inept procedure, Frankfurter appealed privately to Chief Justice White, who ruled that oral argument would be required. This gave Frankfurter the opportunity to present the case so effectively that the Court affirmed it; this victory was nullified later in *Adkins* v. *Children's Hospital*, which Frankfurter argued with cogency but in which Justice Sutherland employed "the most doctrinaire view about 'liberty of contract.'" This case, Frankfurter noted later, "prevented legislation from being introduced and it made still-born legislation which was by way of being introduced," restraining liberal minimum-wage legislation until the advent of the New Deal.

When the United States entered World War I in 1917, Secretary of War Newton D. Baker called Frankfurter to Washington to serve as his assistant. Labor unrest and strikes had begun to hinder the war effort, and a Mediation Commission was formed with Frankfurter as secretary and counsel. In this capacity he went to the Pacific coast, where labor trouble was virulent. Before he left he was asked by President Wilson to look into the Tom Mooney case in California.

His first stop, however, was in Bisbee, Arizona, to investigate the Bisbee kidnapping, which had created national turmoil. Some 1,200 copper miners, most of them members of the Industrial Workers of the World striking for higher wages and better working conditions, had been rounded up by a vigilante posse headed by Jack Greenway, a "rough rider" friend of Theodore Roosevelt, and taken by train to New Mexico, where they were left in the desert without food or drink, until three days later when an Army contingent rescued them. This cruel and brutal act, described by the victims to young Max Lowenthal, Frankfurter's assistant, made him literally sick. In his reminiscences Frankfurter recalled, "This made a great impression on me because that was a just verdict, a just response to, the cruelty, ruthlessness, and callousness that was involved in what was done in Bisbee." Of Greenway he wrote: "He was doubtless a good man in all relations of life in which passion didn't supplant his fairness and reason." The report on the kidnapping, prepared by Frankfurter and Lowenthal, dwelt on the illegality of the deportation and the denial of rights safeguarded by the Constitution. When it was made public, it caused great agitation, chiefly to Roosevelt, whose loyalty to Greenway exceeded his sober judgment. Frankfurter, who considered the report, as many have since, "inoffensive," later declared, "I was certainly in my naive way just doing a lawyer's job, investigating the Bisbee deportations and bringing out the facts and their character."

Frankfurter's report on the Mooney case further irritated antiunion conservatives. He found, what was later firmly established, that the trial had been conducted "in an impregnating atmosphere of guilt," that the "attitude of passion was stimulated by all the arts of modern journalism," and that Mooney had been convicted on perjured evidence. He recommended a new trial.

The report was violently attacked. Roosevelt was almost hysterical in his denunciation. Although he had been favorably inclined toward Frankfurter previously, he now excoriated him in a letter in which he stated that the Bisbee report was "as thoroughly misleading a document as could be written on the subject," and that the Mooney investigation was outrageous: "You have taken, and are taking, on behalf of the administration an attitude which seems to be fundamentally that of Trotsky and other Bolshevik leaders in Russia; an attitude which may be fraught with mischief to this country." Years later Frankfurter intimated that this miscarriage of justice was essentially the responsibility of local lawyers of prominence who had neither sought to prevent it nor made the slightest effort to right it.

> Mooney was incarcerated for twenty years after it was established, demonstrated I think beyond a doubt (Archbishop Hanna told me at the time, "Tom Mooney is a bad man, but he didn't do that") that when he was convicted the chief witness was a demonstrated perjurer. For twenty years this went on, but if six leading members of the California bar had given the governor support and the

strength and the authority of saying, "Do let him go," that would have been accepted. Such is the strength of the bar.

In Washington President Wilson accepted the validity of Frankfurter's reports and prevented Mooney's electrocution.

Frankfurter was soon made chairman of the War Labor Policies Board and dealt with numerous labor problems with notable fairness and liberality. When Judge Elbert Gary, the arrogant head of United States Steel Corporation, refused to appear personally regarding the firm's labor policies, he was forced to do so when threatened with publicity about his obstinacy. In addition, his activities and influence were so widespread that Laski in a note to Holmes remarked facetiously, "Mr. Wilson has charge of foreign policy and Felix seems to sponsor the rest of the Government." In Cambridge, however, Frankfurter was suspected of excessive radicalism, and after the war the danger of his dismissal from Harvard's faculty seemed real enough to cause Justice Holmes to write to President Lowell in praise of his youthful friend.

Before leaving Washington for Cambridge, Frankfurter married Marian A. Denman, the attractive and intelligent daughter of a Congregational minister. Once settled in his teaching activities and relatively certain of tenure despite continued attacks from hostile conservatives, he resumed his libertarian efforts. Frankfurter's liberalism was an amalgam of the different-hued progressivism of his mentors Stimson, Brandeis, and Holmes. He became a founder of the American Civil Liberties Union in 1920, and in the same year he joined eleven other nationally eminent lawyers in a sharp protest against Attorney General Mitchell Palmer's persecution of radicals. At the invitation of United States Circuit Judge G. W. Anderson he and his colleague Zachariah Chafee served as *amicae curia* in cases of detained aliens, and had the pleasure of hearing Judge Anderson say, "I hear from the government no convincing

answer to Mr. Frankfurter's proposition." These and other
of his activities caused J. Edgar Hoover to refer to him later
as one of "the disseminators of Bolshevik propaganda." A
contrary opinion was voiced by Justice Holmes in a letter
to Laski. "He is so good in his chosen business that I think
he helps the world more in that way than he does by becoming a knight errant or a martyr."

Frankfurter risked near-martyrdom when he espoused
the defense of Sacco and Vanzetti. He first paid serious attention to their case in 1925 when he learned that the district attorney admitted to having made one of the expert
witnesses give an unfair impression of the use of the bullet
in evidence. "I was propelled and compelled by the something in me that revolted against this conduct of a district
attorney resulting in the potential death of two people accused of murder." The trial record astounded him by its
prejudiced and illegal aspects. Concerned primarily with
procedural irregularities, which he considered basically
dangerous to the health of our legal system, he met head on
the antagonism of the "best" people in Massachusetts. He
published his findings, later expanded into a small book,
in the *Atlantic Monthly.* In a devastating analysis he stated,

> In 1921 the temper of the times made it the special duty
> of a prosecutor and a court, engaged in trying two Italian
> radicals before a jury of native New Englanders, to keep
> the instruments of justice free from the infection of
> passion or prejudice. . . . In the case of Sacco and Vanzetti
> no such restraints were respected. By systematic exploita-
> tion of the defendants' alien blood, their imperfect knowl-
> edge of English, their unpopular social views, and their
> opposition to the war, the District Attorney invoked
> against them a riot of political passion and patriotic senti-
> ment, and the trial judge connived at—one had almost
> written cooperated in—the process.

He stressed the point that Captain Proctor's evidence
that the fatal bullet was "consistent with being fired from
that pistol" was used by the prosecutor and judge as in-

criminating proof when in fact it was given only after the
prosecutor's vainly repeated urging that he identify the
bullet as coming from Sacco's Colt, so that at the trial
Proctor was merely asked the ambiguous question. Nor was
Proctor cross-examined by the unalert defense attorney.
When questioned subsequently, Proctor stated that he had
found no evidence "that the so-called mortal bullet had
passed through this particular Colt automatic pistol and
the District Attorney well knew that I did not so intend
and framed the question accordingly." Yet neither Judge
Thayer nor the judges on the Massachusetts supreme
judicial court took cognizance of this crucial fact; the highest tribunal in the state, indeed, "was satisfied that throughout the conduct of the trial and the proceedings that followed it. Judge Thayer was governed by the calmness of a
cool mind, free from partiality, not swayed by sympathy
nor warped by prejudice nor moved by any kind of influence
save alone the overwhelming passion to do that what is just."
When the Madeiros confession, exonerating Sacco and
Vanzetti, was brought to Judge Thayer's attention, he
refused a new trial in an opinion which Frankfurter
denounced as "unmatched, happily, for discrepancies between what the record discloses and what the opinion con-
veys . . . "a farrago of misquotations, misrepresentations,
suppressions, and mutilations."

The article struck the Boston Brahmins with the force
of a bombshell. Doing a "lawyer's job" in his presentation
of the case, Frankfurter aimed to prevent what the evidence had persuaded him was a gross miscarriage of justice. He had no interest in or sympathy with the views or
persons of the defendants; all that concerned him, as a
lawyer and libertarian, was to see justice done. But the
passions of the time were too heated for a calm evaluation
of the facts. He was hailed by liberals and denounced by
conservatives. Dean J. H. Wigmore, an eminent traditionally conservative legal scholar, attacked Frankfurter
in two articles distinguished more by excoriation than by
reasoning. "If the Bar of Massachusetts," he fumed, "should

take this body-blow lying down, they would deserve to suffer their profession polluted and their bench bolshevized by agitators financed and led as this one has been." Frankfurter's published rejoinder, exposing the dean's misstatements and bigotry, had no effect on his detractors, who long damned him as an arch radical. Even after the electrocution of the two Italians, Chief Justice Taft wrote to Robert Grant, a member of the governor's committee that vindicated Judge Thayer: "It is remarkable how Frankfurter with his article was able to present to so large a body of readers a perverted view of the facts and then the world-wide conspiracy of communism spread it to many, many countries."

As a result of the article the Harvard Law School failed to obtain sufficient contributions toward a million-dollar endowment fund, but Julius Rosenwald, on learning the reason for this failure, partly countered it with a substantial donation. Indeed, the demand for Frankfurter's dismissal became vociferous, and was ineffective only because good sense finally prevailed. When he was asked at the time if he would resign, he replied, "Why should I resign; let Lowell resign." And such was his interest in teaching that he refused a partnership in a New York law firm at ten times his Harvard salary. What mattered most to him was his ability "to stimulate year after year, influential future lawyers of the country to an understanding of their profession as public servants merely because they were lawyers."

His reputation as a liberal was further enhanced with the publication in 1930 of *The Labor Injunction* in collaboration with Nathan Greene. For years the courts, local and federal, notoriously favored employers over labor unions. In his lectures at Yale early in 1930, Frankfurter declared that in the years between Presidents Grant and Theodore Roosevelt "the Fourteenth Amendment was made the vehicle for writing *laissez-faire* into the Constitution. . . . Members of the Supreme Court continued to reflect the social and economic order in which they grew up. They sought to

stereotype ephemeral facts into legal absolutes." In 1896
liberals had made a rallying campaign cry of "government
by injunction," a slogan coined at the time of the railway
strike led by Eugene V. Debs two years before. For more
than three decades thereafter the injunction was used
freely to thwart the demands of organized labor. State
legislatures and the Congress have from time to time sought
to limit this judicial arrogation, but their efforts were repeatedly nullified by the courts. When Judge J. H. Wilker-
son in 1922, issued his injunction in the railway shopmen's
strike, Frankfurter had written in the *New Republic*, "For
more than thirty years the injunction has been used as a
familiar weapon in American industrial conflicts. It does
not work. It neither mines coal, nor moves trains, nor makes
clothing. . . . The use of labor injunctions has, predominantly, been a cumulative influence for discord in our national life." He reacted equally caustically to Chief Justice
Taft's invalidation of Arizona's law against injunctions:
"From a reading of his opinion the historian of the future
would have to assume that the Arizona legislature withdrew injunctive relief in labor cases out of sheer malevo-
lence or in a spirit of reckless oppression."

Frankfurter's first direct contact with labor injunctions occurred in 1920 when a Rochester clothing manufacturer obtained an injunction against the Amalgamated
Clothing Workers on the charge that it was an "illegal
organization." Sidney Hillman asked Frankfurter to defend the union, which he agreed to do "because public issues are involved." He engaged Emory R. Bruckner and
Max Lowenthal to assist him and arranged for the trial to
take place during his Easter recess so that he would not
absent himself from classes. His argument at court resulted in the union's acquittal.

The Labor Injunction deals with the origin, early use,
enforcement, legislation, and issues underlying the nature
of labor injunctions. It makes clear that by the 1920s conviction had become general that the injunction, in the words

of Justice Brandeis, was usually not sought "to prevent property from being injured nor to protect the owner in its use, but to endow property with active, militant power which would make it dominant over men." It further showed that the Clayton Act was enacted after 20 years of agitation, but was in effect nullified by judges so far as the labor injunction was concerned: "The long-drawn-out battle on the national stage, to withdraw labor tactics from the risks of judicial notions concerning 'restraint of trade,' was fought and lost." It dwelt at some length on the nature of the *Hitchman* case, which permitted "yellow-dog" contracts and furthered the antiunion "American Plan," and stated: "The record of legislative ineffectiveness is the product of more than a temper of hospitality on the part of the judiciary." The final section described how the injunctive power in labor disputes might be modified by Congress and state legislatures. That this advice was not without effect was evidenced by the enactment of the Wagner-LaGuardia Anti-Injunction Act. The book was dedicated, "To Mr. Justice Brandeis. For whom law is not a system of artificial reason, but the application of ethical ideals, with freedom at the core."

Although formal religion had lost its hold on Frankfurter after he was fifteen, he continued to esteem the Jewish tradition in his family. As a student at Harvard he preferred to room with Jews, and he refused to act on the suggestion of his first employer that he change his name to one with a less Semitic connotation. His friendship with and admiration for Brandeis brought him into the Zionist movement, and after 1914 he participated in its activities as one of his mentor's lieutenants. At Versailles in February, 1919, as one of President Wilson's legal aides, he devoted much time to the Zionist cause. At the urging of Brandeis and Judge Mack he conferred with T. E. Lawrence and Prince Feisal about the Arab acceptance of a Jewish homeland in Palestine and received from Feisal a letter which expressed agreement to the Zionist proposals submitted to the Peace Conference and declared Arab amity toward the Jews:

> We feel that the Arabs and the Jews are cousins in race, having suffered similar oppression at the hands of powers stronger than themselves, and by a happy coincidence have been able to take the first step toward the attainment of their national ideals together. We Arabs, especially the educated among us, look with the deepest sympathy on the Zionist movement. . . . We will wish Jews a most hearty welcome. . . . Indeed, I think that neither can be a real success without the other.

In 1920 Frankfurter accompanied Brandeis to the Zionist conference in London. The following year, at the Zionist convention in Cleveland, he defended Brandeis's views in the face of strong opposition, and resigned from administrative activity along with the other members of his faction when the majority of the delegates favored Weizmann. Eight years later, when Jews were massacred in Palestine and Brandeis felt moved to speak out at a protest meeting, Frankfurter vainly pleaded with him not to appear publicly in behalf of the Zionist cause—believing that by this act "he will inevitably entangle himself in public and political controversy."

The British White Paper of 1930, in effect abrogating the Balfour Declaration and closing Palestine to Jewish migration, deeply disturbed Jews everywhere. At a protest meeting in Madison Square Garden Frankfurter, long an Anglophile, condemned it, declaring,

> Lord Passfield has power neither to recall the Balfour Declaration nor to abandon Great Britain's responsibility. His pronouncement on Palestine is less a statement of policy than a revelation of rooted prejudice. . . . The most charitable view to take of the ill-starred White Paper is that oblivion will be its fate. . . . And Jews must continue to proceed on the assumption that Great Britain will honor her international bond.

The following year he published in *Foreign Affairs* "The Palestine Situation Restated," a carefully documented historical evaluation of the increasingly complex problem.

> I speak not only as a Jew, but as one who believes in the wisdom of the policy embodied in the Palestinian Mandate for the establishment of a Jewish National Home in Palestine. . . . I do not wish to over-emphasize the improvement which Jewish endeavor has brought to the lot of the lowly Arab. . . . But the enduring benefits of Jewish capital, enterprise and devotion to the whole of Palestine are incontestable. Those who would lightly throttle the development of the Jewish homeland in Palestine are playing with the future well-being of Palestinian Arab as well as Jew, if indeed not of the entire Near East.

He was further critical of the White Paper because it gave the unknowing reader the impression "that the Jew's coming has been the Arab's woe"—an untruth exploited by economically powerful Arabs. And in 1938, with the Nazi terror on the increase, he had President Roosevelt urge Neville Chamberlain to keep the gates of Palestine open to Jewish refugees from Germany.

His active interest in Palestine, which he visited three times, continued until he took his seat on the Supreme Court. And although he refrained from formal participation thereafter, he exerted his influence in the Roosevelt Administration on behalf of Zionism and Jewish refugees. In 1958 he violated his self-imposed insulation from public affairs to speak at the celebration of Israel's tenth anniversary, at which he said, "I do not think I use the language of hyperbole if I say that history, democracy, and civilization are vindicated by the beginning of the second decade of Israel." It was about this time that he remarked wistfully, "I came into the world as a Jew and although I did not live my life entirely as a Jew, I think it is fitting that I should leave as a Jew." And with no son to say the *Kaddish* prayer at his death, he asked a friend who knew Hebrew to say it.

That Frankfurter continued informally to take a deep and pervasive interest in public affairs after 1938 is attested in the voluminous correspondence between him and President Roosevelt. The two had met casually in 1906. In 1917 they saw each other frequently in Washington on government business. As was usual with Frankfurter, he no sooner met anyone who impressed him favorably than he cultivated his friendship. In 1928, after Roosevelt was nominated for governor, Frankfurter wrote him, "As a Jew I am particularly happy that your nomination prevented the New York contest from degenerating into an unworthy competition for the 'Jewish vote.' Now all good and wise citizens ought to be drawn to your standard." This started a correspondence, interrupted by frequent visits, that continued to the end of Roosevelt's life. As the intimacy of their relationship increased, Frankfurter wrote whenever he felt he could be of help, offering advice and suggestions; Roosevelt responded as often as he was able. And although their relationship remained on a level of personal equality, Frankfurter, to quote Max Freedman, his sympathetic editor, was "an artist of adulation" who sometimes forgot his artistry and "laid on flattery with a trowel."

In 1930 Roosevelt wrote, "I want to talk to you of many things—water power, public utilities, New York City judges, deliberate editorial cads, and other choice subjects." When Governor Ely named Frankfurter to the highest court in Massachusetts in 1932, an office which he declined, Roosevelt wrote from his campaign train, "I wish it were for the Supreme Court of the United States—that's where you belong." Frankfurter persuaded the disgruntled Al Smith to speak in Roosevelt's behalf at a Boston meeting. He also provided issues, facts, and other material for campaign speeches. When his intimate friend Walter Lippmann persisted in criticizing Roosevelt, Frankfurter cooled considerably toward him. Appreciative of this concern in his behalf as well as of the felicitous flattery, Roosevelt wrote, "Your letters are always a joy—saying so much in so few words." On another occasion Roosevelt remarked, "Felix has more ideas per minute than any man of my acquaintance. He has a brilliant mind but it clicks so fast it makes my head fairly spin. I find him tremendously interesting and stimulating."

On assuming the Presidency, Roosevelt offered Frankfurter the office of Solicitor General, saying, "I want you down here, because I need you for all sorts of things, and in all sorts of ways." Frankfurter, with approval of both Holmes and Brandeis, begged off; he had already accepted the Eastman Professorship at Oxford and believed he could be more effective as a free agent. Roosevelt jocularly called him "an independent pig," and added, "You ought to be on the Supreme Court, and I want you to be there."

During his year in England, Frankfurter sent memoranda on various projected bills and on his return saw Roosevelt frequently. He placed some of his former students in key positions, and had a hand in many bills during the first 100 days. Most of the measures he helped formulate were later validated by the Supreme Court, the NRA and AAA, which he avoided sponsoring, were declared unconstitutional. While in England he urged Roosevelt to speak in German to the German people about Hitler's barbarism, and cited precedents for an American protest against anti-Jewish persecution in Austria. While on a visit to Palestine he wrote that "the achievements of the Jewish renaissance [are] almost incredible," and that the Nazis were inciting the Arabs against the Jews.

When Roosevelt decided to present his Court-packing plan to Congress, he exacted from Frankfurter, according to Freedman "a most solemn oath of silence" because he intended one day to put him on the Supreme Court and did not want him entangled in the controversy. Although Frankfurter had long been critical of the Court, which "for about a quarter of a century has distorted the power of judicial review into a revision of legislative policy," he remained neutral to Roosevelt's scheme. He did what he could, however, to keep him from further flagrant blunders and later edited the official version of the Court-packing controversy for *The Public Papers and Addresses of Franklin Delano Roosevelt*. His loyalty to the President caused him to feel distressed that Brandeis let his name be used against the bill, and he was angry with Governor Herbert Lehman for opposing it.

During the 1930s Frankfurter frequently implored Roosevelt to help particular Jews of Central Europe— among them Sigmund Freud and Otto Loewe, the Nobel Prize biologist. Yet he refrained from asking him to secure the release of his uncle, the prominent Vienna librarian, and turned instead to Lady Nancy Astor. He did talk to Roosevelt about Weizmann's views on Palestine, and wrote him all told around 300 notes on the increasingly tragic situation in Europe. Secretary Harold Ickes, less affected, commented at the time that Frankfurter was "really not rational these days on the European situation."

When Justice Benjamin Cardozo died in the summer of 1938, friends of Frankfurter considered him the logical successor to the "Scholar's Seat." Generally known as libertarian, he was particularly favored by New Deal liberals, and a Gallup poll among the nation's lawyers gave him a 5–1 lead over the next likely candidate. Ickes told Roosevelt that Frankfurter "was a legal statesman who stood head and shoulders above every other possible appointee" and that "his ability and learning are such that he will dominate the Supreme Court for fifteen or twenty years to come. The result will be that, probably after you are dead, it will still be your Supreme Court."

Several conservatives in the Senate questioned the nomination and certain wealthy Jews feared that the appointment would increase anti-Jewish feeling in the nation. At first Roosevelt himself hesitated because he thought he should appoint a Westerner, but he was pleased to see the wide sentiment in favor of his friend. On January 4, 1939, he telephoned him that he was sending his name to the Senate. Deeply stirred, Frankfurter responded impulsively, "All I can say is that I wish my mother were alive."

At the Senate hearings he was interrogated especially closely by Senator Pat McCarran on his relation to Harold Laski and communism. "Senator," Frankfurter told him, "I do not believe you have ever taken an oath to support the Constitution of the United States with fewer reservations than I have or would now, nor do I believe you are more attached to the theories and practices of Americanism than I am. I rest my answer on that statement." The audience cheered, and he was afterward confirmed by a unanimous vote.

The friendship between Frankfurter and Roosevelt continued unchanged. Although he had long maintained that a justice of the Supreme Court should keep aloof from political affairs, Frankfurter did not hesitate to advise Roosevelt as often as he was requested, and not infrequently on his own inititative. In 1940 he recommended his old friend Stimson as Secretary of War. When Hitler's armies invaded Russia he exhorted Roosevelt to give Russia all the assistance he could. He also kept him informed on Jewish affairs and suggested speeches to enhance morale. Twenty years later, two days before his own death, he said to Max Freedman, his editor and biographer, "Tell the whole story, let the people see how much I loved Roosevelt, how much I loved my country, and let them see how great a man Roosevelt really was."

For nearly forty years, Frankfurter had steeped himself in the study of the Supreme Court; he not only knew every aspect of its history but also had definite views on its functions and limitations. Following Holmes and Brandeis, he was long critical of the Court for its lack of judicial self-restraint. In an early essay he wrote,

> The veto power of the Supreme Court over the social-economic legislation of the States, thus exercised through the due process clause, is the most vulnerable aspect of undue centralization. It is at once the most destructive

and the least responsive: the most destructive because
judicial nullification on grounds of constitutionality stops
experimentation at its source, and bars increase to the
fund of social knowledge by scientific tests of trial and
error.

By the time he came on the Court in 1939, the political complexion of the majority had changed. As an exponent of judicial self-restraint he aimed to turn the Holmes
and Brandeis liberal dissents against earlier conservatism
into majority rulings, unmindful of the fact that some of
the Justices were inclined to go even further in a liberal
direction. And when the war began, its danger to the United
States affected the attitudes of the Justices, and Frankfurter most of all.

At the time of the *Gobitis* case, pertaining to children
of Jehovah's Witnesses refusing to salute the flag, Germany
had just invaded France and the world outlook was bleak
indeed. Frankfurter considered saluting the flag an appro-
priate means "to evoke that unifying sentiment without
which there can ultimately be no liberties, civil or religious."
He therefore maintained that school boards had the right
to instill patriotism in children by means of the flag salute.
Other justices, equally perturbed by events in Europe,
yielded to his argument, with only Chief Justice Harlan
Stone dissenting. On its face Frankfurter's reasoning
seemed clear and persuasive.

> The ultimate foundation of a free society is the binding
> tie of cohesive sentiment. Such a sentiment is fostered by
> all these agencies of the mind and spirit which may serve
> to gather up the tradition of a people, transmit them from
> generation to generation, and thereby create that continu-
> ity of a treasured life which constitutes a civilization. "We
> live by symbols."

Stone's dissent was unusually sharp, insisting that the
validated law coerced children to express a sentiment which

violated their religious beliefs. He pointed out "that there have been few infringements of personal liberty by the state which have not been justified, as they are here, in the name of righteousness and the public good, and few which have not been directed, as they are now, at politically helpless minorities." To this he was unequivocally opposed.

> The guaranties of civil liberty are but guaranties of freedom of the human mind and spirit and of reasonable freedom and opportunity to express them. . . . If these guaranties are to have any meaning they must, I think, be deemed to withhold from the state any authority to compel belief or the expression of it where that expression violates religious convictions, whatever may be the legislative view of the desirability of such conviction.

News of Frankfurter's majority ruling shocked many liberals. Like Stone, they generally believed that patriotism and national security were independent of the flag symbol. Nor were they impressed with the fact that while Frankfurter personally sympathized with the children, he considered it his duty to uphold the constitutional right of the legislative arm of government to act as it did.

The agitation against the ruling had its effect. Two years later, Justices Hugo L. Black, William O. Douglas, and Frank Murphy not only joined Chief Justice Stone in a dissent in *Jones* v. *Opelika*, but recanted their *Gobitis* vote by proclaiming their error and admitting that "our democratic form of government, functioning under the historic Bill of Rights, has a high responsibility to accommodate itself to religious views of minorities, however unpopular and unorthodox these views may be."

The following year a majority reversed the *Gobitis* ruling in the *Barnette* case, in which Justice Robert H. Jackson held that the local authorities had exceeded their constitutional powers in compelling the flag salute and pledge. Declaring that the "fundamental rights" are not subject to a vote and do not "depend on the outcome of elections," he continued with rare verbal felicity,

If there is any fixed star in our constitutional constel-
lation, it is that no official, high or petty, can prescribe
what shall be orthodox in politics, nationalism, religion or
other matters of opinion, or force citizens to confess by
word or act their faith therein. If there are any circumstances which permit an exception, they do not now occur
to us.

This rebuff by his fellow Justices deeply perturbed
Frankfurter. The personal rebuke apart, he was concerned
not so much for the assertion of legislative authority as for
its breakdown in a time of peril. He feared that judicial
nullification of laws "serves to prevent the full play of the
democratic process," and maintained that judges "should
be very diffident in setting their judgment against that of a
state." Smarting from the hurt to his ego, he rejected the
plea of his colleagues to keep the personal note out of his
dissent.

One who belongs to the most vilified and persecuted
minority in history is not likely to be insensitive to the
freedoms guaranteed by our Constitution. Were my purely
personal attitude relevant, I should wholeheartedly associate myself with the general libertarian views of the
Court's opinion, representing as they do the thought and
action of a lifetime. But as Judges we are neither Jew nor
Gentile, neither Catholic nor agnostic. We owe equal
attachment to the Constitution and are equally bound by
our judicial obligations, whether we derive our citizenship
from the earliest or the latest immigrants to these shores.

In this and similar cases he objected to the mechanical
application of the "clear-and-present danger" formula, the
majority holding that where no imminent danger existed,
the constitutional freedoms must remain inviolate. Taking a
pragmatic view of these freedoms, however, he maintained
that since legislatures were elected by the people, "the
Court's only and very narrow function is to determine
whether within the broad grant of authority vested in legis-

latures they have exercised a judgment for which reasonable justification can be offered." Thus, while he joined the majority in the *Everson* and *McCullum* rulings, which restricted school boards, he continued to be concerned about the possible breakdown of legislative authority.

His constitutional pragmatism also governed his position in labor cases. Long an expert in the subject and a warm sympathizer with the legitimate aims of unions, he nevertheless voted about as often against them as in their favor, his decision depending on the kind of restriction involved and its importance to the community. Thus he approved the loyalty oath in the Taft-Hartley Act and voted against political contributions by unions and against picketing that endangered civic peace. Society, he held, can require competing groups to yield to the public good. He took the position that the Court could not keep legislatures from acting against the union shop, but he also maintained that corporations must respect the rights of the public. In general, he was averse to the Court taking up cases of employee compensation for injuries, stating, "My duty is not to concern myself with a stupid cook who uses a butcher knife to take out ice cream"—the scoop having failed to function.

In holding that the Court should not only exercise self-restraint but also concern itself with law and not with justice—"after all, this is the Nation's ultimate judicial tribunal, not a super-legal-aid bureau"—he ran counter to Justices Black and Douglas, who were equally insistent that the Court must deal with both law and justice. Again, in his strictures against "the tendency to disregard precedents," he tended to cling to precedent for its own sake. Professor Wallace Mendelson wrote, "The Justice's position simply is that the long-settled judicial construction of a statute, and established doctrines which have grown up around a statute, are part of the statute itself. Alteration then is a matter for the legislature."

Frankfurter and Black differed most on matters pertaining to the Bill of Rights and the Fourteenth Amendment. While Black interpreted the freedoms of the First

Amendment as absolute in intent, Frankfurter evaluated them pragmatically. In his *Bridges* dissent, for instance, he declared, "Free speech is not so absolute or irrational a conception as to imply paralysis of the means for effective protection of all freedoms secured by the Bill of Rights." Black, on his part, held that "the unqualified prohibitions laid down by the framers were intended to give to liberty of the press, as to other liberties, the broadest scope that could be countenanced in our orderly society." Both men relied on historical data to substantiate their views of the aims of the Fourteenth Amendment, due process, and incorporation; but while Black tied the first eight Amendments to them, Frankfurter saw no validity in this view: "The Fourteenth Amendment placed no specific restrictions upon the administration of their criminal law by the States."

With the Court constituted as it was in the postwar years, Frankfurter found himself frequently at odds with the majority in cases where there was a conflict between freedom of utterance and the power of the lower courts to punish out-of-court contempts. In *Bridges* and *Times Mirror*, for instance, he accused the majority of, in effect, permitting trial by newspaper. In *Feiner* he joined a more conservative majority because of his respect for the New York court of appeals, which he considered sensitive to civil liberty. In an opinion curbing picketing he held that even when peaceful it was not speech in "its obvious and accepted sense," since it exerted economic pressure.

Frankfurter had difficulty with cases arising from violations of the Smith Act, which he regarded as unwise but constitutional. In the *Dennis* case, which Professor Rodell criticized as "the biggest blot on the Vinson-Court's blot-marked ledgers," he voted with the conservative majority but wrote, "The liberty of man to search for truth ought not to be fettered, no matter what orthodoxies he may challenge. Liberty of thought soon shrivels without freedom of expression. Nor can truth be preserved in an atmosphere hostile to the endeavor or under dangers which are hazarded only to heroes." Yet he had no tolerance for active

Communists, and therefore added that "not every type of speech occupies the same position on the scale of values"; consequently "the interest in protecting speech depends on the circumstances of the occasion." Resorting to his belief in judicial self-restraint, he argued that it was for Congress and not the Court to reconcile the conflicts between freedom and security, that while communism was an external problem, it was not unrelated to its internal aspects.

In the *Sweezy* case it was easier for him to concur with the liberal majority that the powers given to the New Hampshire attorney general were too broad and undefined to relate to state security. Yet he maintained that Chief Justice Earl Warren did not meet the real issue—the claim of the state court that violation of academic freedom was necessary to preserve the government: "Where weighed against the grave harm resulting from governmental intrusion into the intellectual life of a university, such justification for compelling a witness to discuss the contents of his lecture appears grossly inadequate"—especially since the witness had expressly denied advocating the overthrow of the government. He further held that the questions asked Sweezy violated his political freedom. "In the political realm, as in the academic, thought and action are presumptively immune from inquisition by political authority."

In these and other loyalty-security cases he occupied a mildly middle position on the Court, advocating moderation and restraint. He consistently opposed searches and seizures by law-enforcement officers without warrants. He did not, however, believe that the privileges of the Fifth Amendment are unlimited, pointing out that where "the reason for the privilege ceases, the privilege ceases." Nor did he accept the "preferred-position" concept of certain freedoms, stating in the *Ullmann* case that "as no constitutional guarantee enjoys preference so none should suffer subordination or deletion." Yet he did join the liberal minority in a number of alien cases, and his dissent from the

Medina ruling, including a 47-page appendix, was one of his finest judicial opinions.

In *Adamson* he disagreed sharply with Justice Black in the interpretation of the Fourteenth Amendment. Both men claimed to be guided by history yet each used it to bolster his particular preferences. Frankfurter declared that the due-process clause was not "shorthand for the first eight Amendments; that it represented "a living principle . . . that which comports with the deepest notions of what is fair and right and just." Because his approach was empirical, it varied from time to time, but his goal remained constant—the vitality of popular consensus. Like Holmes, he rejected all absolutes and held that the life of law was experience. The security of freedom, he affirmed, ultimately depends on the sentiments and ingrained habits of the people, which come from experience through the painful process of trial and error. Consequently he insisted that judges contribute most when they essay little. Not a few legal scholars were sharply critical of this attitude of restraint. During his last years on the Court, his views lost their influence with his brothers in the Warren-controlled liberal holdings.

In his twenty-three years on the Court, Frankfurter early established himself as one of its most eminent members. Professor A. M. Bickel, one of his former law clerks, expressed a fairly common judgment: "His voice will be heard, and he will influence political thought so long as there is a Supreme Court and so long as men are concerned to make their actions fit American constitutional tradition." The Supreme Court was in truth one of his chief studies. He knew its history and its functions as few men have known it. From early youth a warm libertarian, he instilled in the inner debates of the Court, armed with the ideas and ideals of Holmes and Brandeis, a lofty appreciation of self-restraint which gave pause to tendencies at either extreme. It was ironical that his libertarianism, formed during the Progressive era of an earlier time, should have appeared outdated and conservative against the New Deal liberalism of some of his fellow justices, so that his great scholarship and passion for law were overshadowed by his emphasis on self-restraint.

In 1962, having passed his eightieth birthday, illness forced his retirement from the Court. In a letter of appreciative farewell, signed by all the justices, they wrote,

> Few men in the life of the Supreme Court have made contributions to its jurisprudence equal to your own. As a scholar, teacher, critic, public servant, and a member of the Court for 24 Terms, you have woven your philosophy of law and your conception of our intitutions into its annals where all men may read them and profit thereby.

In July, 1963 Frankfurter was awarded the coveted Medal of Freedom. A month later he was presented with the American Bar Association's Gold Medal "for conspicuous service to the cause of American jurisprudence."

Death came to him on February 22, 1965.

THE UNIONIZATION OF CLOTHING WORKERS

Very few East-European Jews migrated to the United States before 1880. Ruthlessly oppressed and harassed for generations by the Czarist government, and only somewhat less by the governments of adjacent lands, crowded into towns of the Pale of Settlement and greatly limited as to their means of livelihood, most of them clung to their medievally pious way of life with a fatalistic tenacity which kept them intact as a religious and ethnic group, but which long retarded their entry into the modern world. Although a few managed to acquire the education of nineteenth-century "enlightenment," they exerted little influence upon their superstition-fettered fellow Jews until harsh oppression began to drive them into the cities and eventually far from their native lands.

What the intellectual reformer failed to achieve by agitation and preachment, the pogroms of 1881 accomplished by brutality. These government-sanctioned massacres shocked many thousands of Jews out of their complacency and started them toward Western Europe and the United States, which they knew only vaguely as a land of freedom and opportunity. At first a few, but gradually more and more made the arduous journey to New York's East Side. The change from the medievally oriented *shtetl* to the seething modernity of American cities was drastic. Confused, penniless, friendless, ignorant of the language of the land and the mores of the Gentile world, they feared for the opportunity to practice their rituals and for their very existence as Jews. In desperate need and unfitted for hard physical labor, most of them gratefully accepted the offer of employment from Jewish garment manufacturers. Those who were not already skilled tailors were taught the simple tasks within a week or two.

The clothing industry in the United States, as indicated

313

earlier, had developed rapidly after the Civil War. Manufacturers and sub-contractors—ambitious workers without capital who contracted to sew garments from cloth provided by manufacturers—took eager advantage of the increased market, their need for additional workers opportunely filled by the newcomers. These immigrants, loath to venture far from their tenements, gladly accepted work from the sub-manufacturers, Jews who spoke their language and observed the same religious practices. The arrangement was also favorable to the established manufacturers, since it minimized their responsibility for the seasonal factor with its busy periods followed by months of slackness.

The sub-contractors' "factories" were usually converted tenement dwellings; sewing machines were rented or bought on time payments; the kitchen stove was used to heat the pressing irons, and the dining table served as a workbench. In these sweatshops a half dozen or more immigrants were hired to sew the cut cloth into garments. Facing fierce competition, the sub-contractors were often forced to accept prices only slightly above actual cost; in turn they "sweated" their workers to the limit of their physical endurance. A factory inspector reported in 1888, "They usually eat and sleep in the same room where the work is carried on, and the dinginess, squalor and filth surrounding them is abominable." Morris Hillquit, who worked in a sweatshop while studying law evenings and later achieved distinction as a lawyer and Socialist leader, wrote in his reminiscences,

> Mercilessly exploited by their employers and despised by their American fellow workers as wage-cutters, they completely lacked self-assertiveness and the power of resistance. They were weak from overwork and malnutrition, tired and listless, meek and submissive. Tuberculosis, the dread white plague of the tenements, was rife among them.

Yet it was these exploited drudges and their children who in a generation formed the membership of the most successful and enlightened of labor unions—prodded, cajoled, and stimulated by idealistic and dedicated radical leaders.

For along with the many thousands of religiously oriented Jews came scores of emancipated young men and women. They had freed themselves from religious restraints, devoted themselves to secular study, espoused the ideal of social progress—only to be forced to flee from threatened imprisonment. They followed the flow of migration to the United States. Coming to New York without funds or professional training, they were quickly sucked into the maw of the sweatshop. Deeply resentful of their cruel exploitation and spurred by their radical ideals, they formed groups to agitate against this inhuman subjection. Regardless of their political differences—among them were Marxists, anarchists, and social utopians—they jointly appealed to their fellow workers to strike for higher wages and improved working conditions. In their Yiddish newspapers and on dingy platforms, they denounced sweatshop slavery and hailed the glorious possibilities of unionization.

The response was slow and sporadic. The overworked and underpaid clothing employees hugged their skimpy fleshpots with natural timidity. Even when the extremity of their condition forced them to strike for better wages, they let their union memberships usually lapse after their return to work; it took years of persistent agitation to persuade them that the strength of a labor organization depended on the permanence of its membership. This was even true of the more enterprising workers who found jobs in the shops and factories of the larger manufacturers. Thus, although unions in the needle trades began to be formed as early as 1883, they fell apart at the end of each strike and had to be rebuilt anew for the next assault upon employers, with the result that exploitation and strikes were endemic in the clothing industry for many years.

Gradually, however, union organizers became more effective as the partly Americanized workers came to appreciate the values of unionization. The several unions, each limited to a segment of the industry, formed and reformed periodically, gaining strength slowly and unsteadily. In 1910 and later they conducted prolonged and severely taxing strikes, and one after another in time established itself on a solid footing and began to function as an effective and progressive labor organization.

Among their leaders were such men as Joseph Barondess, Benjamin Schlesinger, Morris Sigman, and David Dubinsky in the International Ladies Garment Workers Union, and Sidney Hillman, Joseph Schlossberg, Hyman Blumberg, and Jacob Potofsky in the Amalgamated Clothing Workers Union.

Although most Jews of East-European origin began life in America within the confines of the sweatshop, a good many soon spread out over the continent. Some yearned to make their home on the land and joined communal farms in upstate New York, Connecticut, New Jersey, and as far west as Oregon. Even more found their way to towns and cities west of New York, becoming peddlers, businessmen, and workers in local industries. Everywhere they worked hard, lived frugally, and strove to give their children the best available education. Frequently they met with prejudice and even hostility, and certain doors were closed to them, but they persisted despite these handicaps.

The pogroms in 1903–1905 in Russia and the oppression in Rumania greatly multiplied the number of Jews who migrated from Eastern Europe, and more than a million entered the United States during the following decade. Many of them were more sophisticated than the earlier immigrants, and many went directly to relatives who had settled in various parts of the country. Although they had to undergo much of the ordeal of orientation and acculturation of the earlier newcomers, they more readily adapted themselves to Americanization and manifested an energy and enterprise that in time brought them into the very center of the American economy. Some of their children and grandchildren, educated at great cost and effort, possessed an intellectual alertness and competence which further advanced them economically; not a few, having amassed millions, contributed as generously to philanthropy as did the wealthy German-American Jews. While some of them became executives in large corporations and financial houses, others achieved distinction in the theater, in letters, in music, and in the arts. As professor Allan Nevins has said, "The huge population of East-European Jews was to prove one of the most fertile seedbeds of talent the country has known. From it were to spring many of the best poets, novelists, critics, musicians, architects, painters, and scholars of the twentieth century."

Although East-European Jews have won renown in medicine, law, science, and politics, among them several Nobel Prize winners, on balance the one who best personifies their ideals and individual achievement is perhaps Sidney Hillman.

14
Sidney
Hillman

LABOR
STATESMAN

SIDNEY HILLMAN was born in Lithuania in 1887, the son of a pious merchant and the grandson of rabbis. He received a typical Orthodox education, and at the age of thirteen was sent to Kovno to prepare for the rabbinate. By the time he was fifteen, however, he had become attracted to secular study and walked five miles for a free lesson in Russian. When his father learned of his impiety and threatened to stop his small allowance, the young rebel continued his general studies and managed to keep from starving by working in a chemical laboratory.

In his sixteenth year he joined the Jewish Socialist *Bund* and became active in the local revolutionary movement. Twice he was arrested by the Russian police and imprisoned, first for six months and then for four. In 1906, to avoid further harassment, he left for Manchester, England, where an uncle had established himself in business, but he was not happy in the bourgeois atmosphere, and a year later sailed for New York. Soon after his arrival he went to Chicago at the invitation of a boyhood friend.

For a year and a half he worked as a stock clerk at Sears, Roebuck and Company at a salary of eight dollars a week. In his free time he continued his informal education, reading widely in economics and history. When he was laid off for lack of work, he apprenticed himself as a cutter in one of the suit factories operated by Hart, Schaffner and Marx. When a strike was called in September, 1910, by the newly organized clothing workers of Chicago—provoked by harsh conditions and inspired by the successful outcome of strikes in New York—Hillman left his cutting table along with his fellow-workers.

The strike began without previous preparation or funds to carry it through. News that a few girls had walked out spread through the city's clothing factories with gathering force, driving the workers into the streets, until before long representatives of the 40,000 immigrant workers were picketing factories without organized leadership and in the face of police brutality. When, several weeks later, Thomas Rickert, president of the United Garment Workers, the only existing union in the men's clothing industry, came to Chicago to take charge of the strike and accept an agreement from Hart, Schaffner and Marx, the embattled strikers who by then had developed their own leaders angrily rejected the settlement and held out for better terms. By now they were aided actively by the sympathetic Chicago Federation of Labor and a group of social workers and civic leaders. For sixteen weeks the strikers stayed out despite acute hardship, but in February hunger and cold finally drove them back to the factories. Although defeated, they were not completely beaten, as they felt themselves welded into an active union with an able and aggressive leadership. Moreover, those working for Hart, Schaffner and Marx, the largest of the clothing firms, had gained a relatively satisfactory agreement.

In this settlement two men came to the fore: Joseph

Schaffner and Sidney Hillman. Schaffner, the head of the large company, was a man of enterprise, the first clothing manufacturer to advertise nationally and to make his garments from pure wool and in fast colors. By the 1900's his firm was the country's largest producer of men's clothing, with fourteen basic types of garments in 253 different sizes, shapes, styles, and models. Schaffner was a man of wealth and good will, a ready participant in the philanthropy traditionally incumbent upon Jews of means.

Schaffner had little contact with production and labor conditions in his factories, and no notion of the exploited state of his employees until the strike brought their plight to his attention. His resolve to improve their condition was reenforced by the knowledge that in New York Louis D. Brandeis and Louis Marshall, men he admired, had helped settle the cloakmakers strike by establishing the Protocol of Peace and the preferential union shop. In conferring with their representatives, he found the youthful Hillman most congenial.

In the early stages of the strike the cutters had made Hillman their delegate to the strike committee. His sense of justice had long been exacerbated by working conditions that grievously contravened the American promise of freedom and equity he had read about. Moreover, he had not studied Marx's *Capital* and other socialist works in vain. Eager to do for his fellow workers what his grandfathers had done for the poor in their communities, he gave all his time and thought to furthering the success of the strike. On a later occasion he explained his attitude at the time. "The rabbis in our family were not outstanding, but the rank-and-file kind that are called upon more to help than to lead. Concern in the everyday problems of working people was their job; so I took it for granted it had to be mine."

The strike committee began to lean on Hillman for guidance and stimulation. His clear reasoning, quick intelligence, and deep sympathy impressed all who had dealings with him—Hull House social workers and labor officials, as well as strikers. When Rickert sought to force an unfavorable settlement upon the strikers, Hillman argued against it in his maiden public address. When William D. Haywood of the I. W. W. tried to enlist the strikers in his organization, Hillman perceived the futility of the move and frustrated it. But when Schaffner agreed to install arbitration machinery in his factories without recognizing the union, Hillman urged acceptance because he was persuaded that Schaffner was an honest man and that his terms were the best the strikers could obtain at the time, for he believed that "a constructive labor attitude must be in terms of the achievable."

Schaffner was sincere in his effort to democratize his factories. The board of arbitration received his full support and acted to improve sanitary conditions, provide equal division of work during slack seasons, grant wage increases, establish the fifty-four-hour workweek, and resolve obvious grievances. Clarence Darrow, the eminent lawyer, represented the workers on the board, and his devotion and cooperation served to generate good will among the participants. A labor complaint department was established, headed by Professor Earl Dean Warren to facilitate the removal of causes of dissatisfaction among employees.

Hillman contributed greatly to the smooth and satisfactory functioning of the arbitration machinery. He never hesitated to accept responsibility; he never demanded more than he knew the firm could afford to grant; and he always insisted that the workers abide by the decisions of the arbitrators. Schaffner was impressed with Hillman's tact and gift for friendship, and, in 1914, told the federal Commission on Industrial Relations of his "wonderful influence over all people who came in contact with him on account of his high ideals, his patience under trying circumstances, and his indomitable faith in the triumph of the right methods."

Conditions in other men's clothing factories over the country remained on the sweatshop level. Sporadic strikes failed to achieve any permanent benefits, nor did the officers of the United Garment Workers make any serious effort to improve conditions. In 1912 when the New York workers struck the factories, public sentiment favored them, and a number of manufacturers settled with the union. Then Rickert, as previously in Chicago, disregarded the strike committee and placated the more obstinate employers by arranging for less favorable terms. The strikers rejected the agreement and continued the strike in defiance of the national officers. The terms they subsequently settled on were better than those accepted by Rickert but not so favorable as those of the earlier settlement.

When union members in New York and other cities, incensed at Rickert's behavior, sought to vote him out of office at the next convention, Rickert handicapped the insurgent locals by choosing Nashville for the 1914 convention. Ignoring petitions for a more central location, he also billed dissident locals for dues amounting to $75,000, with notification that their delegates would not be seated unless payment was made promptly. As a result, 105 delegates, representing a majority of the membership, were refused admission to the convention floor. When the protest of the seated Chicago delegates was ignored, they joined the excluded representatives and held their own "regular" convention. Although Hillman had eight months earlier joined the New York cloakmakers union as chief clerk, his admirers knew of his interest in the men's clothing workers and elected him president of the seceding union, with Joseph Schlossberg, New York leader, as secretary-treasurer. Hillman at first hesitated to accept in view of his commitment to his New York post, but his friends were insistent and he yielded.

The new organization was at once attacked by established labor leaders as a usurping dual union. Samuel Gompers, president of the American Federation of Labor, supported Rickert and rejected the appeal of the dissident union for a charter. Hillman and his associates, confronted with the dilemma of either submitting or functioning without the approval of organized labor, took the more risky course and called for a founding convention in New York on December 26, 1914. In issuing the call for the meeting they asserted that their aim was to

> establish such organic laws as will insure to the membership a determining voice in the affairs of the organization. . . . In short the laws and institutions of our organization must be so changed as to permit of the freest and fullest expression of the truly progressive spirit of our membership, and enable it to march unfettered abreast of the Modern Labor Movement.

The officers were re-elected and the organization was named The Amalgamated Clothing Workers of America.

Definitely radical in principle, with Schlossberg a prominent member of the Socialist Labor party and with many others affiliated with the Socialist party, the new union became similar in aim and action to the International Ladies Garment Workers Union. Led by young and exceptionally able officers, the Amalgamated faced not only the antagonism of the conservative leaders of the original United Garment Workers union, but also the opposition of the American Federation of Labor.

The dissident union was forced to handle its first strike before it was formally organized. On October 14, while the rebellious delegates were still in Nashville, a large Baltimore manufacturer locked out his 3,000 employees. Hillman went there and succeeded in arranging a settlement satisfactory to both sides. This minor victory put heart into the organizational efforts of the fledgling leaders. Not long after, in January, 1915, the New York manufacturers locked out their employees, hoping to benefit from the new union's presumed weakness. Without strike funds and betrayed by the Rickert union, The Amalgamated managed to hold fast against severe odds for more than a month, when the employers conceded defeat. The next July, however, they provoked another strike. This time the union was better prepared, and the members left the factories with martial discipline. A week later the manufacturers, fearful of losing the approaching "season," agreed to settle on terms favorable to their employees.

Back in Chicago, Hillman found all employers except Schaffner bitterly antiunion. Together with his associates he worked hard and effectively to increase the union's membership, and by the end of the summer all was in readiness for a strike. When the manufacturers refused to accede to the workers' demands, Hillman struck their plants. The two employers' associations, abetted by police, fought back with unrestrained violence. Two strikers were killed and hundreds were beaten and arrested. John K. Williams, chairman of the arbitration board, stated at the time, "The thing that burned into Hillman's soul and made him a hundred years older was the killing and the slugging. Each murder sent him to bed for a couple of days; his overwrought nerves could not stand it." When he realized that complete victory was unattainable he sought a settlement that gave the workers enough recognition gradually to break down their employers' antiunion policy. The following spring Hart, Schaffner and Marx renewed their agreement with the union, and Williams reported that, "Five years of power, instead of making the union arrogant, has only given it a sense of restraint and responsibility. It has proved that, guided by honest and intelligent leaders, the workers may be trusted with power, that industrial democracy is not a dream, but a potential reality."

When the Amalgamated met for its first biennial convention in May, 1916, it had a membership of 48,000 in 93 locals. Hillman declared, "Success does not come merely by wishing for it. It comes through fighting for it and it necessarily follows that we must be prepared to fight hard when we do fight." This attitude he maintained throughout his years of leadership: one victory became a stepping stone to the next, and no defeat was more than a temporary deterrent.

American participation in World War I greatly strengthened the Amalgamated. The acute need for millions of uniforms tempted many manufacturers to resume the sweatshop system. Hillman aggressively opposed this undercutting of union conditions, cautioning the War Department that uniforms made under unsanitary auspices would endanger the health of soldiers wearing them. Secretary Newton D. Baker cooperated with the union in enforcing sanitary and other working conditions, thereby furthering the unionization of factories.

At the conclusion of the war Hillman began to campaign for the forty-four-hour workweek. When this was met by a lockout in New York, the union fought back with all available resources, and this time the strikers were so well disciplined that the employers soon agreed to arbitration. Felix Frankfurter as chairman of the War Labor Policies Board served with Louis Marshall and Professor W. Z. Ripley as arbitrators and awarded the workers the forty-four-hour workweek and an increase in wages. Thus the Amalgamated was the first industrial union to achieve a reduced workweek.

Hillman now attempted once more to unionize all the men's clothing factories in Chicago. Working carefully and shrewdly, he struck factory after factory. The employers again resorted to every possible weapon to break the strike, but their workers held fast. By May, 1919 the manufacturers acknowledged defeat by recognizing the union and granting its major demands. Unionization in Rochester, the third largest men's clothing center, was achieved in due course. Manufacturers in most other cities, no longer able to resist union pressure and ready to follow the lead of their powerful competitors, likewise cooperated with the Amalgamated. Thus by the end of 1919 more than three quarters of the employees in the men's clothing industry were unionized, adding up to 177,000 members. That year Hillman employed Dr. Leo Wolman, a professional economist, to head the union's research department—the first of its kind in American organized labor.

The economic depression of 1920-1922 brought considerable unemployment in the needle trades. At the 1920 convention Hillman postulated the idea that unemployment was as much the responsibility of industry as were the upkeep of machinery and industrial accidents. The employers, however, used the excuse of bad business conditions to campaign for the "open shop," and in December, 1920 a number of them in several cities locked out their workers. Fully 50,000 tailors in New York alone began to fight for the life of their union. Hillman raised a large strike fund, accumulating nearly two million dollars before the strike ended, and used it effectively. Some of the employers obtained injunctions against the union and sued it for damages. The antiradical Lusk Committee in New York denounced Hillman and his associates as Bolshevik sympathizers and anti-American. For six months the strikers remained steadfast in the face of assaults and suffering until the employers capitulated, agreeing to substantial benefits and control of industrial relations by an impartial chairman. Workers in other cities did not fare so well, but the Amalgamated yielded ground only where unavoidable without lessening either its strength or its prestige.

Once economic conditions improved, Hillman resumed his aggressive activity. In Chicago he projected the problem of unemployment insurance, and an agreement was reached to start an unemployment fund to which both employers and union members would contribute one-and-a-half percent of the total wages. Five years later, employers agreed to double their contribution. Thus workers in Chicago began to receive modest unemployment stipends to tide them over slack periods, until the fund was exhausted during the depression in the 1930s. In 1928 similar plans were started in New York and Rochester.

During the 1920s the Amalgamated launched several social and cultural services for its members. Pamphlets on a variety of subjects were written by competent scholars for workers interested in self-education; lectures were held in public forums. In 1922 the union opened a bank in Chicago, and a year later another in New York, and both specialized in small loans at reasonable interest. The soundness of their various operations kept them solvent during the 1932 bank crisis. In 1926 the Amalgamated began to build cooperative housing, making it possible for hundreds of workers' families to live in comfortable apartments at relatively low cost. In 1928 The Harmon Foundation awarded Hillman a gold medal and $1,000 for "outstanding public service" for his fight for unemployment insurance, labor banking, and cooperative housing.

Hillman was deeply moved by the suffering he saw on a visit to the Soviet Union in 1922. On his return he advocated public assistance to the Russian people and urged the Amalgamated to sponsor the establishment of clothing factories in Russia. A Russian-American Industrial Corporation was formed, capitalized at a million dollars and operated by Amalgamated experts. For several years the corporation functioned successfully under NEP guidelines, but it was dissolved, without financial loss, when the Russian government initiated a change of policy.

Paradoxically, while the Amalgamated was trying to help the Russian people economically, it was attacked by the American Communists for its "class collaboration" because it opposed their party in the 1924 political campaign. Hillman insisted that the union "exists to benefit members by dealing with employers" and was in no position to seek the abolition of the capitalist system. Although for several years the fight with Communist officers of several locals was severe enough to handicap the proper functioning of the union, in time Hillman succeeded in ridding it of disruptive elements.

Meantime Hillman and his associates were chiefly devoted to achieving the full unionization of the men's clothing industry and organizers systematically sought to unionize shops in every part of the country. Firms that refused to deal with the union were fought until they capitulated or went out of business, but the union collaborated with friendly employers to their mutual advantage. Thus it lent $100,000 to an Indianapolis firm in financial difficulties.

For years "Golden Rule" Arthur Nash, the Cincinnati clothing manufacturer, had kept the union out by giving his employees satisfactory benefits, but when he began to be hurt by aggressive competitors, he found it to his advantage to cooperate with the Amalgamated, stating, "I had a job that I could not do, and I just passed the buck to Mr. Hillman. I felt that Mr. Hillman and his organization could do it; and that is why I used him."

The Amalgamated was one of the first unions to use industrial efficiency methods. Cooperative employers, many of them too small to engage their own research technicians, were given the advantage of the union's engineering skill. Union members of course benefited from the successful operation of these manufacturers.

By 1929 only the Philadelphia clothing companies held out against the union, and the city had become known as "the graveyard of the Amalgamated." Strike after strike was defeated by a combination of determined employers, aggressive police, and compliant judges. Now Hillman prepared for the assault with special care. When a particular factory was fully organized, he called the workers out on strike, utilizing all the resources of the union. In this manner most of the smaller firms were forced to capitulate. The large ones fought back with a drastic injunction. Fortunately for the union, the nature of the action came to the attention of Senator Robert M. LaFollette, Jr., and his resolution to investigate the judiciary nullified its effectiveness. Hillman managed to persuade some of the large customers of the struck manufacturers to speak for the union. Anxious to retain their good will, one employer after another settled with the union.

Hillman's successful drive to democratize the men's clothing industry and his initiation of an effective, if necessarily limited, plan to cushion the shock of unemployment had widened his social horizon. In the late 1920s, when the emerging great depression called for constructive thought, Hillman spoke out with a wisdom and realism that brought him to the forefront of eminent Americans. He began to assert the right of all workers to certain benefits and protection. He maintained that if a union was to serve its members effectively it must be able "to share in the responsibilities of management and to participate in the administration of industry."

In the early 1930s, with American business paralyzed and unemployment catastrophic, Hillman was among the few public leaders to present a positive labor program. In an article in the *Atlantic Monthly* he argued for the acceptance of "collective bargaining as a definite and unquestioned element of industrial economics as well as a condition of decent human relations." It was his view that failure to take the welfare of the workers into account was in large part responsible for the depression, and that the government must enact laws to speed economic readjustment. At the 1931 hearings of the Senate Committee on Manufactures he advocated the establishment of a National Economic Planning Council, maintaining that American industry had to plan ahead to avoid economic pitfalls and to make the most of its opportunities.

The Hoover Administration ignored Hillman's counsel. President Roosevelt no sooner assumed office, however, than he called Hillman to Washington to utilize his understanding of modern industrial relations. Although the Amalgamated was not among the largest unions and was unaffiliated with the American Federation of Labor, Roosevelt in effect made Hillman the spokesman for all workers.

Like other unions, the Amalgamated suffered severely from the depression. Few men were buying clothing and thousands of unemployed tailors dropped their union membership. Manufacturers, desperate to avoid bankruptcy, reverted to sweatshop conditions, and workers with families to support reluctantly accepted cut after cut in their wages. To stop this suicidal scramble for business at the expense of workers, Hillman began to fight against unscrupulous employers, most of whom had established nonunion shops in outlying towns. Even in 1932, his organizers enrolled thousands of new members in these sweatshops. That August, Hillman called a strike in New York and its environs and won union conditions within two weeks. This victory soon brought into line manufacturers in other centers and heartened the workers in all needle trades.

The establishment of the Men's Clothing Code Authority in 1933 under NRA placed the industry on a 36-hour work week and started the rise in wages which would ultimately bring members of the Amalgamated into the class of highly paid workers. With the industry again unionized, the Amalgamated began to organize the accessory trades, then still in the sweatshop stage. Under the vigorous direction of Jacob Potofsky, the New York shirt factories were struck successfully. Meantime scores of organizers invaded the sweatshop areas of Pennsylvania, New Jersey, and other nearby states, and their persistent efforts won the confidence of the timid women workers. Strikes were fought to a victorious conclusion despite the frequent opposition of employers, public officials, and local judges. In time wages were nearly quadrupled, the hours of work nearly halved, and working conditions greatly improved. Within two years the shirt makers' locals attained a membership of 40,000. During this period the Amalgamated also attracted related groups of workers, among them neckwear makers, glove makers, laundry workers, and journeyman tailors, and all of them benefited from the support given by the parent union.

The social ravages of the depression convinced Hillman that the strength of the Amalgamated was closely related to the health of the national economy and to the organization of workers in other industries. With New Deal laws favoring labor, he thought it time to challenge powerful antiunion industrialists and to bring unaffiliated workers into unions of their own choosing. Although critical of the leadership of the American Federation of Labor, he tried to work with them for the good of all labor and brought the Amalgamated into their ranks. His aim was to prod the AFL into action in industries still completely unorganized. "To organize the workers of America," he declared in 1936, "is one of my fondest dreams." When President William Green and the Executive Council, however, upheld jurisdictional taboos and showed little interest in the millions of workers in the mass-production industries, Hillman became one of the founders and an active leader of the Committee for Industrial Organization, formed to stimulate the industrial unionization of workers.

Although John L. Lewis, president of the United Coal Miners Union, headed the CIO, Hillman became the driving intelligence of the new organization. Differing from Lewis in both background and point of view, he readily cooperated with him so long as both worked for the good of labor, breaking with him later, when Lewis began to use the CIO as a personal weapon against his adversaries.

In the first few years both men and their unions contributed generously in money and men and inspiration to the organizational drive. The Amalgamated gave $500,000 toward the unionization of the textile industry and its organizers succeeded in raising the membership of the United Textile Workers from 30,000 to 450,000. Lewis and his associates achieved similar successes in the heavy industries. When the AFL leaders panicked at the victories of the CIO unions and threatened expulsion, Hillman sided with Lewis despite his keen desire to keep the labor movement united. In 1939 in "The Promise of Labor," he wrote, "Unity of the right kind is essential if we are to guarantee the gains which we have won in the past and make possible the fullest measure of progress in the future. Yet peace is clearly not worth the cost if it can be purchased only at the price of a return to stagnation and decay."

When Lewis began to act like a blinded Samson in his antagonism to President Roosevelt in the 1940 campaign, Hillman balked. He had long believed that labor must be organized not only industrially but also politically. "Organized labor," he declared, "represents the hard core around which all progressive political action must be built." Acting

on this principle in 1936, he had become one of the founders of the American Labor party in New York. Later, after
personal pique and rising anticommunism caused David
Dubinsky and others to break away and form the Liberal
party, Hillman continued to head the American Labor party
and make it a spearhead in President Roosevelt's New York
campaign. The latter, indeed, continued to depend on his
advice and when Hillman was ill with double pneumonia in
1938, Roosevelt wrote him that "to be deprived of your
counsel, even very briefly, at a time like this is a serious loss
to the labor movement and the people of our country."

The exigency of a desperate world war and the great
need of a wise peacemaker at the end of the actual fighting
caused Hillman to favor a fourth term for President Roosevelt. To this end he organized the CIO Political Action Committee and the National Citizens Political Action Committee
to help re-elect him. The Republicans made much capital
of Roosevelt's remark, "Clear it with Sidney," in connection
with the final choice of his running mate; but their personal attacks upon Hillman had no effect on the labor vote.

Although Hillman gave much time to national affairs,
he always kept close watch upon the activities of the Amalgamated. In 1937 he had succeeded in establishing the
labor-management relations of the men's clothing industry
on a nationwide basis, and later had negotiated industry-
wide wage increases and other improvements with employer
associations. By the time the depression ended in the late
1930s the union and employers found it feasible to effect
the stabilization of the industry and the equalization of
labor costs, which made it possible for the workers to obtain relatively high wages while their employers also made
a fair profit. With this advance in mind, Hillman told the
delegates at the 1938 convention,

> Let us not become too practical. Having realized our
> dreams of yesterday, let us dedicate ourselves to new
> dreams of a future where men and women will be
> economically secure and politically free. Let us dream

these dreams, and let us, with the spirit of the old days as well as with the spirit of the last two years, dedicate ourselves to make these dreams a reality.

The urgency of war brought Hillman to Washington. President Roosevelt turned to him as the man best able to organize the country's labor power for the gigantic task of war preparedness. In 1940 he was made a member of the National Defense Advisory Commission in charge of the mobilization of American workers. This task was broadened by his appointment as joint head of the Office of Production Management. His responsibilities for a time became greater than that of any man save Roosevelt himself. He developed a huge program of work training and refresher courses in order to build up the needed reserve of skilled manpower. Perhaps his greater, if less-known, contribution was his frequent intervention in the resolution of labor disputes, employing on a national scale talents of mediation that had worked so well for the Amalgamated.

With the acceleration of war activity, changes in administrative functions became advisable, and in 1942 the Office of Production Management was transformed into the War Production Board. In the shuffle large industrialists and influential bureaucrats, resentful of Hillman's drive and scrutiny, succeeded in circumventing his powers and responsibilities by persuading Roosevelt that his peculiar talents were no longer essential. With his authority curbed and with representatives of business in the ascendance, Hillman found himself unable to function effectively. Moreover, he suffered the first of several heart attacks. He had no choice but to resign from the Board.

Although his doctors assured him that he could prolong his life by carefully nursing his energy, he recovered only to exert himself to the utmost. For a new vision was stirring his imagination. He perceived that the harrowing war created an opportunity for uniting organized labor everywhere into a single and effective world federation. It was his belief that such a body was the best assurance not only of justice for the mass of workers but also of peace for all mankind. Once the 1944 campaign was over, he began to devote himself to this ideal with what Henry A. Wallace termed "his patient passion for the common good." As chairman of the CIO delegation and as a member of the administrative committee, he labored fervently to reconcile deep-seated differences between radical and conservative labor groups. At preliminary meetings in London and elsewhere he promoted the work of organization, and in September, 1945 the world Federation of Trade Unions, representing 70 million union members from 56 countries, became a reality.

Frequent long trips, several to Europe, coupled with intensive work and his anxiety to complete the major undertaking, finally overtaxed his damaged heart, and when he presided at the fifteenth biennial convention of the Amalgamated in May, 1946, Hillman was a very sick man. His pleasure in reporting the progress of the previous two years was heightened by the vision of the prophet. It was as if he had fully identified himself with his rabbinical ancestors and was counseling his people. With the business of the convention done, his "closing remarks" were less the words of a union president than those of a seer offering his valediction:

> We want a better America, an America that will give its citizens, first of all, a higher and higher standard of living so that no child will cry for food in the midst of plenty. We want to have an America where the inventions of science will be at the disposal of every American family, not merely for the few who can afford them; an America that will have no sense of insecurity and which will make it possible for all groups, regardless of race, creed, or color to live in friendship, to be real neighbors; an America that will carry its great mission of helping other countries to help themselves, thinking not in terms of exploitation, but of creating plenty abroad so that we can all enjoy it here in America. . . . Delegates, I cannot impress upon you too

much that this is going to be a greater, better America, a greater, better world, built by cooperative effort of the common man and women of our own land and of the world.

Two months later, on July 10, 1946, Hillman was dead.

The Amalgamated, bereft of its first and greatest leader, remained dedicated to the policies he had developed during his thirty-two years as president. At its 1948 convention President Potofsky announced the creation in Hillman's memory of a million-dollar medical center for the New York area, a center to be financed entirely by employers. The union also formed the Sidney Hillman Foundation, with a fund of a million dollars to be expended within twenty-five years on educational, cultural, and humanitarian activities.

Sidney Hillman was probably the ablest labor leader this country has yet produced. President Roosevelt told Harold Laski that Hillman "saw the whole range of our economic problems as perhaps only four or five other men in the United States." He possessed a breadth of view and a love of man that caused him to identify his surging personal ambition with the welfare of his fellows. It was natural for him to broaden his goal from the "more, more, now" of the earlier labor leaders to the universal aspect of human betterment.

He was a very skillful negotiator. He approached every labor dispute with the aim not of browbeating his opponent but of narrowing the area of disagreement and of widening the range of concurrence. As he once explained, "The happiest solution in a dispute may be reached before all reserves are drawn into the fight. One is more likely to get concessions while one is on speaking and bargaining terms. Once a fight is on, there develops the desire to win even though victory may mean ultimate defeat for both sides."

He was suave, soft-spoken, quick-witted, persistent, always on the alert for points of advantage. Firm yet fair, he evoked confidence and cooperation from his adversaries at the bargaining table. In 1934 the trade periodical, *The Daily News Record*, explained that the respect employers had for him was based on the fact that "he has never made demands on an industry that it could not meet economically, and he has been known to make concessions when the realities of the situation proved irresistible."

Certain that logic and justice were on his side, that his demands were neither exorbitant nor impracticable, he was willing to let matters be decided on their merits. This insistence on fair dealing made possible the practicality of the impartial chairman—the greatest boon to amity in labor-management relations. From 1911, when the impartial board was established in the factories of Hart, Schaffner and Marx, Hillman always acquiesced in the decisions of the boards of arbitration, resorting to the strike weapon only when manufacturers refused to deal with the union or to honor the decisions of the impartial chairman. Once employers' associations began to cooperate with the Amalgamated the industry became a model of labor-management harmony.

Hillman refused to haggle over words, slogans, or theories. Always concentrating on the main issues and ready to fight hard for the good of the union, he never quibbled over verbal formalities. Fully aware of his worth, he had the greatness of mind readily to admit mistakes. He had no particular pride of opinion, and did not hesitate to change his position when the facts did not bear him out. Like most men of superior ability and practical wisdom, he acted pragmatically, always keeping the chief end in view and seeking to attain it with whatever means he had at his command. When he was uncertain of the next move, he experimented on a small scale by means of trial and error until he found the right direction. To his biographer George Soule he said, "I have made lots of mistakes. Anybody who wants to act at all must make mistakes. If he doesn't act, that is a mistake, too. Any intelligent man must recognize that he will make mistakes, and work out a way to deal with that fact."

This attitude is of course rooted in profound wisdom. He knew men intuitively and loved them despite their foibles and failings. His particular background and early experience broadened his sympathy to encompass all suffering mankind. He hated injustice and abhorred oppression. He was moved not by party labels but my human aspiration. In his teens he dreamt of a better world than the one he lived in, and as a young labor leader he fought for additional pennies in the pay envelopes of his tailors. Once he had built up the Amalgamated and had obtained for its members a fair portion of the earnings of the industry, he came to see that the union could not "do more than conditions in the country will permit it to do." Thereupon he broadened his goals, and his activity included all organized labor. Later, when World War II demonstrated that the United States could not persist in isolation and that its peace and prosperity depended upon the well-being of other nations, he naturally began to work for the unity and amity of all mankind.

It is this lifework, ranging from a single union of sweated workers to an effort at federation comprising the organized labor of the world, that stands as a monument to the greatness of Sidney Hillman.

JEWS IN
SCIENTIFIC RESEARCH

Not until well into the twentieth century did American Jews engage in scientific study and research in any numbers. One of the basic reasons is that institutions of higher learning, where most such scholarship prevails, did not welcome them. The virus of anti-Semitism infected even such eminent intellectuals as Henry and Brooks Adams, Henry Holt, and A. Lawrence Lowell, and their prejudice was shared by many college teachers and administrators. Thus such men as Ludwig Lewisohn, an authority on German and English literature and a gifted writer, and Horace M. Kallen, a favored student of William James and a reputable philosopher, to cite two instances out of many, never obtained teaching tenure consonant with their abilities. Even when a Jewish scholar was admitted to a university because of his special training, he was often slighted. This occasionally led to the bizarre instance of Professor Leo Wiener of Harvard who intentionally kept his son Norbert in ignorance of his Jewish ancestry, until he discovered it for himself at the age of sixteen. Nevertheless a minute number of talented Jews did find their way into the faculties of American universities before World War I, and a few attained international prominence. In the 1930's with academic prejudice dissipating, gifted Jewish refugees from Central Europe and elsewhere were welcomed as teachers and researchers. Brief sketches of a few of these scientists make evident their attainments.

A. A. Michelson (1852–1931) was one of the first Jews to achieve academic eminence in science. Brought to this country from Germany as a child of three he attended the U.S. Naval Academy on an appointment by President Grant and taught physics at the Academy for four years before going to Europe for graduate study in interferometry. As early as 1877 he made a vital improvement in the Foucault method of determining velocity of light. On his return to the United States he taught at the Case School of Applied Science, where he and E. W. Morley began their measurement of the relative velocity of the earth and the ether. In 1889 he went to Clark University, and three years later joined the newly established University of Chicago, where he remained until his retirement in 1929. In 1907 he became the first American scientist to be awarded the Nobel Prize in Physics.

Franz Boas (1858–1942), born and educated in Germany, specialized in the anthropological study of the Eskimos. He settled in the United States in 1886, taught for four years at Clark University, then went to Columbia University in 1896, where he eventually headed the anthropology department until his retirement in 1937. He stressed the influence of environment on physical and mental development and offered proof that even the shape of the skull changes with the environment. In his influential work, *The Mind of Primitive Man* (1911), he asserted that there was no difference in the thinking process between primitive and civilized man and that there were no inborn dissimilarities between blacks and whites. The book was called a "magna charta of self-respect for the so-called lower races." In the 1930's he condemned the Nazi theories of race and headed the American Committee for Democracy and Intellectual Freedom.

Charles P. Steinmetz (1865–1923) was also born and educated in Germany, but was forced, because of his socialist views, to flee to Zurich to complete his university studies. Migrating to the United States in 1889, he worked for an electrical firm in Yonkers until his monographic studies attracted wide attention and in 1893 he became chief engineer in General Electric's Schenectady plant where he spent the rest of his life experimenting with electrical appliances and machinery. Among his discoveries was the law of hysteresis, which made it possible to reduce the loss of efficiency in electrical apparatus resulting from alternating magnetism. He also developed a practical calculation method for alternating current and did important research on the nature of lightning. Throughout his life he retained his belief in socialism, and in his later years favored the ideal of Zionism.

Albert Einstein (1879–1955) was undoubtedly the most seminal scientist in modern times. In 1905, while working as an examiner in the government patent office at Bern, he published four papers which, in addition to postulating the nature of light quanta and the quantum theory of specific heat, announced the revolutionary theory of relativity, according to which matter and energy are not separate and distinct entities but different manifestations of the same reality. He taught at the Universities of Zurich and Prague until 1913, when he was appointed director of the prestigious Kaiser Wilhelm Physics Institute. In 1916 his *Special and General Theories of Relativity* established the greatest intellectual revolution since Newton—unifying the concepts of space and time, matter and energy, gravitation and inertia into an all-embracing cosmic concept. This brought him the Nobel Prize in 1921.

Rising anti-Semitism in Germany caused Einstein to settle in the United States, where he accepted a professorship at the Institute for Advanced Study in Princeton in 1933. In 1953 he completed work on his unified field theory, which attempted to explain gravitation, electromagnetism, and subatomic phenomena in one set of laws. Always an ardent humanitarian and for years an active Zionist, he strongly opposed fascism and in 1940 sent President Roosevelt the letter which initiated work on the atom bomb.

Another German-born Nobel Prize winner, James Franck (1882–1964), was a distinguished teacher and researcher in physical chemistry in Germany, and head of the physics department of Keiser Wilhelm Institute. In 1925 he shared the Nobel prize in physics with Gustav Hertz for their discovery of the laws governing the effect of impact of an electron on an atom. He also did notable work in photosynthesis. With the rise of Hitler, he left Germany and became a visiting professor at the University of Copenhagen and then joined Johns Hopkins University. In 1942 he was appointed director of the chemistry division in the Metallurgical Laboratory at the University of Chicago. A prominent participant in the work on the atom bomb, he sought in vain to stop its use on Japan.

Selman A. Waksman was born in Russia in 1888 and came to the United States in 1910. He studied at Rutgers University and the University of California. Teaching and experimenting in microbiology at Rutgers, he became director of the Institute of Microbiology in 1949. With the aid of associates he isolated various antibiotics, among them actinomycin, clavacin, streptomycin, streptothricin, neomycin, fradicin, and candicidin. In 1952 he was awarded the Nobel Prize in Physiology and Medicine.

Norbert Wiener (1894–1964) was a pedagogically forced child prodigy, who graduated from Tufts College at fifteen and obtained a doctorate from Harvard at nineteen. Long a distinguished member of the faculty of the Massachusetts Institute of Technology, he lectured in several foreign universities. Specializing in mathematics, the theory of probability in particular, he evolved the science of cybernetics and helped develop electronic calculators and computers. His book, *Cybernetics* (1948), made him world-famous. *Ex-Prodigy*, his autobiography, gives a detailed account of his discovery of being Jewish and how he reacted to his parents for his peculiar upbringing and to the idea of Jewishness.

I. I. Rabi, born in Austria in 1898, was brought to the United States in early childhood. A graduate of Cornell University, he did advanced work in modern physics in European universities and at Columbia University. He taught at City College before he joined the physics department of Columbia, which he headed after 1945. He discovered and measured the radiations of atoms and was awarded the Nobel Prize in 1944. When work on the atom bomb was started in 1941, he served in an advisory capacity. After 1945 he became centrally involved in both the further development and containment of atomic weapons, and in 1952 he succeeded J. Robert Oppenheimer as chairman of the General Advisory Committee to the Atomic Energy Commission. He lectured in various universities and was the recipient of many honors, among them the

American Medal for Merit and the King's Medal from Great Britain.

Samuel A. Goudsmid, also a physicist, was born in Holland in 1902. In 1925 he and George Uhlenbeck discovered the electronic spin phenomenon. He came to the United States in 1927, taught at the University of Michigan until 1946, at Northwestern University until 1948, and since then has been professor and chairman of the department of physics at Brookhaven National Laboratory. In 1943 he went to England to serve in the Alsos Mission, whose purpose was to ascertain what German scientists were doing in atomic energy. To his great relief he learned late in 1944 that they had done nothing toward the development of an atom bomb. For this service he was awarded the Medal of Freedom. Since 1951 he has edited *The Physical Review*.

Emilio G. Segré, an Italian Jew born in 1905, obtained his doctorate in physics at the University of Rome. In 1938 he followed his teacher and associate Enrico Fermi to the United States and joined Ernest Lawrence's Radiation Laboratory at the University of California. He was head of the physicists at Los Alamos from 1943 to 1946, when he returned to Berkeley. As the discoverer in 1938 of technetium, the first of the new elements that cannot exist in nature and must be created by man, he was awarded the Nobel Prize in 1959. Other of his discoveries, alone and with others, were slow neutrons, astatine, plutonium, and antiprotons.

Born in Hungary in 1908 and educated in Germany, Edward Teller came to the United States in 1935 and taught physics at Washington University until 1941. A brilliant researcher in atomic physics, he was one of the initiators of the work on the atom bomb, first at Columbia University, then at the Metallurgical Laboratory in Chicago, and finally at Los Alamos, although his contribution was not commensurate with his gifts because of an inability to work well with others. He is known as the "father of the hydrogen bomb," and in 1950 began the research into the technical means which made a thermonuclear fission bomb a reality. Associated with the University of Chicago until 1951, he became a professor of theoretical physics at the University of California the following year and director of the Lawrence Radiation Laboratory in Livermore in 1958. He has made important contributions to chemical, molecular, and nuclear physics as well as to the quantum theory, and has written several books on these subjects.

Jerome B. Wiesner, born in Detroit in 1915, received his doctorate at the University of Michigan, and joined the M. I. T. Radiation Laboratory in 1942. He served at Los Alamos, and returned to M. I. T. after the war. He was a member of President Eisenhower's Science Advisory Committee and President Kennedy's special assistant for science technology. He became dean of the School of science at M. I. T. in 1964 and has been provost of the university since 1966. He is an expert on military technology and a leading proponent of disarmament under international law.

Jonas E. Salk, born in New York in 1914, won chemistry and surgery fellowships while still a medical student. In 1942 he was awarded a fellowship in virus diseases by the National Research Council. After several years with the School of Public Health at the University of Michigan, he joined the University of Pittsburgh and became a consultant to several laboratory staffs. In 1953 he developed the anti-polio serum, and the following year the National Foundation for Infantile Paralysis experimented with it in mass field trials with gratifying results. Soon the Salk vaccine began to be used in other countries, and Salk received many honors. In 1963 he assumed the post of fellow and director of the Salk Institute for Biological Studies at La Jolla, California.

The foregoing representative scientists, because of their notable gifts, were able to overcome the disadvantage of Jewish birth. After World War I conditions in colleges began to change gradually with the increase of student enrollment and with a good many sons and grandsons of Jewish immigrants eagerly entering the field of scholarship. Determined to teach and to do research, and without the handicaps of language and old-country mannerisms, they kept battering away at the walls of the prevailing prejudice until one after another slowly gave way. By 1940, when the need for scientists became acute, Jewish college graduates found a ready welcome, especially on government projects. Five years later, with millions of "G. I." students crowding the colleges, the shortage of teachers opened the doors of most institutions of higher learning to anyone equipped to conduct a class. Thus many hundreds of young Jewish scholars became faculty members. And if vestiges of academic prejudice persist here and there, the present law of the land and current conditions militate against their open manifestation.

15
J.
Robert
Oppenheimer

SUPERIOR
SCIENTIFIC
INTELLIGENCE

J. ROBERT OPPENHEIMER'S father came to New York from Germany and made a modest fortune as a textile importer. He married a girl born in Baltimore and trained in art. Their home had the atmosphere of many cultivated Jewish families of the middle class, and with prosperity came the purchase of paintings by established artists as well as intensified interest in music and books. Julius Robert was a precocious child. At the age of five he began collecting stones, and at eleven he was invited to become a member of the New York Mineralogical Club; a year later he addressed it on the nature of certain rocks. He attended Ethical Culture School, graduating with an outstanding record. The death of his mother when he was ten drew him closer to his father and also developed in him a paternal solicitude for his brother Frank, eight years his junior.

In 1922 he entered Harvard College and took both literary and scientific courses. Aware that fraternities generally discriminated against Jews, he refused an invitation from one of them. He completed his courses in three years, *summa cum laude* and was valedictorian of his class.

That fall he left for Cambridge University to study with Lord Rutherford in the famous Cavendish Laboratory. Influenced by Professor Max Born, a visiting professor, he followed him to the University of Göttingen, where he was awarded a doctorate in 1927. Quickly grasping the meaning and potentialities of the quantum revolution in physics, he wrote papers that contributed to its philosophical aspects. He continued his studies with Niels Bohr at Leiden and with Wolfgang Pauli in Zurich, as well as at Harvard and California Institute of Technology. Later he called this period "a heroic time," with scores of scientists collaborating with and being guided by "the deeply creative and subtle and critical spirit of Niels Bohr."

In 1929 Oppenheimer arranged to give courses at both the University of California at Berkeley and at the California Institute of Technology, choosing this combination so that he could be close to his ranch in the Cristo Mountains of New Mexico. That fall he said, "I have two loves, physics and the desert."

Oppenheimer was a popular teacher and soon attracted advanced students from other parts of the country. Although he made friends easily with most faculty members, he was not long in sensing the hostility of Professor Robert Millikan of Cal Tech. This Nobel Prize winner, according to Raymond Birge, "loathed Oppenheimer . . . and harassed him maliciously"—finding in him something alien and Jewish because of his exceptionally quick mind. Consequently Oppenheimer reduced his stay in Pasadena to four weeks in the spring. Meantime his reputation as a theoretical physicist continued to grow as he published papers that opened up new regions originally discovered by others. His ability to explicate and expand ideas was, according to Birge, tantamount to genius, "His rate of taking in new ideas and his enormous memory are what distinguish him from merely bright people. There is a huge difference between a genius and a bright person." For his own esthetic pleasure he studied Sanskrit and read *Mahatharata* and other works of world literature. The world of events hardly impinged on him, as he read no newspapers and was without a radio or telephone. Before 1936, he stated, "I was interested in man and his experience; I was deeply interested in my science; but I had no understanding of the relations of man to his society."

But even such a sheltered, philosophical individualist was forced to face the world outside his laboratory. The menace of Hitlerism more and more directly confronted him. Until the 1930's he had little experience with anti-Semitism, having only a passive awareness of his Jewishness and having limited his activities to the cloistered science community. For the first time he became conscious of his Jewishness and its tragic significance. His father, alive until 1937, and visiting him periodically, no doubt discussed with him the fate of their relatives still in Germany, and Oppenheimer arranged for some of them to migrate to the United States. Simultaneously he was made aware of the economic depression of the period by some of his graduate students, especially the bright Jewish ones from New York, who suffered from extreme poverty. Years later he explained,

> I had a continuing, smoldering fury about the treatment of Jews in Germany. I had relations there, and was later to help in extricating them and bringing them to this country. I saw what the depression was doing to my students. . . . And through them I began to understand how deeply political and economic events could affect men's lives. I began to feel the need to participate more fully in the life of the community.

About this time, Oppenheimer began to court Jean Tatlock, the attractive but idealistically confused daughter of a professor of English. In her groping for an answer to the social ills of the time she had turned to communism, and through her Oppenheimer met some party members. When the Spanish Civil War broke out, he warmly sympathized with the Loyalists and helped them financially—the death of his father having brought him an ample inheritance. At a benefit for Loyalist Spain he met Haakon Chevalier, a colleague in the French department, and found him intelligent and congenial.

In 1938, through a discussion with three scientists who had lived in Russia, he learned of the Soviet purges and repression. Yet, as he explained later, this "did not mean a sharp break for me with those who held different views." At that time he had no knowledge of the close connection between American communists and the Soviet Union. He further asserted, "I had no clearly formulated political views. I hated tyranny and repression and every form of dictatorial control of thought." Thus he joined organizations which seemed to him consonant with New Deal views.

His wooing of Jean Tatlock was intermittent, largely because of her emotional instability, and by 1939, when he met his future wife, he had stopped seeing her. Katherine Harrison, the young wife of an English doctor, had previously been married to Joe Dallet, a member of the Communist party, whom she met at the University of Wisconsin where she was a student. Dallet persuaded her to join the party in 1934 and do some office work for it. By 1936 she was completely disillusioned with communism and separated from Dallet when he insisted on her continuing in the party. Dallet joined the Abraham Lincoln Brigade and was killed in Spain. Katherine completed her college course, majoring in biology, and went to the University of California, where she married Dr. Harrison, whom she divorced to marry Oppenheimer. They proved a congenial pair, and a son was born to them in 1941. Both associated with people they liked regardless of their political views, and Oppenheimer continued to contribute to liberal causes that appealed to him.

In 1934 Enrico Fermi and Emilio Segré experimented successfully with uranium fission, although without realizing its significance. Four years later Otto Hahn wrote to his friend, Lise Meitner, a German-Jewish refugee in Sweden, that in a repetition of the Fermi experiment he had identified barium in the uranium. She and her nephew Otto Frisch realized the significance of the enormous release of energy and their explanation in *Nature* aroused great excitement among nuclear physicists, along with a fear that German physicists might be working on an atomic weapon. Deeply perturbed by this possibility, Fermi tried in vain to interest an admiral of his acquaintance. Leo Szilard and Edward Teller, Hungarian Jewish anti-Fascists, conceived the idea of having Albert Einstein write to President Roosevelt, apprizing him of the potential danger and urging the United States to start work on an atomic bomb. In March, 1940 the letter was delivered by Alexander Sachs, a Wall Street economist and one of Roosevelt's advisers. When the President was not at first persuaded, Sachs told him how Napoleon had disregarded Robert Fulton's projected idea of a steamship flotilla for the invasion of England and had failed to conquer the world. Roosevelt saw the point at once and appointed an advisory committee on uranium to explore the project.

The fall of France and the air attack on England brought the Nazi menace closer to America. Vannevar Bush, president of the Carnegie Institution in Washington, was asked to form the National Defense Research Committee and soon after, the Office of Research and Development initiated a pilot plant for chain reaction. In Chicago the Metallurgical Laboratory was established to convert uranium into plutonium. When the attack on Pearl Harbor plunged the United States into war, the efforts of these scientists were accelerated into a crash program to produce the atom bomb before the Germans did.

Oppenheimer was of course aware of the work on atomic energy. "Ever since the discovery of nuclear fission, the possibility of powerful explosives based on it had been much on my mind." When his friend Ernest O. Lawrence, an aggressive physicist and a Nobel Prize recipient, asked him to help on the bomb, Oppenheimer readily complied. "I began to think more intensively on my own how to make bombs. I did some calculations on efficiency, design, probable amounts of material, and so on, so that I got into it and knew something about it." With his mind turned in this direction, his interest in liberal causes receded. After Pearl Harbor he even stopped his contributions to Spanish refugees.

In 1941 Arthur H. Compton began calling on him for advice regarding the work on plutonium in the Metallurgical Laboratory and invited him to meetings with other scientists. With secrecy and security paramount, Oppenheimer was necessarily questioned about his political views. "The important thing now," he told Compton, "is the nation's defense. I'm cutting off all my communist connections. For if I didn't the government will find it difficult to use me. I don't want anything to interfere with my usefulness to the nation." Compton was satisfied, and in June, 1942 asked him to take charge of the physics part of the bomb development. Although he had no administrative experience and was not an experimental scientist, Oppenheimer "felt sufficiently informed and challenged by the problem to be glad to accept."

When the Manhattan Engineer Project was assigned to the Army with General Leslie R. Groves in charge, Oppenheimer was the logical choice as scientific director. Compton later stated, "It was my judgment that Oppenheimer's qualifications fitted him to such a post better than any other person who could be made available." This was after a diligent search for about a month, which included consultation with many top-level scientists. When Oppenheimer filled out the security questionnaire, freely listing his previous associations, he was refused clearance. Groves thereupon personally examined his file and issued an order stating, "It is desired that clearance be issued for the employment of Julius Robert Oppenheimer without delay, irrespective of the information which you have concerning Mr. Oppenheimer. He is absolutely essential to the Project." The security officers yielded, but they kept close watch on all of Oppenheimer's movements. Before long they suspected him of spying—while overlooking such men as Klaus Fuchs and David Greenglass.

Oppenheimer became convinced that it was necessary to bring the scattered scientists into a unified laboratory under a single command. Groves agreed, and the two chose Los Alamos, a plateau near Oppenheimer's New Mexico ranch, because of its isolation and yet easy access to trains and an airport. While thousands of workers were erecting buildings and installing facilities to make the site habitable for the scientists and their families, Oppenheimer proceeded on his massive and difficult recruitment program. Most able scientists, already engaged in one war program or another, and apprehensive of the doubtful nature of the new one, were reluctant to live on what they considered a desert wasteland and subject to military supervision. Traveling from one laboratory to another, explaining the urgency of the program, Oppenheimer found that some feared "this was a boondoggle, which would in fact have nothing to do with the war." But so successful was he in exciting their interest, that by the time Los Alamos was ready for occupancy he had a full complement of scientists. The requirements of the crash program made him disregard former Communist connections, provided there were no current involvements. Each scientist, of course, had to obtain clearance, but he himself judged men by their character and not by their associations—sometimes to the chagrin of the security officers. Oppenheimer moved with his family to Los Alamos on March 15, 1943.

His extraordinary ability to learn fast enabled him to direct the work and deal with difficult situations in a manner to elicit the confidence and admiration of both friends and malcontents. He handled Groves "beautifully," to quote I. I. Rabi, and Groves himself later declared, "I came to depend upon him tremendously for scientific advice on the rest of the Project." Even Teller who found Oppenheimer uncongenial, had to admit,

> As chairman, Oppenheimer showed a refined, sure, informed touch. I don't know how he had acquired this facility for handling people. Those who knew him well were really surprised. I suppose it was the kind of knowledge a politician or administrator has to pick up somehow. . . . Oppenheimer's great virtue was that he was intelligent.

Oppenheimer recruited more and more scientists and technologists as he needed them—about 4,000 by July, 1945. Los Alamos had to be built up quickly and its occupants suffered inconvenience and discomfort, but their complaints about the lack of facilities and the strict security regulations dissolved in the presence of his "fantastic brilliance and tremendous power." They perceived not only his complete dedication but also his eagerness to help them in any way he could. He gave them the "impression of a man racked and haggard, alive to a crushing responsibility"; yet he had time for every complaint, showed interest in and sympathy with their personal biases, and played upon their patriotism and vanity to arouse their sense of drive and achievement. He was of course assisted in this morale building by several top scientists who, as antifascist refugees or national leaders, were anxious to produce the bomb before the Germans did. In sum, Los Alamos "was a remarkable community inspired by a high sense of mission, of duty and of destiny, coherent, dedicated, and remarkably selfless."

In June 1943 Oppenheimer visited Jean Tatlock at her request. He found her condition of melancholia acute enough to remain longer than he had expected, missed his train, and had to stay overnight in her parents' home. The security agents following him ascribed the visit to his Communist affiliation, adding the derogatory report to his file. At the hearings eleven years later he stated that he had sought to dissipate her despair, and was saddened some time later to receive a clipping reporting her suicide.

That spring, during a brief stay in Berkeley, he was visited by his former colleague, Hoakon Chevalier and his wife. While in the kitchen preparing drinks, Chevalier told him that an acquaintance of theirs, George Eltenton, had suggested that since Soviet Russia was our ally we should cooperate with her in scientific matters as well as in the war effort. Oppenheimer reacted sharply. In Berkeley again in August, he mentioned to a security agent that Eltenton might be watched, having by this time become more sensitive to security problems. But he was still naive about the concept of security as understood by military intelligence, and the insistence on secrecy troubled him, as it did other scientists. Rabi testified later, "By pointing the finger at Eltenton I think he felt that he had done the necessary thing for the protection of security." But in making the disclosure to get it off his conscience, he did it in such a way as to intensify suspicion of himself.

The following day Oppenheimer was invited for an interview with Colonel Boris Pash, a high-ranking security officer who had for some time suspected him of disloyalty and had secreted a dictaphone in the office. Oppenheimer was told that he must give more information about the Eltenton matter. Unwilling to involve Chevalier, he began to dissemble, deepening his involvement. In his reluctance to name Chevalier, he was led to invent what he later admitted was "a cock-and-bull story" about three scientists who had been approached. "I have told you," he stated to Pash, "where the initiative came from and that the other things were almost purely accident and that it would involve people who ought not to be involved in this." In his innocence he did not realize that in the end he would have to disclose Chevalier's name and that both of them would suffer as a result of his fabrication. After months of intermittent questioning he was compelled by Groves to reveal Chevalier's name, but this did not satisfy Pash: "This office is still of the opinion that Oppenheimer is not to be fully trusted and that his loyalty to the Nation is divided." At the security hearings eleven years later Oppenheimer could only say that he was an "idiot" for having behaved as he did, but it went far to prejudice the men who decided that he was a security risk.

The work at Los Alamos proceeded under great pressure. Oppenheimer continued to attract the scientists he needed, procure difficult materials, pacify dissatisfied or undisciplined workers, imbue everyone with his sense of urgency. By mid-1944 he was close to despair because plutonium was so slow in coming. To ease the strain on him somewhat later, Groves brought the two men who cared most for him to Los Alamos—his brother Frank and Rabi— and both tried to assume some of his responsibilities. Yet, according to Groves, Oppenheimer "worked harder at times than I wanted him to, because I was afraid he would break down under it. . . . I never could slow him down in any way." He lost weight, going down to 116 pounds by July, 1945. Yet he managed to keep the highly complex project progressing, arousing the admiration of all concerned. David Inglis, one of the prominent participants at Los Alamos, later testified,

> I think it was the hardest technical job that had ever been done up to that time. Oppenheimer was not only the administrative head of the laboratory but also the technical head, and this double burden—I was there, I saw it—was a miracle of a performance. The duty and devotion to country—I can't describe to you the pressure the man was under."

In November, 1944 the Allies learned that German scientists were not working on atomic weapons. This news caused many scientists, particularly refugees from fascism, to lose interest in the development of the atom bomb. Niels Bohr wrote to President Roosevelt to urge that work on the bomb be stopped because of the "terrifying prospect of a future competition between nations about a weapon of such formidable character." Leo Szilard and Einstein felt equally strongly, and their letter to Roosevelt early in 1945 was found on his desk after his death. Szilard, unable to see Truman, showed a copy to Secretary of State James Byrnes, but he was unimpressed. The juggernaut was on the move and not to be stopped.

In June, with Germany defeated, a committee of leading scientists headed by James Franck sent a report to Secretary of War Stimson, imploring him not to use the bomb against Japan and advising an international agreement against the use of atomic weapons: "The military advantage and the saving of American lives achieved by the sudden use of atomic bombs against Japan may be outweighed by the ensuing loss of confidence and by a wave of horror and repulsion sweeping over the rest of the world and perhaps even dividing public opinion at home." They proposed instead a demonstration on a desert island. This and other appeals and suggestions were generally disregarded by government leaders—the last one on the ground that according to Oppenheimer there was no certainty of an explosion and a failure would be self-defeating.

A group of eminent scientists, Oppenheimer included, was called to Washington to decide not *whether* but *how* the bomb should be used. Influenced by the information that the planned invasion of Japan might cost a million lives, they agreed that if one or two bombs would make an invasion unnecessary their use was advisable. Ralph Bard, who attended the meeting, commented on Oppenheimer's part in it. "He didn't say drop the bomb or don't drop it. He just tried to do his job, which was to give us technical background. I think he did it well. Certainly he didn't try to influence us in any way." Monsignor Fulton Sheen, no liberal and no pacifist, was not alone in criticizing the decision that it was better to have Japanese killed than Americans: "That was precisely the argument Hitler used in bombing Holland."

Stimson and Groves did not make public the protests of the scientists or inform President Truman about them. Once the decision was made to use the bomb, the only advice they sought was on where to drop it. On Professor Edwin O. Reischauer's plea, Stimson eliminated Kyoto from the designated cities because of its religious and cultural monuments. The tragic truth, of course, is that the decision to use the bomb was based on misinformation. The Japanese code had been broken and military leaders in the Pacific knew that Japan was virtually defeated; that it had urged the Russians and the Swiss to arrange an armistice. Between July 10 and August 6, when Hiroshima was bombed, American forces destroyed or damaged most of the remaining Japanese planes and ships, and Fleet Admiral Nimitz was confident that neither an invasion nor an atomic bomb was needed to produce a surrender. Nevertheless both Truman and Churchill, unaware of this situation, approved the use of the bomb.

Meantime work on the final details of the bomb was carried on. Oppenheimer, up to the very end, feared that the terrible weapon would fail and was equally fearful of its success. He later admitted that he suffered morally during this tense period but felt moved to find out if the bomb was feasible. A half hour before the explosion was to occur he was torn by doubt and irresolution, losing ten dollars on a bet that it would not happen. When the tremendous flash brightened the horizon with "a thousand suns," he thought of the passage from *Bhagavad-Gita*, "I am become death the destroyer of worlds." And when the bomb fell on Hiroshima, he declared, "In some crude sense which no vulgarity, no humor, no overstatement can quite extinguish, the participants have known sin, and this is a knowledge they cannot lose."

With the war ended, Oppenheimer wanted to return to his seminars and laboratory. But as "the father of the atom bomb" he had become a public figure. Although he resigned from Los Alamos in October, saying he was no "armament manufacturer," he was at once drawn into various government committees as adviser and consultant. Fully conscious of his part in developing atomic weapons, he felt it his duty to help curb their further use. He said at the time, "If atomic bombs are to be added to the arsenals of a warring world or to the arsenals of nations preparing for war, then the time will come when mankind will curse the names of Los Alamos and Hiroshima." Later, as he came up against Russian intransigence, he declared, "I had a feeling of deep responsibility, interest, and concern for many of the problems with which the development of atomic energy confronted our country. This development was to be a major factor in the history of the evolving and mounting conflict between the free world and the Soviet Union."

At the end of the war he favored international control and open action on an international scale, even if it meant destroying our available bombs. This was strongly opposed by the military as well as by many members of Congress who feared the Soviet Union. Years later he recalled, "In the winter of 1945–46 hysteria centered on our hypercryptic power and the hope of retaining it. I saw President Truman and he told me he wanted 'help in getting domestic legislation through.'" Oppenheimer expressed the thought that an international agreement was even more important. "I feel we have blood on our hands," he added. But Truman brushed it off: "Never mind, it'll all come out in the wash." Nor could he disabuse the President of a belief that the Russians would never develop an atom bomb. When he left the President he felt completely discouraged. "From the way he looked," William Higinbotham recalled, "I think I could tell that Truman's statement and the incomprehension it showed just knocked the heart out of him."

Out of a sense of responsibility and guilt, Oppenheimer

did not refuse to help government officials struggling with atomic problems. He assisted Dean Acheson and David Lilienthal in preparing their report on international control, a project he favored. But when Bernard Baruch was appointed the American spokesman at the United Nations, he gave up hope. It was only at the urging of both Truman and Acheson that he agreed to advise Baruch at the San Francisco meeting. Knowing that the Russian scientists were capable of developing an atom bomb within a few years, he felt heartsick when Baruch's stipulations made certain the Russian rejection of the proposed agreement. In 1947 Oppenheimer warned Frederick Osborn, Baruch's successor, not to compromise on the issue of control.

Meantime Oppenheimer was perturbed by months of legislative inaction on the management of atomic energy and was ready to accept as a stopgap the May-Johnson bill which favored Army control, thereby antagonizing a number of scientists, who had become a "league of frightened men," by not joining their public fight against it. When Senator Brian McMahon substituted a bill which provided for civilian control and unfettered research, Oppenheimer readily cooperated with him. With the Atomic Energy Commission established under David Lilienthal's chairmanship, President Truman appointed Oppenheimer and eight other scientists to the General Advisory Committee; he was unanimously elected chairman. Again he had to undergo investigation, and his FBI file was fully reviewed by the Commissioners, who also consulted with Bush, Conant, and other top scientists, before giving him Q clearance. For the next five years he worked hard and masterfully in assisting the Commission with its complex and formidable problems.

Lewis L. Strauss met Oppenheimer in 1945 and found him "a man with an extraordinary mind, a compelling, dramatic personality." As a member of the Commission, Strauss familiarized himself with the FBI file before voting to clear him. He also offered him the post of director of the Institute for Advanced Study, of which he was a trustee. After some discussion, Oppenheimer agreed and went to

Princeton in the fall of 1947, continuing, however, as chairman on the General Advisory Committee.

The explosion of an atomic bomb by the Russians caused consternation among government and military officials, and the General Advisory Committee met in October to discuss the problem. Its unanimous conclusion against the advisability of a crash program to develop a super bomb was based on the convictions that we already had a massive amount of atomic weaponry and that the hydrogen bomb was still technically problematical. Fermi and Rabi added that "it is necessarily an evil thing considered in any light," and Conant called it a "folly."

Proponents of the super bomb, headed by Strauss and Teller, strongly objected to the Committee's report. Lawrence, earlier antagonized by Oppenheimer for his refusal to approve a projected laboratory, came to Washington with Teller and several friends to agitate in favor of the crash program, maintaining that the Committee's attitude was endangering the country's security. On January 30, 1950, President Truman ordered work on the super bomb to be started immediately. The General Advisory Committee accepted the directive as a matter of course; Oppenheimer's offer to resign as chairman was not accepted.

Teller, Lawrence, and others expected him to return to Los Alamos and devote himself to the development of the hydrogen bomb. When he did not, their latent hostility, in each case for different reasons, burst into the open. They were joined by leaders in the Air Force who strongly favored the super bomb and suspected Oppenheimer's position as evidence of pro-Russianism. With his loyalty once again in question, General Groves wrote to declare that he considered Oppenheimer completely loyal. Gordon Dean, chairman of the Atomic Energy Commission, also stated that "there never was any doubt as to his loyalty in my opinion. None."

As a matter of fact, Oppenheimer had become definitely anti-Russian when Russia refused to favor international control of atomic weapons. Nevertheless, he wished the United States to set an example by the limitation of its own arsenal and thus arouse the hope of the world for an international agreement. It pained him that "no ethical discussion of any weight or nobility has been addressed to the problem of atomic weapons." As for the super bomb, he hoped emotionally that "the tortured thing" would remain technically unachievable.

In 1951, when Teller discovered the technical means of producing the hydrogen bomb, Oppenheimer in his capacity as chairman of the General Advisory Committee called a meeting in order to arrive at the most expeditious procedure for its completion. As a scientist he realized that it "was technically so sweet that you could not argue about it." But his heart was not in it. In 1952, having completed his five-year term on the Committee, he resigned and limited his connection with it to infrequent assignments as consultant.

In great demand as a lecturer, he accepted many invitations from colleges and professional organizations. He deplored the talk of a preventive war. "I believe that until we have looked this tiger in the eye, we shall be in the worst of all possible dangers, which is that we may back into him. More generally, I do not think a country like ours can in any real sense survive if we are afraid of our people." In November he went to England to deliver the Reith Lectures on the topic of *Science and the Common Understanding*, later published in book form, and to accept an honorary degree from Oxford University. He had received an invitation from Chevalier to visit him in Paris, and he and his wife had dinner with him during their week's stay in that city.

The "cold war," which began shortly after the end of the fighting in 1945, gradually generated an anti-Communist hysteria which intensified in the early 1950s fanned by Senator Joseph McCarthy's irresponsible demagogy. The fear of spies and traitors created a pathological need for national security. President Truman's Executive Order 9835, issued in 1947, stimulated flagrant investigations, insinuations, and accusations on the part of Congressional committees—destroying the careers of numerous liberals and radicals. When Senator Bertram Hickenlooper became chairman of the Joint Atomic Energy Committee in 1947 he did his utmost to expose and vilify New Dealers connected with the Atomic Energy Commission, among them Oppenheimer. The House Committee on Un-American Activities also questioned him. Both of these committees condemned the New Deal freedoms of the 1930s as disloyal. Security officer John Lansdale, no liberal but no witch-hunter, testified in 1954, "I think the fact that associations in 1940 are regarded with the same seriousness that similar associations would be regarded today is a manifestation of hysteria."

In 1947 Truman's Loyalty Order (9835) required that evidence must be strong enough to raise "reasonable grounds" for belief in a person's disloyalty, but in 1951 he issued an Executive Order (10241) requiring only a doubt of a man's loyalty to deprive him of government employment. By 1953 President Eisenhower issued an even more stringent Executive Order (10450) entitled "Security Requirements for Government Employment," that made such employment a "privilege" and shifted the burden of proof on the individual as to whether or not his record "is clearly consistent with the interests of national security."

In June, 1953 Oppenheimer's contract as consultant to the Atomic Energy Commission was renewed for another year, but very little was actually asked of him. The following month Strauss was appointed chairman of the Commission. In November W. J. Borden, secretary to the Joint Atomic Energy Committee and an Air Force enthusiast, having had access to Oppenheimer's FBI file, sent a letter of particulars to J. Edgar Hoover in the belief that the case should be re-examined in the light of the new security order. His letter listed every action and association and insinuation, which might conceivably be considered derogatory, and concluded flatly, "The central problem is not whether J. Robert Oppenheimer was ever a communist; for the existing evidence makes abundantly clear that he was." Borden, in fact, accused him of being "an agent of the Soviet Union."

Hoover sent copies of the letter to President Eisenhower and other top officials. Eisenhower consulted with Strauss and others and directed "that pending a security review of material in the file a blank wall be placed between Dr. Oppenheimer and any secret data," disregarding the fact that Oppenheimer had thrice been cleared on the same charges, and that Strauss was a member of the Commission which had cleared him in 1947. On December 10 the Commission voted "to determine the veracity or falsity of the charges." Oppenheimer, then in England, was as if prophetically expressing in one of his lectures concern for "the increasingly expert destruction of man's spirit by the powers of police, more wicked if not more awful than the ravages of nature's own hand." On his return he was called by Strauss to Washington, told that his clearance was suspended, and that he would have to decide within twenty-four hours whether to resign as consultant or ask for a full hearing. His written response stated in part,

> I have thought most earnestly of the alternative suggested. Under the circumstances this course would mean that I accept and concur in the view that I am not fit to serve this Government, that I have now served for some 12 years. This I cannot do. If I were thus unworthy I could hardly have served our country as I have tried, or been Director of our Institute in Princeton, or have spoken, as on more than one occasion I have found myself speaking, in the name of our science and our country.

General Kenneth Nichols, general manager of the Atomic Energy Commission, sent Oppenheimer a letter itemizing the charges in Borden's indictment and adding the accusation that he had opposed the development of the hydrogen bomb. Oppenheimer's extensive reply explained each item in the light of circumstances at the time of its occurrence, prefaced by a biographical sketch. "The items of so-called derogatory information set forth in your letter cannot be fairly understood except in the context of my life and my work." Aware that the strongest charge against him, from the standpoint of the military and the few scientists led by Teller and Lawrence, was his early opposition to the hydrogen bomb, he asserted, "The unanimous opposition we expressed to the crash program was based on the conviction, to which technical considerations as well as others contributed, that because of our over all situation at that time such a program might weaken rather than strengthen the position of the United States." This opposition, he explained, ended with the directive issued by President Truman, and he cooperated with the program to the best of his ability. He ended his letter with the words, "What I have hoped was, not that I would wholly avoid error, but that I might learn from it. What I have learned has, I think, made me fit to serve my country."

The hearings began on April 12, 1954, and ended on May 6. Gordon Gray as chairman and T. A. Morgan and W. V. Evans made up the Security Board. Roger Robb, a lawyer for Fulton Lewis, Jr., and a friend of Senator McCarthy, was the Commission's aggressive prosecutor, and Lloyd K. Garrison was chief defense counsel. Forty witnesses testified, most of them favoring Oppenheimer, but several definitely hostile. It soon became obvious that the charges were stale and of little significance, dating from the mid-1930s until Pearl Harbor; that even Oppenheimer's untruths in connection with Chevalier were more the result of confused ineptness than of deliberate falsification.

Much of the questioning pertained to Oppenheimer's attitude regarding the super bomb in 1949. Witnesses made clear that he was only one of eight eminent scientists who opposed the crash program; that Conant most vigorously deprecated it; that Oppenheimer's report merely transmitted the Committee's consensus. The highly favorable opinions of Oppenheimer given by many leading scientists and some former government officials were offset by the few scientists known to be hostile to him. Most damaging was Teller's testimony. Admitting that Oppenheimer had cooperated with him after 1951, he asserted that throughout their long association he had no confidence in him.

> I thoroughly disagreed with him on numerous issues and his actions frankly appeared to me confused and complicated. To this extent I feel that I would like to see the vital interests of this country in hands which I understand better, and therefore trust more. . . . If it is a question of wisdom and judgment, as demonstrated by actions since 1945, then I would say one would be wise not to grant clearance.

His criticism was taken at its face value by the Board majority.

In striking contrast was the testimony of the favorable witnesses. W. G. Whitman, a member of the General Advisory Committee, spoke for most of them when he said, "In my judgment his advice and his arguments for a gamut of atomic weapons in air defense of the United States have been more productive than any other one individual." J. J. McCloy, a leading banker who had held high government offices, stated, "He was deeply concerned about the consequences of this awful force that we had released, anxious to do what he could toward seeing that it was not used or did not become a destroyer of civilization." Vannevar Bush, forthright and open-minded, considered Nichols's letter "capable of being interpreted as placing a man on trial because he held opinions, which is quite contrary to the American system." It angered him to see that a man who "rendered service beyond almost any other man, is now being pilloried and put through an ordeal because he had the temerity to express honest opinions."

This resentment was reiterated by a number of scientists. Rabi spoke for them as well as for millions of Americans when he stated that the hearings were "most unfortunate" and should never have taken place. "He is a consultant, and if you don't want to consult the guy, you don't consult him, period. Why do you have to then proceed to suspend clearance and go through all this sort of thing . . . against a man who had accomplished what Dr. Oppenheimer had accomplished."

All the while, day after day, Oppenheimer sat through the hearings. His responses were frank and free, given without guile and with no attempt to save himself. Robert Jungk, who had made a thorough study of the case, wrote, "Rarely can any man of our time have talked so much, with such readiness and in such detail, about himself, his hopes and fears, his achievements and his mistakes." There is no question, however, that he did this at a cost worse than the pain of purgatory; yet doubtless with a sense of having emerged from it with a stoic humility, cleansed and whole —if considerably the sufferer, physically and emotionally. Garrison, in summing up, stressed that for more than a decade Oppenheimer had shared the most secret information on atomic energy without the slightest inkling of any indiscretion. "That in my judgment is the most persuasive evidence that you could possibly have. . . . We submit that the injection into a security case of a scientist's alleged lack of enthusiasm for a particular program is fraught with grave consequences to this country."

Gray and Morgan were not persuaded. Although they were satisfied about Oppenheimer's loyalty, they felt that because of his failure to give "enthusiastic support" to the development of the hydrogen bomb, and for other reasons, it would not be "clearly consistent with the security interests of the United States to reinstate Dr. Oppenheimer's clearance." Professor Evans, in a minority opinion, arrived at the opposite conclusion.

He is certainly less a security risk now than he was in 1947, when he was cleared. To deny him clearance now . . . seems to be hardly the procedure to be adopted in a free country. . . . He did not hinder the development of the H-bomb and there is absolutely nothing in the testimony to show that he did. . . . I personally think that our failure to clear Dr. Oppenheimer will be a black mark on the escutcheon of our country.

General Nichols's letter to the Commission concurring with the findings of Gray and Morgan was much more derogatory. Concerned more with security than with loyalty and fearful of the Communist specter, he found "substantial deficiency" in Oppenheimer's character and associations which might "endanger the common defense or security." On the basis of the record of the case—practically all of it prior to 1942—he concluded that "to reinstate the security clearance of Dr. Oppenheimer would not be clearly consistent with the interests of national security." On June 29, a day before his contract as consultant would have terminated, Oppenheimer was denied clearance by the Commission in a vote of four to one. Lewis Strauss, motivated by a fervid patriotism, influenced by the prevailing anti-Communist hysteria, and mindful of Oppenheimer's negative attitude in 1949 toward his urging of a crash program on the super bomb, found "proof of fundamental defects in his 'character'" in the stale charges which he himself had considered unimportant in 1947. Speaking for the majority, he asserted,

> It is clear that for one who has had access for so long to the most vital defense secrets of the Government and who would retain such access if his clearance were continued, Dr. Oppenheimer has defaulted not once but many times upon the obligations that should and must be willingly borne by citizens in the national service. Concern for the defense and security of the United States requires that Dr. Oppenheimer's clearance should not be reinstated.

Henry D. Smythe, author of the official report on the atom bomb and familiar with the Los Alamos development and with Oppenheimer, dissented vigorously. "The only question being determined by the Atomic Energy Commission is whether there is a possibility that Dr. Oppenheimer will intentionally or unintentionally reveal secret information to persons who should not have it. . . . There is no indication in the entire record that Dr. Oppenheimer has ever divulged any secret information." Although he considered the Chevalier incident regrettable, he found the entire evidence against Oppenheimer "unimpressive." And he added, "Few men could survive such a period of investigation and interrogation without having many of their actions misinterpreted and misunderstood. . . . In my opinion the conclusion drawn by the majority from the evidence is so extreme as to endanger the security system."

Branded publicly as "a security risk," Oppenheimer took comfort in the defense and devotion of many friends. After a brief vacation he resumed his activities as director of the Institute for Advanced Study and was encouraged by the board's unanimous re-election in October—Strauss offering no objection. He continued his research and kept abreast of the work of other scientists. Late in December, 1956 he addressed the Columbia University bicentennial on the subject of the arts and sciences and stated that the university was the proper place for both. In another speech before the Congress for Cultural Freedom in Paris on October 10, 1959, he declared,

> Every time the West, and more particularly my own country, has expressed the opinion that it is legitimate to employ weapons of mass destruction, provided that they are employed against an adversary who has done something evil, we have been wrong. And I think that our unscrupulousness—which developed during the Second World War, by reason of its total nature and the growing callousness of those in power—has done a great disservice to the cause of freedom and free men.

In 1962 he delivered the Whidden Lectures on the three crises in physics. Philosophical of attitude and forthright of speech, he stressed the regrettable lack of understanding in 1945 between Truman and Stalin which led to atomic rivalry and its terrifying consequences. No less easy on the physicists than on the politicians, he said, "The community of physicists is certainly no more than any other free of evil, free of vanity, or free of their own glory; we must expect rather ugly things to happen and they do." He pointed out that although scientists must help governments, they must also work for international cooperation—for "a world which, with all its vanity, freedom, and change, is without nation states armed for war and above all, a world without war."

President Kennedy, aware of the callous injustice done to Oppenheimer by the previous administration, showed his disapproval of the treatment by inviting him to a White House dinner honoring American Nobel Prize winners. The following year President Johnson, acting on the intent of his assassinated predecessor, presented Oppenheimer with the Fermi Award, the highest scientific honor. In response, Oppenheimer replied, "I think it is just possible, Mr. President, that it has taken some charity and some courage for you to make this award today. That would seem to me to be a good augury for all our futures." But if the head of the nation sought to make amends with this gesture of approval, the Atomic Energy Commission persisted in its refusal to remove the "blank wall" between Oppenheimer and secret information, which was hardly secret to a man of his vast knowledge of atomic energy.

A sidelight on this overrated problem of secrecy was offered by Lilienthal. Explaining his discontent in his role as chairman of the Atomic Energy Commission, he stated, "The basic reason for not being happy in so stimulating a job was the fundamental illness of the atomic-energy program: secrecy." In March, 1969, commenting favorably on the public debate concerning the anti-ballistic-missile program, he declared that he had opposed the hydrogen bomb in 1949 and was critical of the security classification which kept the decision from a public airing. He was particularly caustic about scientists and Pentagon officials who "talk about technical solutions as 'beautiful' . . . when the lives of the whole country, of the world are at stake. Let them play with something else."

Oppenheimer's health, never robust, had been deteriorating for some time and he died in February, 1967. At the simple services in Princeton, Professor Smythe commented on the gross miscarriage of justice thirteen years earlier. "In judging the Oppenheimer case, we should remember that the winter and spring of 1954 marked the height of the McCarthy period. It was a horrible period in American history, and we paid horribly for it. . . . Such a wrong can never be righted; such a blot on our history never erased. We can at least be thankful that belatedly an attempt was made to set the record straight."

Bibliography

In addition to various histories, encyclopedias, biographical com-
pilations, dictionaries, and Who's Whos, *I have made use of the fol-*
lowing books and articles in preparation of the book, and hereby
acknowledge my indebtedness to the authors, especially for the pas-
sages quoted from these sources. For the convenience of those
interested, I have listed separately the material used for each chapter.

HAYM SALOMON

Baron, H. S. *Haym Salomon: Immigrant and Financier of the American Revolution*, New York, 1929.

Commission on Revolutionary Claims. Memorial of H. M. Salomon, Report to U. S. Senate, July 28, 1848.

Daly, Charles P. *The Settlement of Jews in North America*, New York, 1893.

Fast, Howard. *Haym Salomon, Son of Liberty*, New York, 1941.

Friedman, Lee M. *Early American Jews*, Cambridge, Mass., 1934.

Hart, Charles H. *Robert Morris: Financier of the American Revolution*, Philadelphia, 1877.

Hart, Charles S. *General Washington's Son of Israel*, Philadelphia, 1936.

Homes, Henry A. Description and Analysis of the Remarkable Collection of Unpublished Manuscripts of Robert Morris, Albany, 1876.

Kohler, Max J. *Haym Salomon, The Patriot Banker of the Revolution*, New York, 1931.

Levinger, Lee J. *A History of the Jews in the United States*, Cincinnati, 1932.

Marcus, J. R. *Early American Jewry*, Vol. I, Philadelphia, 1961.

Morris, Robert, Statement of the Account of the United States of America During the Administration of Finance, 1781–1784.

Oberholtzer, E. P., *Robert Morris, Patriot and Financier*, New York, 1903.

Publications of the American Jewish Historical Society, No. 1, 1893; No. 2, 1894.

Russell, Charles E., *Haym Salomon and the Revolution*, New York, 1930.

Schapes, M. U., ed., *A Documentary History of the Jews in the United States*, New York, 1952.

Wolf, Edwin II, and Maxwell Whiteman, *The History of the Jews in Philadelphia from Colonial Times to the Age of Jackson*, Philadelphia, 1957.

Viernick, Peter, *History of the Jews in America*, New York, 1912.

MORDECAI MANUEL NOAH

Allen, Lewis F. "The Story of the Tablet of the City of Ararat," Buffalo Hist. Soc. Publ., Vol. 25, 1921.

Blau, Joseph H., and Salo W. Baron, eds. *The Jews of the United States, 1740–1840*, New York, 1963.

Cone, G. H., "New Matter Relating to Mordecai M. Noah," Publ. Am Jew. Hist. Soc., Vol. 2, 1894.

Dunlap, Wm., *History of the American Theatre*, New York, 1832.

Friedman, Lee M., "Mordecai Manuel Noah as Playwright," *Historica Judeaica*, Oct. 1942.

Goldberg, Isaak, *Major Noah—American Jewish Pioneer*, Philadelphia, 1936.

Handlin, Oscar, *Adventures in Freedom*, New York, 1954.

Kohler, Max, J., *Judah Touro, Merchant and Philanthropist*, Publ. Am. Jew. Hist. Soc., No. 13, 1905.

Kohut, G. A., "A Literary Autobiography of Mordecai Manuel Noah," Am. Jew. Publ. Soc., Vol. 6, 1898.

Lebowitch, Joseph, "The Jews in Boston, Mass., 1699–1840," *The Menorah*, Jan. 1903.

Lockwood, Samuel, "Major M. M. Noah," *Lippincott's Magazine*, June 1868.

Makover, A. B., *Mordecai M. Noah, His Life and Work from the Jewish Viewpoint*, New York, 1917.

Noah, M. M., *Discourse on the Restoration of the Jews*, New York, 1845.

———, *Gleanings from a Gathered Harvest*, New York, 1845.

———, *She Would Be a Soldier*, New York, 1819.

———, *Travels in England, France, Spain, and the Barbary States in the Years 1813–14–15*, New York, 1819.

Report of the Trial of an Action on the Case Brought by Sylvanus Miller, Esq., Against Mordecai M. Noah, New York, 1823.

Simenhoff, Harry, *Jewish Notables in America, 1776–1865*, New York, 1956.

Trowbridge, J. T., *My Own Story*, Boston, 1903.

Wolf, Simon, *Mordecai Manuel Noah*, Philadelphia, 1897.

JUDAH P. BENJAMIN

Blaine, J. G., *20 Years of Congress*, Norwich, Conn., 1884.

Bradford, Gamaliel, *Confederate Portraits*, Boston, 1914.

Butler, Pierce, *Judah P. Benjamin*, Philadelphia, 1907.

Goodhart, Arthur. L., *Five Eminent Jewish Lawyers of the Common Law*, London, 1949.

Gruss, Louis, ed. & trans., "José Julian Marti on Judah Philip Benjamin," *La. Hist. Quart.*, vol. 23, No. 1, 1940.

Hendrick, B. J., *Statesmen of the Lost Cause*, New York, 1939.

Kohler, Max J., "Judah P. Benjamin, Statesman and Jurist," Publ. Am. Jew. Hist. Soc., vol. 12, 1905.

Korn, B. W., "Judah P. Benjamin as a Jew," Pub. Am. Jew. Hist. Soc., March 1949.

McCall, S. W., *Patriotism of the American Jew*, New York, 1924.

Meade, R. D., *Judah P. Benjamin, Confederate Statesman*, New York, 1943.

Osterweis, Rollin, *Judah P. Benjamin, Statesman of the Lost Cause*, New York, 1933.

Padjett, J. A., "The Letters of Judah Philip Benjamin to Ambrose Dudley Mann, etc.," *The Am. Hist. Quart.*, July 1937.

Pollock, Sir Frederick, "Reminiscences of Judah Philip Benjamin," *Fortnightly Review*, reprinted in *Living Age*, Apr. 23, 1898.

Simenhoff, Harry, *Jewish Participants in the Civil War*, New York, 1963.

Vest, G. G., "Judah P. Benjamin: A Senator of Two Republics," *The Menorah*, Nov. 1903.

JACOP H. SCHIFF

Adler, Cyrus, *I Have Considered the Days*, Philadelphia, 1941.

———, *Jacob H. Schiff, His Life and Letters*, Garden City, N. Y., 1928.

Birmingham, Stephen, *Our Crowd*, New York, 1967.

Cowen, Philip, *Memories of an American Jew*, New York, 1932.

Deutsch, Gotthard, "Jacob H. Schiff," *Am. Israelite*, Jan. 4, 1917.

Resnikoff, Charles, *Louis Marshall, Champion of Liberty*, Philadelphia, 1957.

Schachner, Nathan, *The Price of Liberty: A History of the American Jewish Committee*, New York, 1948.

Schiff, J. H., *Our Journey to Japan*, New York, 1907.

———, "The Need for a Jewish Homeland," *The Nation*, Apr. 26, 1919.

Singer, Isidor, "Mr. Jacob H. Shiff and the Zionists," *N. Y. Sun*, Sept. 4 and 22, 1907.

OSCAR S. STRAUS

Adler, Cyrus, "Oscar S. Straus," *American Jewish Year Book*, vol. 29, 1927.

Creelman, James, "Israel Unbound," *Pearson Magazine*, Feb. 1907.

Hellman, G. S., ed., Record of the Oscar S. Straus Memorial Association, New York, 1949.

Howard, W. W., *Oscar S. Straus in Turkey*, n. d.

Straus, Oscar S., "Citizenship and the Protection of Nationalized Citizens Abroad," *Proceedings* of the U. S. Naval Instit., vol xxx, no. 1, whole no. 9, n. d.

———, *Religious Liberty in the United States*, New York, 1896.

———, *Roger Williams, Pioneer of Religious Liberty*, New York, 1894.

———, *The American Spirit*, New York, 1913.

———, *The Origin of the Republican Form of Government*, New York, 1885.

———, "The Pilgrims and the Hebrew Spirit," *Menorah Journal*, Dec. 1920.

———, "The United States and Russia: Their Historical Relations," *North American Review*, July 1905.

———, *Thomas Paine, Foremost Constructive Statesman of his Time*, New York, 1921.

Strauss, Lewis S., "Oscar S. Straus, An Appreciation," Publ. Am. Jew. Hist. Soc., 1950.

———, "Oscar S. Straus, Father of the U. N." *American Hebrew*, Sept. 22, 1950.

FELIX ADLER

Adler, Felix, *An Ethical Philosophy of Life, New York*, 1918.

———, *Creed and Deed*, New York, 1877.

———, *Incompatibility in Marriage*, New York, 1930.

———, *Life and Destiny*, New York, 1903.

———, *Marriage and Divorce*, New York, 1905.

———, *The Essentials of Spirituality*, New York, 1905.

———, *The Reconstruction of the Spiritual Ideal*, New York, 1924.

———, *The World Crisis and Its Meaning*, New York, 1915.

Analyticus, "Felix Adler," *The Century Magazine*, Sept. 1928.

Blau, J. L., *Modern Varieties of Judaism*, New York, 1966.

Bois, Jules, "Ethical Culture—A Second Reformation," *The Forum*, Feb., 1926.

Bridges, Horace J., ed., *Aspects of Ethical Religion*, New York, 1926.

Davis, Moshe, *The Emergence of Conservative Judaism*, Philadelphia, 1963.

Eckstein, Walter, Felix Adler's Philosophy and Our Times (lecture), 1948.

Elliott, John L., "Felix Adler," *Survey Graphic*, June 1933.

Friess, H. L., "Felix Adler," *Columbia Univer. Quart.*, June 1934.

Hartnett, J. R., *The Origin and Growth of the Ethical Culture Movement in the United States*, (Ph.D. thesis), 1959.

May, Max O., *Isaak Mayer Wise*, New York, 1916.

Morais, S. M., *Eminent Israelites of the Nineteenth Century*, Philadelphia, 1880.

Neumann, Henry, "Half a Century of Ethical Culture," *The Nation*, Aug. 12, 1926.

———, *Spokesmen for Ethical Religion*, Boston, 1951.

Villard, O. G., "Two Americans: Hillquit and Adler," *The Nation*, Oct. 25, 1933.

LOUIS D. BRANDEIS

Bickel, A. M., *The Unpublished Opinions of Mr. Justice Brandeis*, Cambridge, Mass., 1957.

Blau, J. L., et al., eds., *Essays in Jewish Life and Thought*, New York, 1959.

Brandeis, L. D., A Call to the Educated Jew (address), 1914.

———, *Business—A Profession*, Boston, 1914, 1933.

———, *Other People's Money and How Bankers Use It*, New York, 1914, 1932.

———, *The Curse of Bigness*, ed. by O. K. Fraenkel, New York, 1934.

———, The Jewish Problem—How to Solve It (address), 1915.

DeHaas, Jacob, *Louis D. Brandeis*, New York, 1929.

Dillard, Irving, ed., *Mr. Justice Brandeis*, St. Louis, 1941.

Flexner, Bernard, *Mr. Justice Brandeis and the University of Louisville*, Louisville, 1938.

Frankel, Josef, *Louis D. Brandeis*, London, 1959.

Frankfurter, Felix, ed., *Mr. Justice Brandeis*, New Haven, 1932.

Fuchs, L. H., *The Political Behavior of American Jews*, Glencoe, Ill., 1956.

Goldman, Solomon, ed., *Brandeis on Zionism*, Washington, 1942.

Goldmark, Josephine, *Pilgrims of '48*, New Haven, 1930.

Goodhart, A. L., *Five Jewish Eminent Lawyers of the Common Law*, London, 1949.

Harvard Law Review, Nov. 1931, Dec. 1941.

Hellman, G. S., *Benjamin N. Cardozo*, New York, 1940.

Kallen, Horace M., *The Faith of Louis D. Brandeis, Zionist*, New York, 1943.

Konefsky, S. J., *The Legacy of Holmes and Brandeis*, New York, 1957.

Lief, Alfred, *Brandeis: The Personal History of an American Ideal*, New York, 1936.

——, ed., *The Brandeis Guide to the Modern World*, Boston, 1941.

——, ed., *The Social and Economic Views of Mr. Justice Brandeis*, New York, 1931.

Mason, A. T., *Brandeis: A Free Man's Life*, New York, 1946.

——, *Brandeis: Lawyer and Judge in the Modern State*, Princeton, 1933.

——, *The Brandeis Way*, Princeton, 1938.

Nomination of Louis D. Brandeis. Hearings before the Subcommittee of the Committee on the Judiciary, U. S. Senate, Document, no. 409, Washington, 1916.

Pollack, E. H., ed., *The Brandeis Reader*, New York, 1956.

Proskauer, J. M., *A Segment of My Times*, New York, 1950.

United States Report, Cases adjudged in the Supreme Court, 1916–1936, vols. 243–304.

Wise, J. W., *Jews Are Like That*, New York, 1928.

ADOLPH S. OCHS

Barnett, J. W., *Joseph Pulitzer and His World*, New York, 1941.

Bent, Silas, *Ballyhoo*, New York, 1927.

———, *Strange Bedfellows*, New York, 1928.

Berger, Meyer, *The Story of the New York Times, 1851–1951*, New York, 1951.

Davis, Elmer, *History of the New York Times, 1851–1921*, New York, 1921.

Goran, G. E., and J. A. Livengood, "Adolph S. Ochs, The Boy Publisher," *East. Tenn. Hist. Soc. Publ.*, no. 17, 1945.

Hinkel, J. V., *The Contributions of Adolph S. Ochs to Journalism*, New York, 1931.

Johnson, G. W., *An Honorable Titan, A Biographical Study of Adolph S. Ochs*, New York, 1946.

Richin, Moses, *The Promised City*, Cambridge, Mass., 1962.

Rittenberg, Louis, "Ochs at Seventy-five," *American Hebrew*, March 10, 1933.

Stolberg, B., "The Man Behind the *Times*," *Altantic Monthly*, Dec. 1926.

Villard, O. G., *Some Newspapers and Newspaper-Men*, New York, 1923.

JULIUS ROSENWALD

Cohn, David L., *The Good Old Days*, New York, 1940.

Embree, E. R., and Julia Waxman, *Investment in People*, New York, 1949.

Emmett, B., and J. E. Jenck, *Catalogues and Counters*, Chicago, 1950.

Howser, Th. V., *Big Business and Human Values*, New York, 1957.

Rosenwald, Julius, "The Burden of Wealth," *Saturday Evening Post*, Jan. 5, 1929.

Werner, M. R., *Julius Rosenwald*, the Life of a Practical Humanitarian, New York, 1939.

ABRAHAM FLEXNER

Flexner, A., *A Modern College and a Modern School*, New York, 1923.
——, *A Modern School*, New York, 1916.
——, *An Autobiography*, New York, 1960.
——, *Henry S. Pritchett*, New York, 1943.
——, *I Remember*, New York, 1940.
——, *Medical Education in Europe*, New York, 1912.
——, *Medical Education in the United States and Canada*, New York, 1910.
——, *Prostitution in Europe*, New York, 1914.
——, *The American College: A Criticism*. New York, 1908.
——, *The Burden of Humanism*, Oxford, 1928.
——, *Universities—American, English, and German*, New York, 1930.
Gardner, John W., "Abraham Flexner, Pioneer in Educational Reform," *Science*, Feb. 26, 1960.

STEPHEN S. WISE

Janowsky, O. I., ed., *The American Jew, A Reappraisal*, Philadelphia, 1964.
Polier, Justine W., and J. W. Wise, *The Personal Letters of Stephen Wise*, Boston, 1956.
Silver, Abba Hillel, *Religion in Present-Day Jewish Life*, Cincinnati, 1939.
——, *Religion in a Changing World*, New York, 1930.
Strawn, Arthur, "Stephen S. Wise—Prophet a la Mode," *The Reflex*, Jan. 1928.
Voss, Carl H., *Rabbi and Minister, The Friendship of Stephen S. Wise and John Haynes Holmes*, New York, 1964.

Wise, James W., *Jews Are Like That*, New York, 1928.
Wise, S. S., American Israel and Democracy (address), 1916.
———, An Open Letter, Portland O., Jan. 5, 1906.
———, *As I See It*, New York, 1944.
———, *Challenging Years*, New York, 1949.
———, *How to Face Life*, New York, 1917.
———, The Case of the Jewish People (address), 1922.
———, and Jacob DeHaas, *The Great Betrayal*, New York, 1930.

HERBERT H. LEHMAN

Bellush, Jewel, "Roosevelt's Good Right Arm: Lieut. Governor Herbert H. Lehman," *New York History*, Oct. 1960.
Herbert H. Lehman, Director General, United Nations Relief and Rehabilitation Administration, 1943–46, Stamford, Conn., 1946.
Lehman H. H., Creeping McCarthyism (address), 1953.
———, Faith of a Fighting Liberal (address), 1949.
———, "Giant Business Expands," *The New Leader*, Apr. 29, 1957.
———, "In Defense of Principles," *Congress Weekly*, July 27, 1956.
———, Liberalism: A Personal Journey (2 addresses), April 9, 16, 1958.
———, "Liberalism and Judaism," *Jewish Heritage*, Spring, 1958.
———, The Challenge of 1953 (address), 1953.
———, The Problem of Present-Day Civilization (address), 1936.
———, The Straitjacket of Fear (address), 1953.
Levitt, Saul, and Allan Chase, "Herbert Lehman: Silent Dynamite," *Am. Mercury*, Sept. 1934.
Nevins, Allan, *Herbert H. Lehman and His Era*, New York, 1963.
Powell, Hickman, "Profile of Herbert H. Lehman," *The New Yorker*, May 2, 9, 1936.

Rodell, Fred, "Our Languid Liberals," *The Progressive*, March 1951.

Simenhoff, Harry, *Saga of American Jewry, 1865–1914*, New York, 1959.

FELIX FRANKFURTER

Aronson, M. J., "The Juristic Thought of Mr. Justice Frankfurter," *Jour. of Soc. Philos.* Jan. 1940.

Felix Frankfurter Reminisces, ed. by Harlan B. Phillips, New York, 1960.

Frankfurter, Felix, *Law and Politics*, ed. by Archibald McLeish and E. F. Pritchard, New York, 1939.

———, ed., *Mr. Justice Brandeis*, New Haven, 1932.

———, *Mr. Justice Holmes and the Supreme Court*, Cambridge, Mass., 1961.

———, *Of Law and Men*, ed. by Philip Elman, New York, 1956.

———, *The Case of Sacco and Vanzetti*, Boston, 1927.

———, "The Palestine Situation Restated," *Foreign Affairs*, Apr. 1931.

———, *The Public and Its Government*, New Haven, 1930.

———, "Why Young Men Go to Washington," *Fortune Magazine*, Jan. 1936.

———, and Nathan Greene, *The Labor Injunction*, New York, 1930.

Gilkey, R. C., *Mr. Justice Frankfurter and Civil Liberties* (Ph. D. thesis), 1957.

Grossman, James, "A Note on Felix Frankfurter," *Commentary*, March 1966.

Howe, Mark D., ed., *Holmes-Laski Letters, 1916–1945*, Cambridge, Mass, 1953.

Ickes, Harold L., *The Secret Diaries of*, New York, 1953–1954.

Jacobs, C. E., *Justice Frankfurter and Civil Liberties*, Berkeley, 1961.

Josephson, M., "Profile of Felix Frankfurter," *The New Yorker*, Nov. 30, Dec. 7, 14, 1940.

Mendelson, Wallace, ed., *Felix Frankfurter: A Tribute*, New York, 1964.

———, *Justices Black and Frankfurter: Conflict in the Court*, Chicago, 1961.

Rodell, Fred, "Felix Frankfurter, Conservative," *Harper's Magazine*, Oct. 1941.

———, *Nine Men*, New York, 1955.

———, The Complexities of Justice Fortas," N. Y. York *Times* "Magazine," July 28, 1968.

Roosevelt and Frankfurter: Their Correspondence, 1928–1945, ed. by Max Freedman, Boston, 1967.

Thomas, Helen S. *Felix Frankfurter, Scholar on the Beach*, Baltimore, 1960.

SIDNEY HILLMAN

Advance, 1917–1948.

Book of the Amalgamated of New York, 1914–1940, New York, 1940.

Budish, J. M., and George Soule, *The New Unionism in the Clothing Industry*, New York, 1920.

Cort, John C., "Hillman, CPA and PAC," *The Commonweal*, Oct. 20, 1944.

Documentary History of the ACWU, 1914–1948, New York, 1948.

Foster, W. Z., *American Trade Unionism*, New York, 1947.

Gollomb, Joseph, "Sidney Hillman," *Atlantic Monthly*, July 1938.

Hardman, J. B. S., ed., *The Amalgamated Today and Tomorrow*, New York, 1939.

———, ed., *American Labor Dynamics*, New York, 1928.

Hardy, Jack, *The Clothing Workers*, New York, 1935.

Hillman, Sidney, "Labor in the United States," St. Louis *Post-Dispatch* 50th-Anniversary Edition, 1928.

———, "The Promise of American Labor," *The New Republic*, Nov. 8, 1939.

———, "Unemployment Reserves," *Atlantic Monthly*, Nov. 1931.

Hillquit, M., *Loose Leaves from a Busy Life*, New York, 1934.

Josephson, M., *Sidney Hillman, Statesman of American Labor*, Garden City, N. Y., 1951

Kopald, Sylvia, *Rebellion in Labor Unions*, New York, 1924.

Pope, Jesse, E., *The Clothing Industry*, Columbia, Mo., 1905.

Saposs, David J., *Left-Wing Unionism*, New York, 1926.

Scholossberg, Joseph, *The Workers and their World*. New York, 1935.

Seidman, Joel, *The Needle Trades*, New York, 1942.

Soule, Geo., *Sidney Hillman*, New York, 1939.

Strong, Earl D., *The Amalgamated Clothing Workers of America*, Grinnell, Iowa, 1940.

Wolman, Leo, *The Clothing Workers of Chicago, 1910–1922*, Chicago, 1922.

Zarets, C. E., *The Amalgamated Clothing Workers of America*, New York, 1934.

J. ROBERT OPPENHEIMER

Bethe, Hans, "J. Robert Oppenheimer, 1904–1967," *Bull. of Atomic Scientists*, Oct. 1967.

Cahn, Robert, "Behind the First A Bomb," *Saturday Evening Post*, July 16, 1960.

Cohen, H., and I. J. Camin, eds., *Jews in the World of Science*, New York, 1956.

Chevalier, Haakon, *Oppenheimer: The Story of a Friendship*, New York, 1965.

Curtis, C. P., *The Oppenheimer Case*, New York, 1955.

Davis, N. P., *Lawrence and Oppenheimer*, New York, 1968.

Groves, Leslie, R., *Now It Can Be Told*, New York, 1962.

In the Matter of J. Robert Oppenheimer, Texts of Principal Documents and Letters, May 27-June 29, 1954, Washington, 1954.

In the Matter of J. Robert Oppenheimer, Transcript of Hear-

384   BIBLIOGRAPHY

ings before Personnel Security Board, April 12 to May 6, 1954, Washington, 1954.

Johnston, Marjorie, *The Cosmos of Arthur Holly Compton*, New York, 1967.

Jungk, Robert, *Brighter than a Thousand Suns*, New York, 1958.

Knebel, F., and C. W. Bailey II, *No High Ground*, New York, 1960.

Kugleman, J. A., *J. Robert Oppenheimer and the Atomic Story*, New York, 1953.

Millikan, Robert A., "Albert Abraham Michelson," *Scientific Monthly*, Jan. 1939.

Oppenheimer, J. Robert, *Science and the Common Understanding*, New York, 1954.

———, *The Flying Trapeze: Three Crises in Physics*, Oxford, 1964.

———, *The Open Mind*, New York, 1955.

Price, Don K., "Oppenheimer," *Science*, March 3, 1967.

Rouzé, Michael, *Robert Oppenheimer*, New York, 1965.

Strauss, Lewis L., *Men and Decisions*, New York, 1962.

Index